LAWYERS AND JUDGES

LAWYERS AND JUDGES

The ABA and the Politics of Judicial Selection

Joel B. Grossman
University of Wisconsin

John Wiley and Sons, Inc.   New York · London · Sydney

Some of the material which appears in Chapter 4
is reprinted from "Federal Judicial Selection:
The Work of the ABA Committee," *Midwest
Journal of Political Science*, Vol. VIII, No. 3
(August 1964). Copyright 1964 by Wayne State
University Press.

Library of Congress Catalog Card Number: 65-16409
Printed in the United States of America

To my parents

PREFACE

The impact of the behavioral revolution in the social sciences on the world of the political scientist has been profound. It has prompted him, at the very least, to reexamine many propositions about the political arena which had seemed to be no longer open to question. It has caused him to examine aspects of politics which had previously rested almost exclusively in the domain of sister disciplines; and it has caused him to examine these aspects with a variety of innovative methodological approaches more or less squarely in the tradition of scientific inquiry.

Nowhere is this contrast better seen than in the work of those political scientists who, for want of a better term, have recently toiled under the label of "judicial behavioralists." Expanding outward from the traditional public-law focus on the major decisions rendered by appellate court judges, new emphasis has been placed on other aspects of the judicial process such as the consequences of judicial decisions and the roles which judges play in the political process. And focusing inward, these political scientists have sought to explain and predict judicial decision-making patterns in dynamic rather than static terms—in terms of the types of behavior exhibited by judges as individuals rather than simply in terms of cases and precedents.

But regardless of the focus of specific research efforts, the overall goal has been to relate the actions of judges and of the judicial process to existing and developing knowledge about all forms of political relationships. Although as yet there is no reason to be especially sanguine about the prospects of ultimately developing a reliable empirical theory of judicial decision-making, there is very good reason to orient most research in that direction. To be sure, most of the data available and much of the methodology in use are only pale approximations of what is needed to achieve the goal of a reliable empirical theory. But the prospect of developing such a theory and the notion of what is needed to achieve it is likely to have the beneficial effect of guiding and limiting our inquiries to those questions that appear to promise the greatest return.

This study of the role of the American Bar Association in the recruitment of federal judges is focused on questions of this type. Although the judicial-selection activities of the ABA remain the focus of attention throughout the book, they are described and analyzed in a manner that will permit future scholarship to expand on what has been done here. Patterns of behavior extending beyond the available data are implicitly or explicitly articulated. Attention is given not only to what the ABA has been doing, but to why it has been doing it and to the possible consequences of its actions for the institutionalization of the judicial role and the socialization of prospective judges. This book will fulfill my objectives if it raises more questions than it answers.

Any study of this length is inevitably the product of many hands, and no formal acknowledgment could possibly capture the exact nature of their contributions. But my indebtedness is too real to permit any easy escape from such a ticklish—though obviously pleasant—problem, and so in a spirit of genuine humility I shall begin the customary countdown.

Foremost, I am indebted to Professors John R. Schmidhauser and Vernon Van Dyke of the State University of Iowa; to Professor Schmidhauser for stimulating my interest in the problems of judicial selection with his thoughtful and realistic approach to the judicial process and also for directing the research for an earlier version of this manuscript; to Professor Van Dyke for bringing to bear upon this version his unsurpassed faculties of critical analysis. Without John Schmidhauser this particular book would probably not have been written, and without Vernon Van Dyke it would have been a different book.

A large vote of thanks must go to Professors Lane Davis, Robert Boynton, Donald Johnson, Samuel Patterson, and Deil Wright of the State University of Iowa, Richard Wells of the University of Oklahoma, Jack Walker of the University of Michigan, Stuart Nagel of the University of Illinois, and to my colleagues at the University of Wisconsin, Herbert Jacob and David Fellman, for reading the manuscript in its various stages and making useful comments on it. They may not have made this a good book, but it is certainly a better one for their efforts.

In addition to those already mentioned, several persons proved indispensable to my research efforts. Deputy Attorney General Nicholas deB. Katzenbach and Assistant Deputy Attorney General Joseph Dolan generously provided the facilities of their offices for my comfort. Mr. Dolan especially devoted a considerable amount of time to answering my questions with great candor. Mr. Bernard Segal of Philadelphia, former chairman of the Committee on Federal Judiciary of the American Bar Association, talked very frankly with me and at great length about the operations of his Committee, as did Messrs. Robert Meserve of Boston, Cloyd Laporte of New York City, Preston King, Jr., and Edgar Goodrich of Washington, D. C., and Roy Willy of Sioux Falls, South Dakota, all members of the Committee, and Mr. John Randall of Cedar Rapids, Iowa, past president of the American Bar Association.

Former Deputy Attorney General Lawrence Walsh was very helpful in describing for my benefit the liaison between the ABA Committee and the Attorney General during the Eisenhower Administration. And, by letter, former Deputy Attorney General Ross Malone described the role of the Truman Administration in establishing the initial liaison with the ABA in 1952. Also by correspondence, former Committee members Ben Miller of Baton Rouge, Howard Burns of Cleveland, and Loyd Wright of Los Angeles provided invaluable original and corroborative information on some aspects of the Committee's work. Mr. William Barnes, Personnel Section Director of the Administrative Office of the United States Courts, graciously allowed me to inspect some of the files on all federal judges appointed since 1946, and Mr. Joseph Davis, Clerk of the Senate Judiciary Committee, gave me access to the transcripts of Committee hearings on judicial nominations which had not been published.

Thanks must also go to Mrs. Margaret Sherlock for typing the manuscript and Miss Judith Starnes for editing it. And, finally, a word must go to my wife, Mary, whose indispensability in the final stages of preparing this book far exceeded her proof-reading and index-constructing chores.

Some of the material used in this book has already appeared in article form, and I am grateful to the editors of the *Midwest Journal of Political Science* (Vol. 8, No. 3, 1964) and the *Vanderbilt Law Review* (Vol. 17, No. 3, 1964) for permission to use that material again here.

In the course of my investigations, I was given access to some information which, for obvious reasons, cannot—and should not—be made public at this time. In using this information I have omitted those names that would serve to identify either the source or principals involved. And where necessary, I have altered minor details to strengthen the shield of anonymity.

Needless to say, the interpretations set forth herein, except as otherwise indicated, are my own, as is the responsibility for any errors of fact.   I doubt whether my interpretations of the judicial-selection process as a whole, and of the ABA's role in it, will conform precisely to the notions of any of the principals just named.   But I do earnestly hope that the composite picture afforded me by their sometimes conflicting views has enabled me to paint an accurate picture of the ways in which federal judges are recruited today.

JOEL B. GROSSMAN

Madison, Wisconsin
December 1964

CONTENTS

xi

LAWYERS AND JUDGES

INTRODUCTION

The final check on public acts, in our democratic system, is the vigorous expression of public opinion in behalf of worthy ideals. It is essential to our free society that the American people, lay and professional alike, hold the judgeship in the highest esteem, that they regard it as the symbol of impartial, fair, and equal justice under law. The selective process has had enough of political pressures and partisan enthusiasms in the past. Public opinion, determined that the best men of law in each community should be persuaded to accept the most critical and demanding posts of the law, could effectively uphold the hands of all who strive to achieve this result.

It is the lawyers' task to lead in this public campaign. To foster understanding, respect, and support of our courts is one of the most solemn duties of the Organized Bar. It can have no greater interest than the judicial system of the Country, no more pressing activity than participation in the selection, the work, and the well-being of the bench.

I enlist you all in this cause—the next great step that lies ahead for the Organized Bar! [1]

Bernard G. Segal

---

[1] Bernard G. Segal, "Federal Judicial Selection—Progress and the Promise of the Future," 46 *Massachusetts Law Quarterly* (1961), 150–151.

One phenomenon of recent American politics has been the growth of the American Bar Association as a vital and often influential force in the political process as well as in the legal profession. There is no better illustration of this than the ABA's assumption of a leading position in a professionwide campaign to gain a measure of control over the several processes of judicial selection. The successes that the ABA has had in this venture are of great interest to many students of politics. The central importance of the judge in our society underscores the importance of understanding the ways in which prospective judges are trained and selected and of knowing the groups or individuals most deeply involved in that process. And the training and reasons for selection determine in part the type of judiciary we will have.

The role that the judiciary has played in different historical eras has depended as much on the type of men who became judges as it has on the constitutional rules that appear to set at least the outer limits of judicial action. No political institution can survive if it fails to change with the society around it, and when no specific provisions for change have been made—as they have not been for the judiciary—change must come in part with the infusion of new blood.

Until now the available information has enabled scholars to describe the judicial-selection process in broad but discernible outlines. But the inner workings of the process, while the subject of much commentary and some description, have not yet been accorded the systematic analysis that their significance demands. And the impact of the recruitment process on the socialization of judges has received even less attention. The need for such analysis has only been compounded by the recent development of the American Bar Association's role in the process of selection. The ABA's activities over the last decade have created a new balance of forces which has already had, and is likely to continue to have, important consequences for the ways in which federal judges are chosen and the types of judges selected.

Now, for the first time, there are enough data available to permit the development of interesting and significant propositions on these subjects. This book will concentrate on the impact of the ABA's activities on the process of selecting federal judges; work now in progress by other students will continue to add to our knowledge of the judicial-recruitment process.

Thus, although this book is primarily a study of the ABA's activities in the process of federal judicial selection, it is not simply a description of those activities. Rather, it is an attempt to take a fresh look at the entire selection process by demonstrating how the work of the ABA has affected the traditional patterns of judicial recruitment. What was it in the existing selection process that the ABA found unsatisfactory? What is the particular interest of lawyers in judicial selection? How were the ABA's claims made and how were they received? How different is the selection process today from the process antedating the efforts of the ABA? What have been the consequences of these alterations in the selection process for the types of judges chosen, or likely to be chosen in the future?

A study such as this should also have important, though indirect, bearing on the question of the relationship between judicial selection and the entire process of judicial decision making. If the ultimate theoretical goal of political science is to understand why, how, by whom, and with what consequences political decisions are made, the decision as to who will sit for how long a period on a particular court is of great importance. There is some evidence that the ways in which judges are chosen affect the types of judges selected,[2] and more convincing data to indicate that the type of judge chosen will make a difference in the types of decisions courts will make.[3] But the exact relationship between method of selection and type of judge chosen and between type of judge and patterns of decisions remains elusive. The data presented here should help clarify the first of these two relationships and thereby broaden the base for explaining the second.

One final set of questions with which a book such as this must deal, if only in passing, could be considered normative rather than empirical. The quest for political power by an organization such as the ABA inevitably raises the question: "what is the legitimate role of a private group dealing with important public policy matters?" The term "legitimate" is not used here in any legal sense, but rather to indicate a high degree of congruence between the operations of the group and generally accepted norms of behavior. The ABA is not the first group

---

[2] The evidence here is still sketchy but nonetheless suggestive. See Herbert Jacob, "The Effect of Institutional Differences in the Recruitment Process," 13 *Journal of Public Law* (1964), 104–119. See also Bancroft Henderson and T. C. Sinclair, *Judicial Selection in Texas: An Exploratory Study* (Houston, Tex.: University of Houston Studies in Social Science, 1964). And see Richard Watson, Rondal Downing, and Frederick Spiegel, "Lawyers and Judicial Selection under the Missouri Plan," and Harold Chase, "Federal Judges: The Appointing Process," both papers delivered at the 1964 Annual Meeting of the American Political Science Association, Chicago, Ill.
[3] See John R. Schmidhauser, "Judicial Behavior and the Sectional Crisis of 1837–1860," 23 *Journal of Politics* (1961), 615–640, and "Stare Decisis, Dissent, and the Background of the Justices of the Supreme Court of the United States," 14 *University of Toronto Law Journal* (1962), 194–212. See also Stuart Nagel, "Ethnic Affiliations and Judicial Propensities," 24 *Journal of Politics* (1962), 92–110.

to hold a quasi-formal position of considerable power in the political system—although it is the first in the federal judicial-selection process—and it undoubtedly will not be the last. The problems of legitimacy which the ABA's present activities raise are recurring problems in our society. They are not likely to disappear without substantial formal changes in our constitutional apparatus. But that they are common and recurring problems does not obviate the necessity of dealing with them anew *as* they recur. And that they are essentially problems of normative political theory does not require or permit that they be ignored in a book primarily concerned with contributing to the construction of an empirical theory of politics. Normative theory, after all, is often but a reflection of existing behavior and, perhaps as often, conditions that same behavior.

What is it, therefore, about the ABA's role in the selection of federal judges that raises the question of legitimacy? Most obviously, we must inquire whether any of the basic notions of prevailing democratic theory have been offended; in particular has the notion of public accountability and political responsibility for important political decisions been compromised? Recognizing that the exercise of controlled power by a private group may not, per se, violate these basic canons of democratic theory, we must inquire further if the group has made, or is likely to make, a contribution to the stability or efficiency of the political system.

In other words, even if there has been a departure from the norm of political action exercised by politically responsible officials, is it not possible to justify recourse to a private group if that group can make a unique contribution to the system? May it not be that exclusion of this particular group from exercising formal power in the selection process will produce results more inimical than if the group was permitted to exercise this power? And in a system such as ours where considerable political power is exercised, albeit informally, by a multiplicity of private groups, is there not some case to be made for legitimating—and hence controlling—the exercise of such power? The questions posed here are clearly not susceptible to answering by recourse only to dogmatic assertions of traditional theories. A dynamic political system can never be preserved, or permitted to develop, on such a basis. When we return to these questions in the final chapter, it will be with the benefit of a fuller picture of the ABA's present role in the selection process, of the rational alternatives to such a role, and of the judicial-selection process as a whole. Our equipment for answering the questions posed here will then be more adequate.

As a guide to the pages that follow, it is advisable here to sketch very briefly the judicial-selection activities of the American Bar Association, which constitute the core of the book.

Beginning in 1946 the American Bar Association has attempted to exert a continuous, quasi-formal influence on the process of recruiting federal judges. Operating through a small committee of eleven lawyers, it has sought to be recognized as an integral and indispensable part in the selection process in a role that would enable it to exercise considerable influence in setting the standards to be followed in selecting judges, in promoting the nomination of the "best" judges available, and in barring the selection of judges who fall below these standards. In the pursuit of these objectives, the ABA has been aided by the decentralized nature of the selection process, by the postwar increases in its own prestige, due in part to its increased membership and fuller representation of the legal profession, and by a generally favorable climate of public opinion. On the other hand, that same decentralization of power in selecting federal judges has impeded the fulfillment of some of the ABA's objectives. It has had to settle for the lesser goal of guardian of minimal standards of selection, rather than its maximum objective of promoting the nomination of the "best" men available. And its ability to gain access to some points in the decision process, that is, its liaison with the Attorney General, has been matched by its inability to gain much of a foothold in the Senate, the final important stage in that process.

The results of this study indicate that the ABA has had a diffuse impact on the selection process. It has been responsible for some fairly significant changes in the early stages of the recruitment process but has had little impact on the senatorial role of confirmation. There is some evidence that the patterns of recruitment since the formation of its liaison with the Attorney General reflect ABA influence. And there is a good basis for predicting that the sum total of the ABA's judicial-selection activities might encourage different kinds of career patterns by lawyers aspiring to positions on the federal bench. It is true, of course, that the ABA's impact on various aspects of the selection process has varied with changes in presidential administrations. But these variations are symptomatic of the dynamism of the American political process and should not be thought a bar to analysis of phenomena that must change accordingly. As with any political force that derives its strength from the indulgences of the President or the Senate, the ABA will occupy a role that reflects the needs of the officials who indulge it. But even so, the evidence presented here would indicate that within certain flexible limits the ABA's role in the selection of federal judges has become institutionalized.

One further preliminary note: this book is an attempt to describe and analyze the impact of the judicial-selection activities of the American Bar Association on the federal judicial-selection process. These activities are only a very small slice of the total enterprises in which the ABA constantly engages, and as such afford only a segmented picture of the ABA as a whole. And though these activities of the ABA are sufficiently important to justify treating them in depth and detail, they are not intended to convey an accurate picture or evaluation of the totality of the ABA's operations.

1

⚜

JUDICIAL SELECTION
AND THE JUDICIAL PROCESS

The process of recruiting judges is a fascinating aspect of our political life. The federal judgeship has become, among other things, an index of political success; the very thought of a judgeship as a reward for political activity can attract able and ambitious lawyers to the ranks of party workers. But despite the fact that a federal judgeship frequently caps a career in politics, it carries with it and bestows upon its holder a degree of prestige and immunity from criticism that accompanies no other office in our political system.[1] It is, in short, very close to the apex of our occupational hierarchy. The contrast between the types of career preparation sometimes needed to obtain a federal judgeship and the high dignity and nonpartisanship of that office is a striking paradox.

The reasons for this paradox are deeply rooted in our political traditions. On the one hand, it reflects our veneration of "law" as an instrument of justice and social order, our "recognition" of the legal profession as a desirable source of political leadership,[2] our symbolic devotion to constitutionalism as a "way of life," and our sense of security at being governed—at least in theory—by "laws and not men." On the other hand, it reflects our good political sense that judges are important political decision makers and our realization that for most types of judgeships some prior involvement in politics is a desirable

---

[1] See William C. Mitchell, "The Ambivalent Status of American Politicians," 12 *Western Political Quarterly* (1959), 688.
[2] See Donald R. Matthews, *The Social Backgrounds of Political Decision-Makers* (New York: Random House Studies in Political Science, 1954), pp. 30 ff., and Joseph A. Schlesinger, "Lawyers and Politics: A Clarified View," 1 *Midwest Journal of Political Science* (1957), 26–39.

prerequisite. Though paradoxical because of the way in which judges are chosen, high status and prestige for occupants of judicial office are obviously quite functional for the judge's position in the system.

The process of recruiting judges is an intimate part of the judicial decision-making process. Despite the understandable tendency of many people to glorify the "rule of law" as the characterizing aspect of our political system, the fact remains that laws are made by men and carried out by men. Laws are at least as much a reflection of the prevailing political balance of power as they are an embodiment of an objectively and externally determined "right." Nowhere is this contrast between myth and reality better seen than in the function of judging. It is the judge whose duties and actions symbolize the convergence of law and politics.

In focusing our attention on the process by which judges are selected, we are bringing into view one aspect of a process by which important political decisions are made. The importance of judicial selection lies primarily in its relation to a larger segment of the political process. And, conversely, an understanding of the selection process generally, and of the work of the American Bar Association in particular, must rest on a comprehension of the relationship between judicial selection and judicial decision-making. Briefly demonstrating that relationship will be the major purpose of this chapter.

THE FEDERAL COURTS AND THE
EXERCISE OF POLITICAL POWER

The federal courts exercise vast political power. By "political" is meant the authoritative allocation of values or the authoritative determination of certain norms of behavior.[3] The courts make political decisions, however, in a manner distinct from the way in which similar decisions are made by executive and legislative agencies. The style of

---

[3] This definition is built, in part, on a definition by David Easton, who defines political science as "the study of the authoritative allocation of values as it is influenced by the distribution and use of power."—*The Political System* (New York: Knopf, 1953), p. 146. For other attempts at definition, see Lewis A. Froman, Jr., *People and Politics* (Englewood Cliffs, N. J.: Prentice-Hall, 1962), pp. 80–102; Herbert Jacob, "The Courts as Political Agencies—An Historical Analysis," in Jacob and Kenneth Vines, *Studies in Judicial Politics* (New Orleans: Tulane Studies in Political Science, 1963), pp. 9–50; Jack W. Peltason, *Federal Courts in the Political Process* (New York: Random House Studies in Political Science, 1955), pp. 3–6; and Robert A. Dahl, "Decision-Making in a Democracy: The Supreme Court as a National Policy-Maker," 6 *Journal of Public Law* (1957), 279–295.

judicial decision-making, from the honorific rituals attending the operations of a courtroom to appearances of continuity and rationality which give form to the decision, is purposely set apart from the style of other types of political decisions. This distinction in style is, in and of itself, quite functional. It serves to emphasize the basic symbolic concerns of the judicial process with conservation rather than change, with stability rather than progress, with reasoned rather than impulsive choices, and with "independent" and "objective" rather than "representative" thought.

There are also differences of content and method between judicial and other species of political decision-making. Judges do not usually initiate the actions leading to a judicial decision; the decision whether or not the judiciary will participate in the solution of a particular problem rests largely on a decision to litigate taken by a private party or another governmental agency. By contrast, the identification of problem areas and the raising of issues is a primary function of executive and legislative decision-makers. An equally fundamental distinction concerns the scope of the proposed solution to a problem. The judiciary is limited, partly by constitutional and legislative rules and partly by self-imposed limitations, to the decision of narrow rather than broad-ranging problems, whereas legislators and executives can define the scope of their actions and frequently opt for the broad rather than the narrow. Although judicial decisions frequently have wide-ranging consequences, they are expressed as (and frequently confined to) solutions to discrete problems. A third major distinction revolves around the function of law as an ingredient in judicial or executive-legislative decisions. Although it is no longer fashionable (and was never true) to argue that "judges only interpret laws and legislators make them," it is quite accurate to state that law does have a special role in judicial decision-making which it does not have in executive-legislative decision-making. The functions of the judiciary are not only to settle problems, but to settle them with reference to established rules (or laws).

These distinctions between judicial and nonjudicial decision-making processes are quite real, but they frequently obscure the fact that there are also great similarities. For a variety of reasons our political system frequently allows major public-policy issues—such as racial integration and legislative apportionment—to be resolved by judicial bodies. When the courts are faced with such broad questions, for which there may not be adequate legal grounds for decision, their job cannot be merely to interpret an existing law or apply an existing precedent. In such cases it must be "to a very large extent the task of weighing competing practical considerations and forming a practical judgment." [4]

Furthermore, the Supreme Court is clearly an important cog in the public policy-making process. It is not always a detached "observer" of the workings of the political system. Throughout its history the Supreme Court has been an active participant in the important political controversies of the era. The Marshall Court was concerned and quite active in behalf of the forces of nationalism,[5] the Fuller and White Courts were very active in behalf of the forces opposed to social-welfare experiments,[6] the Hughes (post-1937) and Stone Courts were important cogs in the legitimation of social-welfare legislation,[7] and most recently the Warren Court has dramatically taken the helm of a social revolution designed to secure the political and social rights of a variety of minority groups.[8]

Although the immediate focus of the business of the Supreme Court remains "legal"—that is, the deciding of cases or controversies involving discrete parties in conflict by recourse to legal criteria—its work cannot be understood out of the context of the larger political and social system of which it is a part. Apart from the specific roles that different courts have appeared to play, as just summarized, the Supreme Court has occupied certain generic roles in the political system. By its decisions the Supreme Court has frequently acted as a catalyst in the political system, unleashing some powerful forces while restraining others. By changing the legal rules which had theretofore governed a particular type of activity, the court has laid the groundwork for political change; and by ratifying (legitimating) such changes it has channeled new patterns of behavior within stable limits. It has also symbolized the primacy of law in the constitutional system, acted as a moderator of group conflicts within the society, acted as the final decision-maker in conflicts over the powers exercised by the other agencies of the government, acted as the guardian of the purity of the political process, acted as umpire of the federal system, provided an alternative route

---

[4] Thomas Reed Powell, "The Logic and Rhetoric of Constitutional Law," 15 *Journal of Philosophy* (1918), 654.

[5] See, among others, Wallace Mendelson, *Capitalism, Democracy and the Supreme Court* (New York: Appleton, Century, Crofts, 1960), Chs. 1 and 2.

[6] *Ibid.*, Ch. 4.

[7] See C. Herman Pritchett, *The Roosevelt Court: A Study in Judicial Politics and Values* (New York: Macmillan, 1948).

[8] See, among others, C. Herman Pritchett, *The Political Offender and the Warren Court* (Boston: Boston University Press, 1958).

of access to political power, and acted to legitimate the decisions of the legislative and executive branches.

The interplay between the process of selection and the process of judicial decision-making is best illustrated by the Court's "legitimating" role. Through constant infusion of new judicial blood, the Supreme Court is, in Robert Dahl's words, "inevitably a part of the dominant national alliance," excepting only in periods of transition such as 1933–1937, where the Court is still representative of a politically discredited administration.[9] Dahl argues quite convincingly that the "policy views on the Court are never for long out of line with the policy views dominant among the lawmaking majorities of the United States [President and Congress]."[10] This does not mean that the Supreme Court is simply a servant of that alliance, or that it can never depart from the policies of the alliance. If it does so, however, it will be at great risk to its prestige and powers except when the alliance itself is in a state of flux or stalemate and is unable to muster the necessary strength to effectively thwart the Court's actions.[11] The *Brown* decision of 1954, in which the Court clearly sought to lead the alliance rather than legitimate its decisions, was just such an action. And the recent efforts by the Supreme Court to alter the basis of both congressional and state legislative apportionment are equally in the same mold.[12] (In fact, it could be said that *Brown* represented the Court's view that the *inaction* of the law-making majorities on a matter of great national importance was not to be considered legitimate—or permanent.)

As contrasted with the Supreme Court, judges of the lower federal courts are not *primary* makers of public policy. But they do occupy a position in the judicial bureaucracy which enables them to significantly influence the making of judicial policy ostensibly determined at the higher levels. Through their responsibilities for fact finding at the trial stages of litigation, lower-court judges can shape the judicial policies determined at higher levels. Although the Supreme Court's supervisory power over the federal courts is extensive, its capacity for supervision is strictly limited, and there is evidence to suggest that

---

9 Dahl, *op. cit.*, p. 285.

10 *Ibid.*, p. 293.

11 *Ibid.*

12 See *Brown v. Board of Education*, 347 U. S. 483 (1954); *Baker v. Carr*, 369 U. S. 186 (1962); *Wesberry v. Sanders*, 376 U. S. 1 (1964); and *Reynolds v. Sims*, 377 U. S. 533 (1964).

the lower courts may handle different types of policy questions than those which ultimately get to the Supreme Court.[13]   Chief Justice Vinson noted in 1949 that

The Supreme Court is not, and never has been, primarily concerned with the correction of errors in lower court decisions. . . . The function of the Supreme Court is, therefore, to resolve conflicts of opinion among the lower courts, to pass upon questions of wide import under the Constitution. . . . If we took every case in which an interesting legal question was raised, or our prima facie impression is that the decision below was erroneous, we could not fulfill the constitutional responsibilities placed upon this court.[14]

Not only do the lower courts handle many types of cases free of supervision, but through their responsibilities for implementing Supreme Court decisions they exercise considerable power and discretion in determining the outcomes of political conflicts.   Except in rare instances the Supreme Court does not render either the initial or final decision in a case.   Even the general policy which the Supreme Court is charged with formulating is often vague and ambiguous and permits varying applications in different circuits.   Often, by distinguishing the facts of a particular case from Supreme Court policy for cases of the same genus, the lower courts can and do evade the control of the Supreme Court—on occasion with impunity.[15]

The picture that emerges, therefore, is of the lower courts as quasi-independent centers of power.   As the implementers of judicial policies, for example, integration, lower-court judges often act as a buffer between the Supreme Court and the litigants in particular cases.   The decision of the Supreme Court in the second *Brown* case to turn over to the lower courts the initial responsibility of supervision of the desegregation process was a tacit recognition of this "buffer" function.[16] In general the principle of integration was "generously" received by the lower federal courts in the southern states, which extended it from schools to other areas within a relatively short period of time with direct Supreme Court instructions.   Yet there were still definite

---

13 See Kenneth N. Vines, "The Role of Circuit Courts of Appeal in the Federal Judicial Process: A Case Study," 7 *Midwest Journal of Political Science* (1963), 305–319, especially 305–307.

14 Quoted in Fowler V. Harper and Arnold Leibowitz, "What the Supreme Court Did Not Do in the 1952 Term," 102 *University of Pennsylvania Law Review* (1953), 461–462.

15 See Walter F. Murphy, "Lower Court Checks on Supreme Court Power," 53 *American Political Science Review* (1959), 1017.

16 349 U. S. 294 (1955).

instances of resistance at the district court level both to the application of *Brown* and its extension.[17]

THE JUDICIAL ROLE AND JUDICIAL DECISION-MAKING

With the passing of the now discredited "mechanistic" interpretation of the role of the judge in the judicial decision-making process, there still remains the question of ascertaining what the real function of the judge is. There has always been at least a tacit understanding that judges are products of their environments and do not become, upon accession to the bench, impersonal vehicles of revealed truth. "The decision as to WHO will make the decisions affects what decisions will be made." [18] This is not to say that judges do not operate within certain predictable and required frames of reference. There is some truth in the "effect on a judge" attributed to the donning of the judicial robe. But such factors do not, themselves, constitute the essence of the judicial role. As David B. Truman has observed, "judges do not cease to be human when they don their robes. They do not derive all their premises from the courtroom." [19]

Although the propositions of mechanistic jurisprudence and syllogistic reasoning have generally been replaced with hypotheses emphasizing the social and psychological nature of judicial decision-making, there is still disagreement over the relative importance of a variety of influences on, and the extent of, the exercise of judicial discretion.[20] To what extent is a judge free to select the premises and mode of a decision? What are the sources of the values that the judge may find most congenial and influential? What are some of the factors that limit not only his choice among decision alternatives, but his choice *of* decision alternatives?

---

[17] Paul H. Sanders, "The Warren Court and the Lower Federal Courts," in John R. Schmidhauser, *Constitutional Law in the Political Process* (Chicago: Rand-McNally, 1963), pp. 423–435. Also see "Judicial Performance in the Fifth Circuit," 73 *Yale Law Journal* (1963), 90–133.

[18] Peltason, *op. cit.,* p. 29.

[19] *The Governmental Process* (New York: Knopf, 1951), p. 490.

[20] Perhaps the earliest attack came from Oliver Wendell Holmes, in his treatise, "The Common Law" (1881): "The life of the law has not been logic; it has been experience." The social nature of judicial decision-making has been emphasized by such men as Roscoe Pound, Benjamin Cardozo, and Underhill Moore; the psychological basis by Jerome Frank, Karl Llewellyn, and others of the legal "realist" school.

It is entirely too simple an explanation to suggest that judges make these sorts of decisions on the basis of their value preferences. Of course values enter the picture. But to simply trace values is to ignore entirely the process by which they are internalized and the reasons why and how they are called upon in particular case situations. We must ask not only what are the dominant values that guide the actions of a judge, but how they operate to produce certain behavior patterns as well.

The obvious fact that judges holding similar values can make different decisions in the same case suggests that it is not the values themselves as much as it is the way in which they are ordered and brought to bear on a particular problem that best explains judicial decision-making. In simple language, different judges will *approach* a single case differently. It is quite conceivable that a case involving prosecutions for the same act by both federal and state authorities, for example, *Bartkus v. Illinois*,[21] would be viewed by Justice Douglas as a civil-liberties deprivation and a violation of a fundamental human right, by Justice Black as these plus a misreading of the Fourteenth Amendment and its alleged incorporation of the guarantees of the Bill of Rights, by Justice Frankfurter primarily as a question of achieving a federal balance in criminal proceedings, and by Justice Clark as a question of the efficacy of certain types of law-enforcement procedures. Clearly, each of these justices mentioned viewed the consequences of the decision differently because to each it posed a different problem. Each judge was responding to a different variable emphasizing what he thought the Supreme Court's role in such a case ought to be.

To explain the contrasting approaches of the justices to a case such as *Bartkus* as simply reflecting their basic value commitments for or against "civil liberties" is to say very little.[22] A better explanation would come from a determination of the role that each judge had determined to play. This would involve exploring the various role alternatives which have been institutionalized in the political system, exploring the judge's perception of these institutionalized role alternatives, suggesting the relevant variables most likely to determine his choice, and determining if the role or cluster of roles the judge

---

[21] 359 U. S. 121 (1959). The Court decided, 5–4, that a person acquitted in a federal court of robbing a federally insured bank could later be tried and convicted in an Illinois court for the same offense.
[22] See Joel B. Grossman, "Role-Playing and the Analysis of Judicial Behavior: The Case of Mr. Justice Frankfurter," 11 *Journal of Public Law* (1962), 285–309.

has chosen result in identifiable and meaningful patterns of decision-making.[23] The basic hypothesis of this sort of analysis is that the judge's actual behavior will represent his conception of the nature of his "role" or function in the political system.[24]

It is important to remember that there is no necessary identity between the institutionalized role of "judge" and the actual role behavior of a particular incumbent of a judicial office. The institutionalized role certainly is an important force in determining the judge's actual role behavior. No judge is likely to depart significantly from the contours of that role—particularly from those norms concerned with surface aspects of his behavior as a judge. But within these broad outlines judges may have significant latitude in selecting an appropriate role behavior. The tendency to assume an identity between the institutionalized role and the behavior of an individual judge was the source of many of the sterile explanations of judicial behavior of former generations.

Such surface norms are, of course, quite functional in terms of the needs of the greater political system of which the judiciary is a part. They frequently include some of the more common ritualistic elements that give at least the appearance of continuity and stability; they serve to remind the judge as well as the public of the appropriate behaviors involved in the judicial process. A good example of this sort of "norm" is the minimization of appearances of judicial discretion.

The judiciary is charged with the task of regulating controversial human relationships (in fact the Constitution prohibits the federal courts from hearing "noncontroversial" cases). That a case reaches a high appellate court would indicate that the conflict has not appeared previously in the same form, was not governed by existing precedent, or was governed by a precedent no longer tenable. And the very fact that a conflict must be resolved by the judiciary might indicate that it has proved insoluble by other means. In "arriving at a viable regulation of human relationships," [25] the courts are inevitably expressing their own preferences as to value priorities—values that will change as new judges begin to reflect the newer values of each generation. But our courts have the equally traditional but contradictory function of conserving established values and insuring that the operative rules governing human relationships are both orderly and

---

23 *Ibid.*
24 *Ibid.*, p. 294.
25 Truman, *op. cit.*, p. 487.

predictable.[26]   And the resolution of these conflicting functions is eased if it appears that judges are really the voice of some neutral and impersonal force, that is, "the law," rather than that they make decisions (or "legislate") according to their own predilections. Some scholars have gone so far as to argue that the Supreme Court of the United States should not make decisions except insofar as they can be based on some "neutral principles of constitutional law." [27]

Although the expectation that decisions of the Supreme Court ought only to be based on "neutral" principles is illusory, the expectation that most decisions must appear to have such a basis is not. The opinions of the judges are rarely expressed in terms of candid value preferences. They are, instead, articulated as necessary conclusions reasoned from constitutional premises, notwithstanding the fact that these premises themselves may be ambiguous or controversial. It is interesting that there has been very little challenge to this type of surface norm; the challenges have come mainly to the traditional assertion that judicial behavior could be adequately explained only in such terms.

It is *within* these surface norms that the most important explanations of judicial decision-making are to be found. Here again we find a series of institutionalized norms about what judges can and cannot do. But one of the relevant norms itself is responsible for judicial latitude at this inner core of the decision-making process. With the trial judge, the latitude is primarily one of fact finding.[28] And with the appellate judge, the latitude is one of choosing the criteria by which a conflict is to be resolved.[29] Again using the *Bartkus* case, is this primarily a question of individual rights, a question of the rights of competing jurisdictions to punish for a criminal act, or a question of determining acceptable practices for law-enforcement officials? The case is subject to at least these three approaches. The judge's choice

---

26 *Ibid.* For an interesting commentary on the illusions of judicial certainty, see Jerome Frank, *Law and the Modern Mind* (New York: Tudor, 1936), especially his description of Oliver Wendell Holmes as "the completely adult jurist," pp. 253–260.
27 Herbert Wechsler, "Toward Neutral Principles in Constitutional Law," 73 *Harvard Law Review* (1959), 1–35. See also Arthur S. Miller and Ronald F. Howell, "The Myth of Neutrality in Constitutional Adjudication," 27 *University of Chicago Law Review* (1960), 661–695.
28 See Jerome Frank, *Courts on Trial: Myth and Reality in American Justice* (Princeton, N. J.: Princeton University Press, 1949), pp. 23–24.
29 See Karl Llewellyn, "Remarks on the Theory of Appellate Decision," 3 *Vanderbilt Law Review* (1949–1950), 395–406, and also *The Common Law Tradition: Deciding Appeals* (Boston: Little, Brown, 1960).

of approach is likely to be determined by his view of what the Supreme Court's role ought to be—one of champion of individual rights, one of umpire of the conflicts of the federal system, one of overseeing the process of law enforcement. And it is within the framework of the approach he has chosen (itself a value preference) that a whole range of substantive values can be brought into play.

The four steps by which the judicial role is institutionalized, by which future and present occupants of a judicial role are trained (or socialized) to accept these behavior norms, by which incumbent judges perceive the imperatives and latitudes of the institutionalized role and enact their own role behavior, and by which "acceptable" role behavior is reinforced and deviant role behavior sanctioned, are all keys to the process of judicial decision-making. Each of these four factors provides a means of indirect access to the judiciary, a means of indirect control over the scope, style, and inevitably, content, of judicial decisions.

The relative importance of these indirect access routes is heightened by the unavailability of the more direct means of access found to other parts of the political system. Limitations on direct access to the judiciary are mandated not only by institutional and constitutional requirements, but by the requirements of the institutionalized judicial role. Types of pressures effective on other political bodies are out of bounds insofar as the courts are concerned. The traditions of judicial independence and insulation from political conflict effectively bar such approaches. There are, of course, some approaches such as the filing of an amicus curiae brief which are "less indirect" than others. But the direct personal access which so frequently characterizes the decision-making of other political bodies is not present in the judicial process.

This bar to direct access to the judiciary is strengthened by the conditions under which federal judges are selected. Unlike the selection of officers of the executive and legislative branches, whose terms of office are of short duration, the selection of federal judges is for an indefinite period. Of course, judicial tenure is limited by natural factors and could not be called "permanent." But in one sense it does have a political permanence since the original choice is neither reviewable nor revocable by ordinary political means. Extraordinary means do exist for removing a judge from office, but these are rarely invoked except in cases of extreme deviant behavior. Impeachment as a political weapon was effectively discredited by the failure of the Jeffersonian attack on Justice Samuel Chase in 1805, and impeachment as a control of judicial corruption has long proved inadequate.[30] Efforts to legitimate the recall of judges failed to achieve more than a temporary and limited acceptance, although the same effect is accomplished by having judges popularly elected for short terms.

Furthermore, not only is the selection of a federal judge irrevocable by ordinary means, it is unconditional as well. The new judge takes office on his own terms, so to speak, and he need only respect the institutionalized conventions and expectations of his office to enjoy unlimited tenure. His actions on the bench can be taken without reference to the predilections of his one-time supporters. By obtaining the appointment of a friend for the federal bench, one does not normally receive the opportunity to informally consult or advise the judge on cases pending in his court. Just the opposite is true, of course, in the case of the selection of nonjudicial political officials, where one campaigns in the definite expectation of future rewards in the event of victory. These rewards may be tangible benefits such as patronage, or intangibles such as the right to consult or advise on key issues. On the other hand, any attempt to "follow up" one's support of a successful judicial candidate would be considered a serious infraction of the rules of the game, and for the judge to be receptive to such advances would be a gross violation of his judicial role.

JUDICIAL SELECTION AND THE SOCIALIZATION OF JUDGES

Although in some ways the norms of the judicial-selection process help to insulate the courts from a variety of direct pressures, judicial selection does provide a primary (though not exclusive) means of indirect access to the judiciary. This access may result, in individual instances, from the selection of a judge whose values and approaches to the cases in question are consonant with those who have pushed his candidacy. But this type of access is likely to be haphazard, since no single group can expect uniform control over all nominations. More effective access can be obtained by controlling or influencing the process by which all prospective judges are socialized or trained for the specialized role of "judge" in the political system. And the means

---

[30] The difficulties in formally removing a corrupt judge are effectively stated in Joseph Borkin, *The Corrupt Judge* (New York: Potter, 1962), pp. 189–204. See also Albert P. Blaustein and Charles Porter, *The American Lawyer* (Chicago: University of Chicago Press, 1954), pp. 267–268, and Joseph Harris, *The Advice and Consent of the Senate* (Berkeley: University of California Press, 1953), pp. 30–33.

of controlling this process of socialization rests largely in the recruitment function.[31]

"All members of societies go through common socialization experiences."[32] But these experiences do not prepare them for the specialized roles that every society must have, including the roles of political leadership. It is the recruitment function to draw members of a society out of particular subcultures and "induct them into the specialized roles of the political system, train them in the appropriate skills, provide them with political cognitive maps, values, expectations, and affects."[33] Recruitment thus consists of special role socializations built on the foundation of general socialization.

As used here, recruitment is a generalized description of a variety of activities designed to produce judges with certain types of training, certain sets of values, and certain sets of expectations. The socialization of judges necessarily involves a variety of factors. After the obvious ones such as adequate legal training and experience, basic honesty, and judicial temperament, we can identify such basic role-expectation alternatives as devotion to procedure versus concern for substantive issues, judicial self-restraint versus judicial activism, concern for "the law" as an abstract doctrine versus concern for arriving at "just" settlements of individual cases, and a view of the courts as instruments for social change versus a view of the courts as conservators of the status quo. Judicial selection, considered as one part of the overall recruitment process, is not the only means by which judges are socialized. Thus, the subject of this book, the American Bar Association, does not limit itself to seeking influence via the selection of judges. Through its canons of legal and judicial ethics, and through its influence and control over legal training and bar membership, it seeks to set some of the norms of the institutionalized judicial role and seeks to orient lawyers toward these norms. In its meetings and journals it provides forums for evaluation of judicial actions; and through these same media it tries to educate judges as well as lawyers and the lay public as to proper handling of great constitutional questions or proper responses to judicial actions.

In one sense judicial selection comes "near the end" of the judicial-recruitment process. It acts to reinforce the socialization process by

---

[31] See Gabriel Almond, "A Functional Approach to Comparative Politics," in Almond and James Coleman (Eds.), *The Politics of the Developing Areas* (Princeton, N. J.: Princeton University Press, 1960), pp. 26–31.

[32] *Ibid.*, p. 31.

[33] *Ibid.*

choosing those lawyers who have conformed to the established norms and who therefore give promise of fulfilling the judicial role in an expected manner.   But though the act of selection may contribute little to the socialization of the new judge, it demonstrates visibly and effectively the types of behavior to which prospective judges ought to conform.   If a particular selection system appeared to favor a high degree of prior political involvement rather than intensive legal experience as a necessary prerequisite, the types of preparatory activities in which prospective judges would engage would vary accordingly. At first, these changed patterns might be latent rather than manifest. But they would be very real indeed!   Thus, in another sense, the act of selection could be considered the "initial" act in the process of socializing would-be judges.   The norms of selection give the initial cues as to the type of training and preparation which might lead to the federal bench.

The ways in which prospective judges are socialized depends partially on the nature of the selection process.   And that process is not susceptible to simple categorization or description.   Rather it consists of a variety of forces whose interaction produces a phenomenon called the "selection process."   But what are these forces?   And which among them is responsible for particular aspects of the process?   Which, if any, dominate the process, or make most of the important decisions?

The process of political socialization is necessarily a dynamic one. As the values or conditions of a society change, the training of its future leaders must change accordingly.   Thus, any attempt to describe the process by which federal judges are socialized through recruitment is at once limited by the dynamics of the situation.   Any description of it must recognize that change itself is a constant factor.

The responsibility for selecting federal judges, particularly those below the Supreme Court level, is quite decentralized, and it is impossible to isolate one individual or group of individuals who control the process in its entirety.   There is a wide gap between the formal, constitutionally created, process and the actual selection process. Nonetheless, it is possible to identify the several most important forces involved and to determine the role that each plays in the overall process.

2

⊰⊱

THE POLITICS OF JUDICIAL
SELECTION: AN OVERVIEW

To further prepare for our detailed exploration and analysis of the American Bar Association's role in the process of selecting federal judges, it is necessary to describe that process in some detail. We have already suggested the relationship between judicial selection and judicial decision-making. Here we shall focus on the individuals and groups who are most concerned with and involved in the recruitment of federal judges. We shall pay particular attention to those aspects of the process that are most conducive to the influences of groups such as the American Bar Association.

THE CONSTITUTIONAL BASIS OF JUDICIAL SELECTION

Perhaps we should return briefly to the constitutional basis of the selection process, since an understanding of the competing aims and opposing forces institutionalized by the Constitution of 1787 is necessary. Although constitutional rules often fail to tell the whole story about a particular aspect of the political process—a maxim especially true in this instance—they do provide the framework within which the political process operates, and usually manage to condition the course and content of that process. Constitutional rules can have the effect of giving an advantage to particular groups or interests in the political process; moreover, at least initially, they may generally structure the nature of political leadership and influence.

The rules for selecting federal judges were the subject of extensive debate at the Constitutional Convention. Although the delegates were certainly concerned with securing as judges men of integrity and ability, they were equally aware that the method of selection chosen would also have to satisfy implicit requirements of political stability and balance. The question of selecting federal judges was discussed in relation to the greater issues of the Convention—large state-small state rivalry, executive-legislative checks and balances, and so on—and was ultimately settled in the light of the compromises which resolved these basic issues.

The Convention considered first the selection of the national judiciary by the legislature, a proposal which was included in the Virginia Plan used as a basis for discussion. Opposition to selection of judges by the legislature centered primarily on the fear that Congress could not select men of high qualifications. James Wilson argued that "experience shewed the impropriety of such appointments by numerous bodies. Intrigue, partiality, and concealment were the necessary consequences." [1] Madison did not favor appointment by the legislature, but it was not until the last days of the Convention that he supported appointment by the executive. He then stated that it was important to secure "the responsibility of the executive who would in general be more capable and likely to select fit characters than the legislature, or even the second branch of it, who might hide their selfish motives under the number concerned in the appointment." [2] Those who favored an executive role in the selection process, either independently or in conjunction with the legislature, believed that the President would be most likely to secure able judges.

With Madison's plan of selection by the executive contingent upon a Senate veto failing of adoption, the previous agreement on appointment by the Senate (proposed earlier by Madison) stood through the report of the Committee on Detail. The latter, in its report of August 6, gave the President the power to appoint all officers not otherwise provided for in the Constitution, and gave the Senate the power to appoint Supreme Court judges and ambassadors. However, the Special Committee on Postponed Matters, reporting on September 4, gave the sole appointing power to the President, with the advice and consent of the Senate called for in all cases. It was this compromise—originally offered by Hamilton and rejected—which was written into the final document. [3] Thus, reflecting the checks and balances

---

[1] Quoted in Joseph P. Harris, *The Advice and Consent of the Senate* (Berkeley: University of California Press, 1953), p. 20.

[2] *Ibid.*, p. 22.

[3] *Ibid.*, Ch. 2. See also Charles Warren, *The Making of the Constitution* (Boston: Little, Brown, 1928), pp. 213, 327–329, 531–532, 640–642.

orientation of the framers, the rules for selecting federal judges institutionalized a high degree of conflict.

Furthermore, the Constitution, as it was written in 1787 and as it stands today, made no provision for establishing minimum qualifications of judges as a guide to executive choice. Although the special position and great importance of the judge in western cultures was recognized and embodied in other clauses of the Constitution, the framers chose not to specify the patterns of education, training, and occupation preparatory to assuming judicial office. Even the requisites of citizenship and minimum age imposed on officers of the executive and legislative branches were not applied to the judiciary.

In choosing to follow neither the Continental model, in which judges constituted a separate vocation and received separate training,[4] nor even the British model, in which judges were almost always chosen from a select group of barristers,[5] the framers left a void which could have been—but was not—filled by either Congress or the executive. It is true that Congress, in the Judiciary Act of 1789, created the principle of geographical distribution of Supreme Court justices by assigning them to circuit duty. But Congress has set no formal qualifications for the federal bench. It is tradition alone which has dictated that District Court judges are usually residents of the state and district area in which they serve and that all prospective judges are lawyers.[6] And it is also true that the framers *assumed* that at least the judges of the Supreme Court would be chosen from among the best trained men available—at that time a very small number. In Number 81 of *The Federalist,* Alexander Hamilton predicted that Supreme Court judges would be "selected for their knowledge of the laws, acquired by long and laborious study."

This lack of constitutional guidance on the qualifications of judges never proved to be a serious "handicap" to the appointing authorities. As if by general agreement, the gentry class provided the occupants for every Supreme Court vacancy until 1829, and from that date until the present the vast majority of Supreme Court appointees have been

---

[4] Carl J. Friedrich, *Constitutional Government and Democracy* (Boston: Little, Brown, 1941), p. 106.

[5] Morse Erskine, "The Selection of Judges in England: A Standard for Comparison," 39 *American Bar Association Journal* (1953), 279.

[6] Formal legal training is demanded by custom today, although this was not true in centuries past. Title 28, 134(b) of the United States Code requires federal district judges to be residents of that district before they are appointed to the bench. The nomination of persons living outside the district (provided they do live in the state) is not infrequent.

from "economically advantaged" backgrounds.[7]   In every period of American history, Supreme Court justices have been drawn from the "better" classes of society.[8]   Furthermore, Presidents have only occasionally appointed men of the opposite political party to any federal court, and then usually only to satisfy other tacit requirements of geographical and ethnic balance or political representation.   The standards of selection grew out of the pressures of a variety of forces in the political system.

One result of the lack of constitutional guidance was that the process of judicial selection came to reflect the political standards and balances of each generation.   The process was an "open" one, which was vulnerable at a number of points to a variety of individuals and groups, each of which would strive to have its "own" standards accepted by the appointing agents.   The impact of the selection process on the socialization and recruitment of judges was necessarily dynamic.   The selection process became an effective conduit of forces seeking to reshape the institutionalized judicial role, and through it, the style, scope, and substance of judicial decisions.

THE MAJOR PARTICIPANTS IN THE SELECTION PROCESS

Who are the main actors in the process of selecting federal judges? Although for purposes of analysis we shall consider each of these actors more or less independently, we should keep in mind that it is the interaction between them, rather than occasional individual actions, which make up the essence of the selection process.   But identifying the major actors, the roles they seem to play, and the key decisions they make in the selection process is the necessary base for analysis in depth.

The President, the Attorney General, and the Senate

The constitutional responsibility for selecting justices of the Supreme Court, "by and with the advice and consent of the Senate," rests with the President.   Inferior federal court judges need not be chosen in this manner.   Congress could vest selection of lower-court judges in the "Head of a Department,"—presumably the Chief Justice or even the entire Supreme Court.[9]   But, traditionally, the power to appoint lower-court judges has also rested with the President.

---

[7] John R. Schmidhauser, "The Justices of the Supreme Court: A Collective Portrait," 3 *Midwest Journal of Political Science* (1959), 14.
[8] *Ibid.*

In the exercise of this function, the President could depend on the advice of any person or group. He could—as some have suggested he should—create an independent commission of lawyers and laymen to suggest names; he could delegate the recruitment work to any of his White House staff, or to any Cabinet or other officer of the government. Prior to the Pierce Administration, the clearance function for federal judges, as for all federal officials, rested with the Secretary of State. Pierce's Attorney General, Caleb Cushing, was able to effect a transfer of that responsibility to his own department, where it has since remained.[10]

The Attorney General theoretically recommends to the President, in a formal letter, that "John Doe be appointed to the United States District Court for the Eastern District of Wisconsin," and the President decides whether or not to accept that recommendation and make the nomination. But in practice the Attorney General's letter is a formality. In most cases the choice of a federal judge is the Attorney General's to make—provided only that he makes it within the framework of the relevant norms of behavior which operate on the selection process. No President could devote the time needed to personally consider even all *serious* candidates for each vacancy, although Presidents do vary in the degree of interest they show in judicial-selection problems. Generally, Presidents will control Supreme Court nominations and exhibit some interest in a few of the more important lower-court vacancies.[11]

---

[9] Burke Shartel, "Federal Judges: Appointment, Supervision, and Removal—Some Possibilities Under the Constitution," 28 *Michigan Law Review* (1930), 485, 723, 870.

[10] Rita Cooley, "The Department of Justice and Judicial Nominations," 43 *Journal of the American Judicature Society* (1958), 86.

[11] President Taft had an unusual interest in selecting federal judges himself, and continued this interest when he later became Chief Justice. See Walter Murphy, "Chief Justice Taft and the Lower Court Bureaucracy: A Study in Judicial Administration," 24 *Journal of Politics* (1962), 453.

President Eisenhower is reported to have frequently talked with each candidate before submitting a nomination.—William Rogers, "Judicial Appointments in the Eisenhower Administration," 41 *Journal of the American Judicature Society* (1957), 40. President Kennedy was reported to occasionally overrule the recommendation of his Attorney General, presumably where a powerful senator or other political personage was supporting a candidate whom the Justice Department could not accept.—Interview with Deputy Attorney General Nicholas deB. Katzenbach, November 7, 1962.

Although the Justice Department is primarily responsible for the bulk of the judicial appointments in any administration, the President is often "represented" in the recruitment process by his congressional liaison people, and occasionally through the national party machinery. Senators who are "rebuffed" at the Justice Department can appeal to the White House; and some senators will always operate through the White House staff initially.

Depending on his own personal interests, the Attorney General may or may not play an active role himself in the judicial-selection process. Traditionally, the Deputy Attorney General and *his* staff have handled the recruitment chores, and it is they who establish the foundation of information and recommendations on which the eventual choice is based. The decisions they make, at early stages of the process, in determining which names will be given further consideration and which will be dropped from contention limit the alternatives which the Attorney General has in making his formal recommendations to the President. With the exception of those few nominations that are likely to become major public issues, recruiting judges is essentially a staff operation in the name of the Attorney General—and ultimately in the name of the President.

In addition to the obvious limitations that a staff operation places on the President's prerogatives, his choices are even more circum-scribed by the traditional assertion of senatorial prerogative. In fact, the role of the President in the selection of federal judges is a sub-stantial modification of the plain words of the Constitution. Those of the framers who favored a strong role for the executive in the selection of all public officials appeared to have won their point in the Constitutional Convention. Alexander Hamilton interpreted the Constitution on that point as follows:

. . . It will be the office of the President to NOMINATE, and with the advice and consent of the SENATE to APPOINT. There will, of course, be no exertion of choice on the part of the Senate. They may defeat one choice of the Executive and oblige him to make another; but they cannot themselves CHOOSE—they can only ratify or reject the choice of the President. They might even entertain a preference to some other person at the very moment they were assenting to the one proposed, because there might be no positive ground of opposition to him; and they could not be sure, if they withheld their assent, that the subsequent nomination would fall upon their favorite, or upon any other person in their estimation more meritorious than the one rejected.[12]

In his book, *The Advice and Consent of the Senate,* Professor Joseph Harris supports Hamilton's interpretation. Harris argues that

the phrase "advice and consent" was used in the Convention as synonymous with such terms as "approval," "approbation," and "concurrence," and it was held that this provision gave the Senate a "negative" on appointments by the President. The debates in the Convention do not support the thesis since advanced that the framers of the Constitution intended that the Presi-

---

[12] *The Federalist* (New York: New American Library, Mentor, 1961), p. 405.

dent should secure the *advice*—that is, the recommendation—of the Senate or of individual members, before making a nomination.[13]

It would appear that the power given to the Senate was intended as a safeguard against bad appointments and a salutary influence on the President—a test of the *fitness* of judicial nominees rather than a significant limitation on executive choice. But in delegating to the Senate the power to advise and consent, the framers opened the door to a perversion of the principle of executive responsibility.

The extent of this senatorial limitation on executive choice has varied with particular administrations. Few Presidents in the twentieth century have accorded senators as much leeway as did President Harding, who stated that "he would look to the Republican . . . Senators from the state to give final judgment as to the wisdom of the appointment." If, according to Harding, the senators were to recommend men "who prove to be unworthy or lack the ability to perform the duties of the offices to which they are appointed, the President will place upon them the responsibility for whatever trouble arises through this means."[14] But on the other hand, no President has found it possible—or perhaps even desirable—to ignore the advice of individual senators.

Professor Harris has concluded that historically the effective power over a majority of judicial nominations has rested with the Senate.[15] But more recent data—including some presented later—indicate that there has been at least a slight move of the pendulum toward the President. With the growth of the Presidency as an institution, the vastly increased prerogatives of that office, and the widespread acceptance of the President as *the* responsible national leader, the judicial selection process has, like many others, become more centralized.

Of the three levels of federal courts, the President's latitude for choice is greatest with regard to nominations to the Supreme Court and least (but not nonexistent) concerning nominees to the District Courts. With rare exceptions Presidents have considered Supreme Court appointments to be *their* personal prerogative, and senators of the same party as the President have always considered District Court appointments to fall within *their* sphere of responsibility. Nominations to the Courts of Appeals and (formerly) nonconstitutional courts appear to "go either way," depending on the case at hand. The choice more often than not is the President's, but senatorial opposition and

---

[13] Harris, *op. cit.*, pp. 28–38.
[14] Quoted in *ibid.*, p. 116.
[15] *Ibid.*, p. 20.

prerogative cannot be discounted. Occasionally, the President will circumvent certain opposition and invocation of senatorial courtesy by appointing a resident of one state to a Circuit Court in another area, or occasionally to the District Court in the District of Columbia.[16] Where there is no senator of the President's party in a particular state, the President may rely on the state party officials to suggest prospective candidates for a judicial vacancy. Although no state party official can exercise the pressure in behalf of a candidate that a senator could, the President usually relies on those who are "close" to the local situation.

The reasons why Presidents have chosen particular men for the Supreme Court vary. Ideology has often played an important role in determining the nominee, but often other factors appear to have been just as decisive. Political rewards, personal friendships, party service, and even prior judicial experience have been the major justifications for Supreme Court appointments.

TABLE 2.1

SUPREME COURT APPOINTMENTS BY POLITICAL PARTY,
1933–1962

President	Democrat	Republican	Per Cent Own Party
Roosevelt (Dem.)	8	1	88.9
Truman (Dem.)	3	1	75.0
Eisenhower (Rep.)	1	4	80.0
Kennedy (Dem.)	2	0	100.0

All Presidents have made most of their Supreme Court selections from among the members of their own political party. But it is also customary to have at least one member of each major political party on the high bench, and to satisfy this "requirement" Presidents have at least occasionally chosen "out-party" judges. As Table 2.1 indicates, three of the last four Presidents have each chosen one "out-party"

---

[16] Illustrative of this situation was the 1962 appointment of Louisiana Federal District Judge J. Skelly Wright to the Court of Appeals for the District of Columbia. As a result of a series of strong pro-integration decisions, Wright was unpopular in his home state, and Senator Russell Long reportedly told the President that he could not expect to be reelected to the Senate in 1962 if he did not veto Wright's promotion to the Fifth Circuit Court of Appeals. President Kennedy then appointed Wright to the Court of Appeals for the District of Columbia, thus making a merited promotion and not antagonizing a powerful senator.

judge, and at no time during the period 1933–1963 has the Supreme Court consisted exclusively of justices belonging to one political party. The principle of religious and geographic balance has also been influential, although no President has seemingly considered himself absolutely bound by it. President Truman replaced Catholic Frank Murphy with a non-Catholic, and the "Catholic" seat on the court was vacant until 1956 when President Eisenhower appointed William Brennan. The "Jewish" seat, which began with the appointment of Louis Brandeis in 1916, has never been vacant; in fact, President Hoover's appointment of Benjamin Cardozo in 1930 to replace Oliver Wendell Holmes temporarily doubled the "Jewish representation" on the Court. Questions of geographic balance have also been considered appropriate and each of the major regions of the country has been represented in recent years.

Ideology appears to have been a frequently important factor. For example, Grant's two appointments in 1871 were made on the basis of the known views of the appointees on the legal-tender issue, whereas all of Franklin Roosevelt's Supreme Court appointees were New Deal supporters. Ex-President Taft raised the issue of the ideology of prospective Supreme Court appointees during the 1920 campaign:

Mr. Wilson is in favor of a latitudinarian construction of the Constitution of the United States, to weaken the protection it should afford against Socialist raids upon property rights.

He has made three appointments to the Supreme Court. He is understood to be greatly disappointed in the attitude of the first of these [Mr. Justice McReynolds] upon such questions. The other two [Mr. Justices Brandeis and Clarke] represent a new school of constitutional construction, which if allowed to prevail, will greatly impair our fundamental law. Four of the incumbent Justices are beyond the retirement age of seventy, and the next President will probably be called upon to appoint their successors. There is no greater domestic issue in this election than the maintenance of the Supreme Court as the bulwark to enforce the guarantee that no man shall be deprived of his property without due process of law. . . .[17]

But on the other hand, ideology has appeared to be a minor factor in other instances, such as Eisenhower's appointment of William Brennan, Wilson's appointment of McReynolds, and Hoover's selection of Cardozo.

Supreme Court "politics" can also be important. In at least one instance in the twentieth century, the selection of a Chief Justice (Vinson) was apparently determined in part by an internal situation

---

[17] Quoted in Archibald MacLeish and E. F. Prichard, Jr. (Eds.), *Law and Politics: Occasional Papers of Felix Frankfurter* (New York: Harcourt, Brace, 1939), p. 37.

on the Court—the raging feud between Justices Black and Jackson.[18] Vinson, also a close personal friend of President Truman and a former circuit judge, was chosen ostensibly for his ability to bring together the warring justices whose battle had brought the Supreme Court into considerable disrepute.

The power to make nominations to the lower federal courts, unlike the power with regard to the Supreme Court, is not entirely the President's own. It must be shared with individual senators and selected leaders of the President's party. The party acts as a mediate for the recruitment of judges of the lower courts. It performs the important functions of testing and sifting prospective judicial candidates by making them perform a variety of tasks. Although it could be argued that some of these tasks are not relevant to the training of a judge, many of them do provide the future judge with an indispensable "cognitive map" of political society. In fact, the initiative for a judicial nomination in a particular state will often pass to the senator(s) of that state if he is of the party of the President. If there is no senator of the President's party, the state party committee will normally be asked to suggest prospective candidates.

Where there is neither a senator of the President's own party nor an available and trusted party leader, the President could ask a leading congressman or other elected public official to perform this "service." In 1961 President Kennedy referred much of the judicial patronage from New York City to Congressman Emanuel Celler, chairman of the House Judiciary Committee and dean of the New York City congressional delegation. Kennedy had refused to consult with either the Tammany Hall leadership or the Reform Democratic organization led by the Mayor until they had resolved their heated feud.[19]

If the President decides to appoint a member of the opposition party (frequently in a state with no senators from his own party or in a state with multiple-judge courts), he may consult with a variety of sources. President Kennedy used Republican Minority Leader Everett Dirksen as a liaison between the White House and Republican senators. Dirksen was asked to solicit suggestions from the senators in those states which had two Republican senators, though suggestions of names made directly by the senators were accorded equal treatment.[20] Appointing an "out-party" judge involves very delicate ma-

---

[18] *New York Times,* June 7, 1946, p. 1.
[19] U. S. Congress, Senate, Committee on the Judiciary, *Hearings on the Nomination of Irving Ben Cooper,* 87th Cong., 2nd Sess., 1962, p. 3.
[20] Interview with Assistant Deputy Attorney General Joseph Dolan, November 2, 1962.

neuvering, since the state party officials of the President's party are not likely to acquiesce willingly in this "loss" of prime patronage. Although the President will not always choose the candidate suggested by a senator or leader of his own party, he will more than likely select a name that is satisfactory to these people. If there are no senators from his own party in a particular state, the President will probably have greater flexibility of choice, since no party leader with whom he deals could actually veto a nomination in the way a senator could. Thus, a President whose party dominates the Senate has to contend with more senators than a President—such as Eisenhower—whose party controls but one-third of the Senate.

Not all senators feel equally strongly about the responsibilities of the Senate in "advising"—as opposed to "consenting"—in the judicial-selection process. There have been at least a few senators who have opposed any senatorial participation whatever, suggesting that instead of being considered as typical executive appointments, judgeships be handled under a different set of rules:

After long experience and close observation, I have reached the conclusion that senatorial meddling with judicial nominations is an unmixed evil. If the senators from a state are to enjoy the prescriptive right to indicate to the President the man whom he is to nominate, the calibre of the nominee is apt to be determined by the quality of the senators. If they are responsive to a corrupt local political organization or are themselves incapable of estimating judicial fitness and if the President accepts their choice, he may inflict lasting injury upon the entire judicial system.[21]

Other senators have continued to "suggest" names to the Attorney General for investigation and consideration as possible federal judges. But they have not insisted on these choices to the exclusion of all others. If, however, a senator makes "his" choices public prior to any consultation with the Attorney General, it is a good bet that he will adamantly insist on these appointments. He has staked his prestige, and if the man is at least minimally qualified he will probably receive the nomination. Consider as typical the following letter from the two Democratic senators of a southern state to President Kennedy in 1961:

We have, after most serious and thorough consideration of many candidates and recommended persons, come to agreement on our recommendations for a number of Federal appointments in _____.
We realize, of course, that some of these appointments are contingent upon

---

21 George Wharton Pepper, as quoted by Harris, *op. cit.*, p. 302.

creation of the posts, which has not taken place yet, but which is anticipated in the near future.

In other cases herein mentioned, flexibility is needed to permit incumbents and recommended successors alike to arrange their affairs.

However, our action in making public our recommendations prior to the accomplishment of these and other procedures was governed by two main factors: (1) the need for early preparation for the tackling of our heavily over-burdened federal dockets in _____, and (2) the need to advise others interested in these appointments of a decision so that they might pursue other courses in which they are interested.

[Here follows a list of names, one for each present and prospective vacancy in the state.]

It will be greatly appreciated by us both if favorable action can be taken on these recommendations as soon as the proper time arrives in each instance.[22]

Of the names listed in this letter, all were subsequently appointed to the federal bench despite a borderline report on the qualifications of one of them.

Although in this instance the two senators from a state teamed up to make recommendations, they frequently alternate (assuming they are both of the President's party), with each senator responsible for filling every other vacancy with the concurrence of his colleague. There is evidence in at least several recent cases that a second senator has publicly approved of the choice of his colleague and privately tried to sabotage the nomination through intercession with the Attorney General or the local bar association.[23]

For the obvious reason that the source of a lower-court nomination may not be readily identifiable, the motivations of choice are more obscure than with Supreme Court nominations. Personal friendship with the sponsoring senator appears to be a major factor, whereas political ideology (to the extent that a senator's friends may not share his values) does not. Where the nomination originates with the Justice Department, the selection may be from the ranks of United States attorneys and other federal officials. In either case, there is about an even chance that the nomination will go to a state or federal public

---

[22] By agreement with Assistant Deputy Attorney General Dolan, the anonymity of the authors of letters such as this will be preserved.

[23] This is true not only of senators, but of other public figures as well, who are asked by a candidate or friends of a candidate to write a letter of recommendation. Such letters, with a copy usually sent to the candidate, are usually discounted by the Justice Department as being unreliable. Several members of the Attorney General's staff have reported that as often as not writers of such letters privately communicate with the Justice Department to give a more honest—and usually less favorable—appraisal of the candidate.

or party officeholder,[24] as opposed to a lawyer who has been engaged primarily in private practice. But even if the nominee holds no public office at the time of his selection, there is a strong likelihood that he will have performed some substantial service for the party organization, for the individual senator, or for the nominating President.[25]

Two factors which appear to be about as important in determining the selection of lower-court judges as in the selection of Supreme Court judges are party label and geographic and ethnic balance. The re-

TABLE 2.2
LOWER-COURT APPOINTMENTS BY POLITICAL PARTY, 1933–1962

	President and Party			
Court	Roosevelt (Democrat)	Truman (Democrat)	Eisenhower (Republican)	Kennedy (Democrat)
Courts of Appeals				
Democrat	50	24	3	17
Republican	4	3	42	0
(Per cent own party)	(92.6%)	(88.9%)	(93.3%)	(100.0%)
District Courts				
Democrat	138	92	6	83
Republican	2	6	123	8
(Per cent own party)	(93.6%)	(93.8%)	(95.3%)	(91.2%)

quirement of party consistency insures that a very high percentage of a President's appointments to the lower federal courts will be given to men or women who are at least nominally identified with the President's party. As Table 2.2 demonstrates, 90 per cent is a floor beneath which few Presidents go in choosing federal judges.[26]

---

24 See Table 7.6, Chapter 7, infra.
25 Illustrative of the general practice, a survey made of twenty-eight appointments during the last three years of the Truman Administration showed the new judges to have the following backgrounds: a brother of a United States senator, a son of a United States senator, a former United States senator (interim appointee), two former state Attorneys-General, one former governor, one manager of a successful gubernatorial campaign, two delegates to the Democratic National Convention, six state legislators, and two party officials. Thirteen of the remaining forty-eight were taken from the ranks of the Justice Department.—Compiled by Ben R. Miller, "Politics and the Courts," 42 American Bar Association Journal (1956), 939.
26 Since the first administration of Grover Cleveland, no President has made less than 82.2 per cent of his judicial appointments from the ranks of his own party.— "Report of the Standing Committee on Federal Judiciary," 81 Annual Reports of the American Bar Association (1956), 439. (Hereinafter cited as ABA Reports.)

Even when so inclined, all Presidents have found that deviation from party consistency is very difficult. The pressure for patronage is one that few Presidents can completely withstand, no matter how good their intentions. When President Kennedy assumed office in 1961, the federal bench was almost evenly divided between Republicans and Democrats, and there was considerable pressure on him from bar groups and Republicans to preserve this balance. Counterbalanced against these pressures was the fact that the Democrats had been out of the White House for eight years, two-thirds of the Senate was Democratic, and the Democratic congressional leadership had gambled in the eighty-sixth Congress and had not passed a new judgeship bill pending the outcome of the 1960 presidential election. Thus, when it became evident that Kennedy would have to fill perhaps as many as one hundred judgeships in his first year in office, all "good" intentions of bipartisanship were simply tabled. Of his first eighty-five original appointments, eighty-four were Democrats and one was a member of the New York State Liberal Party—a close relative of the Democratic Party. President Kennedy did resubmit the names of three Republicans whose nominations had been pending, and the Congress even rejected one of these.

President Kennedy did select a number of Republicans, but it was late in 1962 before these appointments began coming through. According to Assistant Deputy Attorney General Joseph Dolan, it was always Administration policy to make a number of "out-party" appointments, but because of patronage and other pressures these naturally take longer.[27]

The requirement of ethnic and geographic balance is also important at the lower-court level. It is illustrative that despite their inability to agree on the same three candidates for the District Court in Illinois in 1950, President Truman and Senator Paul Douglas each planned to choose a Protestant, Catholic, and Jew—conforming to that area's notion of "balance."[28] In 1956 President Eisenhower's appointment of Solicitor General Simon Sobeloff ran into opposition from South Carolina's senators, who felt that their state and not Maryland, from which Sobeloff came, was "entitled" to that vacancy on the Fourth Circuit Court of Appeals.[29] Since both of the South Carolina senators

---

27 Interview with Assistant Deputy Attorney General Joseph Dolan, November 2, 1962.

28 Harris, *op. cit.*, pp. 321–323.

29 *Congressional Quarterly Weekly Report*, May 11, 1956, p. 536. Sobeloff was also opposed because he had written the government's brief, later adopted by the Supreme Court, in the second *Brown* decision.

were of a different party than the President, they were unable to block the Soboloff nomination by invoking senatorial courtesy, but did manage to prolong the hearings for an embarrassing length of time.

In the frequent "conflict" that occurs between the President and a powerful senator of his own party over filling a judicial vacancy, each has certain weapons at his disposal, any of which might prove decisive in a particular case. If the President can show, for example, that *his* choices are substantially better qualified, or have received higher professional endorsement than those of the senator, the latter may be reluctant to continue supporting his candidate. Increased public receptivity to bar groups publicly evaluating judicial candidates has become a strong weapon for the President. If the senator's choice has not yet been made public (and there is still room for negotiation), the Attorney General (or Deputy or Assistant Deputy Attorney General) is often able to dissuade the senator from backing a man who will probably be rated as not qualified by the Standing Committee on Federal Judiciary of the American Bar Association. Through the informal report on each candidate made by the Committee, the Attorney General is aware of facts—often derogatory to the candidate—which the senator may not know about. Furthermore, the Attorney General is privy to the complete FBI report made on each serious candidate, a report which could uncover information embarrassing to the senator endorsing the candidate. The FBI report itself is not made public, but whatever information it obtains is as likely as not to be eventually uncovered. Thus, although this type of pressure may well cause considerable resentment by the senator toward the administration, it is very effective. For no senator wishes to acquire the reputation of "selecting" mediocre or unqualified men for high public office.[30] Despite frequent observations to the contrary, the pressure to appoint well-qualified judges is understood and accepted by most participants in the selection process. In the long run, and with very few exceptions, "good" appointments are good politics.

Another presidential weapon is, of course, that only he can make the nomination; the senator may block it through the invocation of senatorial courtesy, but no senator could, in the last instance, "force" the appointment of any particular candidate. Delays of many months, and even years, are not unknown when a President wishes to pressure

---

[30] The uses of the ABA Committee by the Attorney General as an intervening "third force" and the possible responses of senators so pressured are discussed at length in Chapters 5 and 6.

a recalcitrant senator. No senator likes to accept responsibility for a heavy backlog of cases in the courts of his state.

A final weapon which the President has at his disposal if he wishes to insist on a certain nomination is the recess appointment. By having his candidate assume judicial office while Congress is not in session, the President forces the Senate and its Judiciary Committee to consider not only the qualifications of the nominee, but the effect of removing him from participation in cases in which he is already involved—to the detriment and cost of the litigants. Furthermore, if the candidate's qualifications are challenged, his interim service is an opportunity to disprove such allegations. Of course, this is not a very potent weapon in the face of a forceful assertion of senatorial courtesy, but it is an advantage. This advantage is greatest when a Supreme Court or key Circuit Court nomination is at stake. Hearings on nominations at this level are usually more concerned with the ideology and political beliefs of the candidate, and a nominee of the President may effectively parry embarrassing questions—such as his stand on integration or "communism in government"—because they purportedly bear resemblance to questions that might be litigated before his court.[31] This potential does not usually exist at a subcommittee hearing on a nomination to the District Court, since these sessions are often perfunctory and concerned primarily if not exclusively with questions of professional qualifications, and rarely with interrogations into political belief. If the qualifications of the candidate *have* been challenged, however, interim service could be an advantage.

The senator who is of the same party as the President has a number of opportunities to block a nomination he opposes, although as we have seen he is not as effective in overcoming strong presidential resistance to his own choices. He can persuade the Attorney General to refrain from making a certain nomination by proving that *his* candidate is superior. Prior to the establishment of the liaison between the American Bar Association and the Attorney General, a senator could turn a favorable local bar association recommendation to *his* advantage and "demonstrate" that his candidates were superior.[32] This

---

[31] See U. S. Congress, Senate, Committee on the Judiciary, *Hearings on the Nomination of William Brennan*, 85th Cong., 1st Sess., 1957.

[32] By polling the Chicago and Illinois bar associations in 1951, Senator Paul Douglas was able to gather considerable support for "his" two candidates for District Court vacancies in Illinois, as opposed to two selections by President Truman. The President had not consulted Douglas at all, but had acted on the advice of Scott Lucas, a personal friend and United States senator recently defeated for reelection, and of Representative Adolph Sabbath of Illinois, whose nephew was one of the nominees. See Harris, *op. cit.*, pp. 321–323.

"weapon" has now been preempted, as it were, by the President, and to all intents and purposes is no longer "available" to the senator except in the unusual case of complete disagreement between the local or state bar association of his state and the American Bar Association Committee on Federal Judiciary, and this possibility, as we shall see later, is remote.

A powerful senator, of course, need not attempt to justify his backing of a particular candidate. If he is solidly entrenched politically in his own state, and knows that the President can ill afford to challenge him, he is in a good position to have his candidate nominated. Concerning his support of a man for district judge in 1930, Senator Reed of Pennsylvania offered the classic claim for the exercise of this senatorial privilege: ". . . I thought for awhile that I had found a good man in Luzerne County, which is where Wilkes-Barre is, and then I thought I had found a man in Tunkhannock. . . . All of these men I considered. I wanted to get the best one. . . . So far as this being somebody else's choice, it is not. It is my choice. It is my free choice. . . ." [33]

This position brought Reed into conflict with the Hoover Administration's "new" policy of appointing only qualified people to the federal bench. Albert Watson, the senator's choice, had been opposed by most of the bar on the ground that he failed even to approximate minimum standards. After months of waiting, Senator Reed delivered an ultimatum that if the President did not appoint Watson, "he could expect no support from the Pennsylvania delegation in Congress." [34] Hoover made the nomination and, after considerable debate, it was approved by the Senate.

Hoover's capitulation—unusual only in the degree of publicity which the dialogue received—indicates that no President can frequently afford to alienate key senators as the price for a particular nomination to the District Court bench, or even to the Circuit bench. A spokesman for the Kennedy Administration has commented privately that after all the negotiation and pressuring is completed, "we simply can't turn down _____ [an important Committee Chairman and Southern Moderate] provided his candidate meets minimum specifications."

Appointments to the federal district court are not isolated instances of judgment, but are intimately involved in a vortex of political decisions of greater as well as lesser importance. Franklin Roosevelt's attitude, as described by Joseph Harris, bears out this maxim:

---

[33] Quoted in Harris, op. cit., p. 315.
[34] Ibid., p. 318.

President Franklin D. Roosevelt was evidently less impressed with the importance of maintaining high standards for judicial appointments than his predecessor, and as a result, he had fewer conflicts with the Senate over nominations to the Bench. He appointed a number of eminent attorneys to the circuit court of appeals, in which he had a freer hand; but for district judgeships he ordinarily accepted the nominee with political backing without insisting on high standards of qualifications. He followed a policy like that of Lincoln, who did not hesitate to appoint incompetent men to lesser posts when larger policies were at stake.[35]

Yet what may have been true in the 1930s is not necessarily true in the 1960s, and both the President and the senator may find their freedom of choice in judicial selection circumscribed by increased public and professional concern, a concern which may limit the President but is a greater impediment to the senatorial prerogative. Assuming that occasional capitulation by the President to the demands of an important senator is an *unavoidable* concession, the administration will normally try to work these "borderline" nominations into slots where they will do the least damage, for example, multiple-judge courts where there are already a number of capable judges sitting. To be avoided is the choice of a "barely qualified" judge for a single-judge court where he may operate—"free of benevolent influences"—for a long time. It must be emphasized that though such concessions to senatorial pressure *are* occasionally unavoidable, they come only after extended bargaining between the Attorney General and the "recalcitrant" senator has taken place.

If the senator is unsuccessful in reaching an accord with the administration over a judicial nomination, and it selects a person whom he opposes, he may redirect his efforts toward the Senate Judiciary Committee. Prior to considering any nomination, the chairman of the Committee writes to each of the senators from the state in which the candidate resides—regardless of their party affiliation—and requests that each senator reply within one week on his "blue slip" if he opposes the nomination in question. The senators queried are invited to sit with the Committee considering the nomination, either to support or oppose the nomination. If the blue slip is returned with an unfavorable comment, or if the senator publicly invokes senatorial courtesy and declares the candidate "personally obnoxious" to him (and he is "eligible" to invoke such privilege), the nomination will normally be rejected. A senator can frequently delay confirmation by not returning the blue slip or requesting "more time" to consider

---

[35] *Ibid.*, p. 320.

it. This delay could result in the lapse of the nomination in question
if the Senate adjourns in the meantime.

The Sitting Judiciary

The sitting judiciary has no official role in the selection of federal
judges, but it is not surprising that in virtually *all* cases the views of
some judges are solicited or offered. There is no uniform manner in
which judges can express their opinions on judicial nominations.
Harlan Fiske Stone is reported to have been very influential in the
selection of both Frankfurter and Cardozo, and was himself recommended for promotion to Chief Justice by outgoing Chief Justice
Charles Evans Hughes.[36] William Howard Taft is reported to have
been instrumental in the selection of Pierce Butler and Edward Sanford
to the Supreme Court and of a number of lower-court judges.[37] When
a recent proposed nomination to the Circuit Court of Appeals was
delayed for two years because of an intraparty dispute between the
senators and the Attorney General, a number of prominent jurists
sought to break the deadlock. One Supreme Court justice wrote to
Attorney General Brownell in 1957 that ". . . _____ is one of those
rare creatures whose talents and capabilities so far exceed those even
of able men that in talking of him one must indulge in conscious
understatement in order to avoid disbelief on the part of those who
have not had intimate experience with his capacities." [38] A year later
another justice wrote to Deputy Attorney General Walsh:

. . . if the situation as to filling the existing vacancy in the CA . . . has
become any more fluid, I strongly urge your consideration of _____.
He is superbly qualified for the position, and I am sure that his appointment
would be regarded by the Bar as an outstanding one reflecting great credit
on the Administration.

I need hardly say that I write without _____'s knowledge and only
because of my high regard for him as a lawyer and as a man. It is not often
that such a "natural" for this important job comes to hand.

---

[36] Alpheus T. Mason, *Harlan Fiske Stone: Pillar of the Law* (New York: Viking
Press, 1956), p. 566.

[37] Walter F. Murphy, *Elements of Judicial Strategy* (Chicago: University of Chicago
Press, 1964), pp. 73–78, 113–120. See also David J. Danelski, *A Supreme Court
Justice Is Appointed* (New York: Random House, 1964).

[38] This nomination was entangled with the proposal to create new judges. The
senior senator's choice was a Democrat already sitting on the District Court who
was rated almost as highly as _____ by the ABA Committee. The senator's
choice was elevated to the Court of Appeals by the succeeding administration.

P.S. _____ possesses the other qualifications which I suppose are also factors in the discussion.[39]

In 1959 Retired Circuit Judge Learned Hand wrote to President Eisenhower:

I think there have been not more than two occasions during the long period I have served as a judge when I felt it permissible to write a letter in favor of anyone for a judicial appointment. However I feel so strongly that the . . . Circuit would be greatly benefited by the appointment of Mr. _____ that I cannot forbear writing to you to express my hope that you may see fit to fill the vacancy now existing in the circuit by selecting him. I have not the slightest doubt that as a Circuit Judge he would be an addition to [the] Court, as great as, if not greater than, any one else you could choose; not only because of his unblemished reputation and high scholarship, but because of his balanced wisdom and wide outlook.

_____ was appointed to the Circuit Court shortly thereafter!

Sitting judges can also play a negative role. In 1952 a number of judges of the Federal District Court for the Southern District of California appeared at a subcommittee hearing to oppose the nomination of Ernest A. Tolin (later confirmed) on the grounds that he was inexperienced and had an "unclean reputation" as United States attorney.[40]

When a judge is serving via recess appointment pending confirmation, inquiries can be made of his colleagues regarding certain of his qualifications or deficiencies which have been drawn into question. Such was the case in 1961 when Judge Sylvester Ryan, presiding judge of the District Court for the Southern District of New York was asked to comment on the judicial temperament—or lack of it—of Judge Irving Ben Cooper, yet to receive confirmation. Ryan's letter stated that he found Cooper to be "most industrious, cooperative, and competent. His work as a judge has been of exceptionally high character and he has disposed of a large number of suits by trial and settlement." [41] In obvious allusion to the charges filed by the Association of the Bar of the City of New York and the American Bar Association, that Cooper was lacking in judicial temperament and had a long record

---

[39] The "other qualifications" mentioned are _____'s religious affiliation—Jewish —and party affiliation—Republican. The other candidate was also Jewish, but, alas, a Democrat!

[40] U. S. Congress, Senate, Committee on the Judiciary, *Hearings on the Nomination of Ernest Tolin*, 82nd Cong., 2nd Sess., 1952, pp. 13–31.

[41] U. S. Congress, Senate, Committee on the Judiciary, *Hearings on the Nomination of Irving Ben Cooper*, 87th Cong., 2nd Sess., 1962, pp. 18–19.

of hostility toward court personnel, Ryan stated that no evidence of this trait had presented itself while Cooper sat as a federal judge. (Other aspects of the Irving Ben Cooper case will be considered in Chapter 6.)

Very clearly, the amount of influence a sitting judge can exert on the nomination depends on his personal stature, his degree of access to the appointing authority, and the stage of the process at which he acts. A Chief Justice, like Taft, who has the ear of the President, may indeed become a "judge maker," but even Taft's efforts in this area were not uniformly appreciated by the men who served as President during his Chief Justiceship.[42] Judicial influence at the Senate stage is least likely to be effective, since the momentum *toward* confirmation of a nominee is usually overpowering. Unless the judge who speaks in opposition to a nominee has specific facts or evidence of dishonesty or incompetence to support his argument, his battle is an uphill one. Judicial *support* of a nomination at the Senate stage, except when there is a serious doubt about the nominee, is just frosting on the cake, since most senators believe that the most powerful argument in behalf of any judicial candidate is that he was selected by the President. The Cooper case, which is an exception to many of these "rules," was the rare instance when the favorable testimony of a judge (Ryan) was an effective solvent of the considerable adverse testimony.

In the past decade, the sitting judiciary appears to have acquired a more formal role in the judicial-selection process. The Attorney General's office regularly communicates with sitting judges in the area where a vacancy is to be filled, receives confidential evaluations of lawyers being considered for possible appointment and also suggestions of other possible candidates. Although little publicized, this source is of great value to the Justice Department.

The sitting judiciary is also in a position to exert considerable influence through the medium of local bar groups and the Standing Committee on Federal Judiciary of the American Bar Association. In evaluating each prospective judicial nominee, the Committee interviews lawyers and judges from the candidate's home area—with whom and before whom he has practiced. Adverse confidential reports from judges are likely to adversely affect the ABA Committee's recommendation, and ultimately perhaps the candidate's chances of receiving the nomination. Given the predisposition of President Eisenhower and,

---

[42] See Walter F. Murphy, "Chief Justice Taft and the Lower Court Bureaucracy: A Study in Judicial Administration," 24 *Journal of Politics* (1962), 453.

to a lesser extent, of President Kennedy to heed at least the negative recommendations of the ABA Committee, the influence of the sitting judiciary in the selection of federal judges through the medium of the organized bar appears to be substantial.

The Judicial Candidate

The judicial candidate himself often plays a much larger role in the selection process than is customarily recognized. Although the American myth of the "office seeking the man" is applied to all public offices, it is perhaps most influential in setting the norms of behavior for candidates for judicial office. Aspiring presidential candidates never "announce" their obvious intentions until a short time before the quadrennial campaign year begins. But there *is* a time at which such an announcement is proper. On the other hand, the relevant folklore does not accommodate, at any stage in the process, a similar announcement by a judicial candidate.

Nevertheless, although refraining from publicly throwing their wigs in the ring, candidates for federal judgeships (particularly District Court positions) often wage extensive campaigns. In fact, except insofar as there is no necessity to make a public appeal for votes, as is required of a state judge who must seek election, there is a similarity between the efforts of all aspiring judges, regardless of the jurisdiction in which they serve and the type of selection process.

Most frequently, the campaign of an aspiring judicial candidate is directed toward the senator(s) of his state who are of the President's party, or to the state party organization if there are no senators of the President's party. He may write to inform the senators or party officials of his availability, his credentials, and often of his meritorious service in behalf of the party or in the personal organization of the senators of that state. Occasionally, the candidate (privately, of course) directs his efforts toward the Attorney General, although the Justice Department would still ask for "clearance" from the senators or party officials of his state. Frequently, the campaign will include the solicitation of letters of recommendation from public figures, including judges. Despite the intensity of some campaigns, the candidate will never publicly admit that he is doing something as unseemly as "running" for a judgeship. But running he is, and with the exception of a few well-known lawyers or political figures who may literally be "chosen" by the recruiting agents, the candidate who does not make at least a minimum effort in his own behalf is likely to remain a private citizen.

Interest Groups

In the complex process of federal judicial selection, various kinds of interest groups become involved in a number of ways and at a number of points in the process. A group may seek to suggest candidates of its own, but this has to be done discreetly, since a candidate "belonging" to a particular group may be bypassed or attacked as not likely to be an impartial judge. Much more likely, the group will attempt to exert pressure at either the prenomination or confirmation stages, which will result in the selection of judges who, although they may not be the group's "own" men, probably will be sympathetic to its values. "Group membership need not be formal to be effective," [43] and a judge with no formal connections with a group may hold an intellectual commitment that dominates his thoughts.

In either case, the pressure may be explicit, in the form of an attempt to veto or engineer a particular nomination, or it may be implicit, in the form of having certain criteria of selection accepted by the appointing authority. The type of pressure exerted, and the point in the process to which it is directed, will depend on the nature, size, resources, and goals of the particular group as well as on the type of decision-making process in which influence is sought.

The approach or combination of approaches is determined by three factors: (1) the available avenues of access as determined by the formal structure and norms of the particular process; (2) the peculiar resources of the group which lead it to favor certain courses of action over others; and (3) the perception by the group's leaders of the most effective way to translate the group's resources into effective political action.

Approaches to the federal judicial-selection process are numerous. Since at one time or another decisions are to be made by individual senators, state party officials, local bar groups, judges, the President, the Attorney General, and finally the Senate itself, each of these "points" in the process becomes the potential object of group forays. Approaches are also governed by certain norms, such as the nonuse of mass-propaganda techniques (except in terms of general objectives), emphasis on professional qualifications rather than political values, and the construction of a "candidate-draft" image of the prospective nominee. But even these norms are not always followed. A group reduced to the position of seeking only to block the confirmation of a particular candidate does not normally feel constrained to bypass the

---

[43] David B. Truman, *The Governmental Process* (New York: Knopf, 1951), p. 489.

less-subtle approaches. It has, after all, nothing more to lose. Clearly, if at all possible, the advantage lies with the group that can exert its influence at the earliest point in the process—that is, at the prenomination stage.

Depending on their peculiar resources and interests, different groups have gained access to different stages in the selection process. The Chamber of Commerce, for example, could not be said to have gained, in 1964, a high degree of access to the presidential stage. But, on the other hand, the Chamber has a host of supporters in the Senate, any or all of whom might be persuaded to take up its fight in the legislative arena. The Chamber, of course, could send its own representative to testify at the hearings on a nomination it wished to block. But senatorial manpower would have to be enlisted to carry on the fight in (1) interrogating favorable witnesses at the hearings, (2) stating its case at the executive session of the Committee at which all decisions on confirmation are made, and (3) arguing against the nomination on the floor of the Senate if necessary.

Of course, any group that has a foothold in the Senate stage only is reduced to fighting a defensive battle. The odds against defeating any single nomination are distinctly unfavorable, and, even in the slight chance of victory (that is, rejection of the nomination), the battle may have to be refought if the next nominee is equally objectionable to the group involved.

Despite this poor chance of success, most groups are likely to exercise overt pressure on individual senators. Access in any form is more difficult at the presidential level, and, even if achieved, is likely to be diluted. This is not to say that groups do not try to exert influence at the presidential level; there is ample testimony to such efforts in the voluminous files of letters in the Justice Department for the many candidates for each judicial vacancy. But the process of recruitment has become so routine and the depths of investigation so thorough that one or a thousand letters from a group with no direct contact with the judicial process and no new evidence to offer is not likely to be effective.

Unless the group is in the happy position of already having its "standards" of selection embodied in the values of the appointing authority, it will have to work primarily through the senators involved or through the organized bar. This might be considered covert rather than overt pressure-group activity.

No such impediments to group activity exist at the Senate level, either at the recruitment or confirmation stages. Group activity is particularly effective in exerting influence on a senator who is himself recruiting for a District Court judgeship. One of the keys to the success of an interest group is the amount of pressure it can sustain, and public-opinion support it can gain, by enlisting the aid of other groups with related or similar orientations. The individual senator who claims responsibility for recruiting federal judges in his state is in a peculiarly vulnerable position, particularly if he must soon campaign for reelection.

Although the *confirmation* stage of the selection process is also an open forum, it is less vulnerable to pressure-group influence. Because of the improbability of successfully *opposing* a nomination already made and subject only to confirmation, overt pressure-group activity even at this level has become spasmodic and is customarily initiated only in "hard" cases.[44] The opposition of conservative groups to the nomination of Louis D. Brandeis in 1916 and the successful opposition of labor groups and the National Association for the Advancement of Colored People to John J. Parker in 1930 are illustrative not only of the techniques of such pressure-group activity, but of the uniqueness of the situation in which such activity might have a chance of success.[45]

The relative scarcity of such major campaigns since 1937, excepting the more general efforts of the organized bar, suggests that these groups have increased their covert influence—as already noted—at the presidential stage, that as the selection process has "closed" and become more stabilized they have been effectively excluded, or that they have been effectively displaced by the organized bar. Presidents wary of stimulating organized group opposition—and its consequent political penalties —normally take the views and prejudices of such groups into account and do not appoint anyone clearly hostile to such interests. (Depending on their party affiliation and political philosophy, different Presidents are more concerned about some groups than others.) Such means of covert influence may actually constitute a more effective strategy than overt opposition, particularly in view of the strongly held (and widely accepted) position of the organized bar that only the legal profession can have a legitimate and overtly expressed interest in the selection of judges.

The organized bar, although an interest group in every sense of the

[44] Richard Burke, *The Path to the Court: A Study of Federal Judicial Appointments* (unpublished Ph.D. dissertation, Department of Political Science, Vanderbilt University, 1958), p. 31.

[45] John R. Schmidhauser, *The Supreme Court: Its Politics, Personalities, and Procedures* (New York: Holt, Rinehart and Winston, 1960), p. 13. Also Harris, *op. cit.*, pp. 99–114, 127–132.

word,[46] must be treated separately in this context because of its distinct proprietary attitude toward the judicial-selection process. Leaders of the bar have always considered their profession uniquely competent to select judges at all levels of government. They stipulate that since "lawyers are better able than non-lawyers to appraise accurately the qualifications of candidates for judicial office," they have a positive duty to speak out. This concept is regularly communicated to lawyers in the editorial sections of the *American Bar Association Journal* and other similar publications. A recent editorial stated that "because lawyers are the only group of citizens that are in daily contact with the courts, they are the only group that are really able to judge the qualifications necessary for good judicial material." [47] It has long been the policy of the American Bar Association to "stamp the system of judicial selection through the medium of the Bar as an accepted institution in our political life—accepted by the people we mean—with the like force of law itself." [48]

To what degree has this policy been effectuated? How much access has the organized bar gained to the councils of those who choose our judges? How much popular acceptance is there of the concept of deference to the legal profession in the selection of judges? On the state and local level, which is not a major concern of this study, the successes of the organized bar have been moderate. After nearly thirty years of campaigning, the ABA has seen versions of its Plan of Judicial Selection adopted in whole or in part in seven states and pending in about four others. Under variations of this plan, the Governor of a state nominates judges from a list of names submitted by a panel of laymen and lawyers. The panels are previously selected and usually consist of an equal number of laymen and lawyers, with the Governor choosing the lay members and the state bar association choosing the lawyer members. The state Chief Justice or senior member of the highest state court normally presides. Local panels, drawn in the same manner, are usually constituted to recommend names for district judgeship vacancies. After the Governor selects one

---

[46] Defined here as a group of persons who, on the basis of shared interests and attitudes, make certain claims on public officials or other groups in the society. See Truman, *op. cit.*, Ch. 1.

[47] Editorial comment on Edward J. Fox, Jr., "The Selection of Federal Judges: The Work of the Federal Judiciary Committee," 43 *American Bar Association Journal* (1957), 685.

[48] "Report of the Committee on Judicial Selection," 14 *American Bar Association Journal* (1928), 617.

name from the list drawn up by the panel, that person serves as a judge for a short period of time, after which his name appears on the ballot for voter approval. If he is approved then he serves a substantial number of years and at succeeding intervals is "approved" or "disapproved" by the voters.[49]

Bar association involvement at the municipal level is probably even more substantial. But even in states or cities where the organized bar plays no formal role in the selection process, it usually wields significant influence and, by the use of accepted methods of publicity and campaigning, can secure the selection of approved candidates.[50] Another interesting application of this "Bar Ethic" can be found in Congress and many of the state legislatures. Membership on the Judiciary Committees of both the House of Representatives and the Senate is restricted to lawyers, presumably on the theory that only lawyers are competent to investigate the qualifications of judicial candidates or (in the case of the House) able to adequately consider measures concerning judicial reform.

On the federal level, the American Bar Association and its Standing Committee on Federal Judiciary have gained a degree of access to the processes of judicial selection which is of a quasi-official character, and which, in effect, recognizes the special competence of the legal profession to assist in the choice of judges which the American Bar Association and other legal groups had long advocated. By agreement with the Attorney General, the Committee on Federal Judiciary investigates the qualifications of every person considered by the Attorney General as a possible candidate for judicial office. It first makes an informal report on each name under consideration and then, after a vote of the members of the Committee, follows up with a formal recommendation on the candidate picked by the Attorney General. If the Attorney General recommends, and the President actually nominates, a person rated unqualified by the Committee, it still has an opportunity to

---

[49] "Status of Non-Partisan Appointive-Elective Plans for Selection of Judges," *American Judicature Society Information Sheet No. 1,* November 12, 1962.

[50] See, among others, Edward M. Martin, *The Role of the Bar in Electing the Bench in Chicago* (Chicago: University of Chicago Press, 1936); Edward T. Butler, "Cleveland Bar Association's Plan for Judicial Campaigns," 30 *Journal of the American Judicature Society* (1946), 42–44; Laurence M. Hyde, "Missouri Method of Choosing Judges," 41 *Journal of the American Judicature Society* (1957), 74–77; Glen R. Winters, "How Should Judges be Chosen?," 29 *Wisconsin Bar Bulletin* (1956) , 7–8, 63–66; and Samuel Rosenman, "A Better Way to Select Judges," 48 *Journal of the American Judicature Society* (1964), 86–92.

oppose the nomination in the Senate, but it has no special priority or prestige with that body and must operate in the manner of every other group.

Both from the nature of its tactics and long-range objectives and from its high degree of success, the ABA must be regarded as a special case.   It has a special interest not only in exercising influence over the types of persons selected for the federal bench, but in exercising that influence on a regular, and semiformal basis.   The reasons for that special interest, the ways in which it has been expressed, and the impact which it has had on the selection process will be the focus of the remaining chapters.

3

⬥

THE DEVELOPMENT OF THE ABA'S

ROLE IN JUDICIAL SELECTION

In the preceding chapter we indicated briefly the role which the ABA—through its Standing Committee on Federal Judiciary—had come to play in the process of selecting federal judges. Here we shall suggest some of the most important reasons for its interest in judicial selection and describe in some detail the formation and development of the Committee on Federal Judiciary. The evolution from the ABA's episodic involvement in judicial selection to its present status of formal advisor to the Attorney General is, in and of itself, an interesting historical phenomenon. But it is only one aspect of our study. Further chapters will explore in depth the work of the ABA Committee and its impact on the judicial-selection process.

THE ABA'S TRADITIONAL INTEREST
IN JUDICIAL SELECTION

Through its activities and major policy pronouncements, the ABA has demonstrated a continuing interest in the selection of judges. Although the selection of "good" judges was not specifically enumerated as an objective of the newly formed Association in 1878, it is fair, in the light of the early activities of the ABA, to consider this objective as immanent in the "promotion of the administration of justice"— always a major articulated goal.[1] The first official statement of the ABA's interest in judicial selection apparently came in 1908, when the

---

[1] 33 *Annual Reports of the American Bar Association* (1908), 575. (Hereinafter cited as *ABA Reports*.)

Committee on Professional Ethics listed "The Selection of Judges" as the second Canon of Professional Ethics:

It is the duty of the Bar to endeavor to prevent political considerations from outweighing judicial fitness in the Selection of Judges. It should protest earnestly and actively against the appointment or election of those who are unsuitable for the Bench; and it should strive to have elevated thereto only those willing to forego other employments, whether of a business, political, or other character which may embarrass their free and fair consideration of questions before them for decision. The aspiration of lawyers for judicial position should be governed by an impartial estimate of their ability to add honor to the office and not by a desire for the distinction which the position may bring to themselves.[2]

With the addition of only two clarifying "opinions," this statement of the lawyer's position vis-à-vis the selection process has remained unchanged.

But neither this nor any other canon of the Association provides guidance for the specific goals to be achieved, the standards of qualification for "good judges," or the expected or desired role which the ABA was to play in securing such judges. How were these goals to be achieved?

The working policy goals of the Association were left to be determined by the contemporary leadership. Typical of the frequently enunciated policy statements was the following Report of the 1924 Committee on Judicial Selection:

Certain postulates we accept as basic. It is both the right and the duty of the Bar to act in this selection process. The right springs from that inherent privilege which entitles one to demand that he who is chosen from his fellows to sit in judgment of the case must needs bear worthily that distinction and meet four square the traditional tests of an exalted professional attainment. Born of this, society in turn, has rightfully to require a recognition and performance of the correlative obligation. That duty is fulfilled only when the Bar, offering for its aid and counsel, has registered in full measure its conception of judicial fitness, founded, as it must be, upon a discernment of those qualities of mind and heart, those traits of poise and patience that mark in man the true judicial temperament. To the extent that society accords recognition of this right and that the Bar exerts its duty will results be achieved.[3]

Beneath the flowery rhetoric the point was abundantly clear. The bar, as the representative of the legal profession, had not only the

---

[2] "Opinions 189, 226," *Opinions of the Committee on Professional Ethics and Grievances* (Chicago: American Bar Association, 1957).

[3] 10 *American Bar Association Journal* (1924), 820. (Hereinafter cited as *ABAJ*.)

right but the duty to actively offer its services in the judicial-selection process. Furthermore, the implication is clear that the choice of judges by a process which excludes the voice—or voices—of the organized bar is to be condemned.

Missing from this statement, however, was any indication of what precise standards of qualification were to be sought. What was it about prospective judges that other lawyers were especially adept at perceiving and evaluating? Was it legal scholarship, courtroom ability, capacity for philosophical thought? "No," said the American Bar Association that same year. "It would, of course, be ideal if every judge were a profound jurist and yet it is probably better that he should have a listening ear than that he be too sure of the correctness of his own conclusions."

The prime requisites of a judge are . . . integrity and a keen sense of justice. With these qualities and a willingness to hear all that is to be said on both sides of a debatable proposition, little more is required than the faculty of perception, and that type of intellectual serenity which for want of a better name we call the "judicial temperament." [4]

These broadly stated goals of the ABA regarding the selection of judges have not materially changed in the intervening years. The claim is still made that "because lawyers are the only group of citizens that are in daily contact with the courts, they are the only group that are really able to judge the qualifications necessary for good judicial material." [5]

The American Bar Association's continuing interest in judicial selection was in keeping with the bar's venerable tradition of political leadership and public service. But as many friendly critics perceived, this continuity of formal objectives was a facade which concealed the changing nature of the bar's concept of public service. Justice Harlan Fiske Stone, writing in 1934, declared that ". . . candor would compel even those of us who have the most abiding faith in our profession, and the finest belief in its capacity for future usefulness, to admit that in our own time the Bar has not maintained its traditional position of public influence and leadership." [6]

Nowhere was this change better seen than in the efforts of the ABA to influence the process of judicial selection and in its obvious motives in so doing. One of the underlying reasons for the formation of the

---

4 *Ibid.*, p. 176.
5 Editorial comment on Edward J. Fox, Jr., "The Selection of Federal Judges: The Work of the Federal Judiciary Committee," 43 *ABAJ* (1957), 685.
6 "The Public Influence of the Bar," 48 *Harvard Law Review* (1934–1935), 1.

American Bar Association in 1878 was the felt need to "do something" about a trend of judicial decisions illustrated by *Munn v. Illinois*.[7] Committed as they were to the growing industrial empire, the bar leaders saw the judiciary as the last bastion of defense against encroachments on the entrepreneurial prerogative, and intensified their efforts to assure the recruitment of judges who shared their own views of society. These efforts strengthened the public leadership consciousness of the bar; but the forms of such leadership rested on values and assumptions that were at considerable variance with the new progressivism of the twentieth century. An inevitable "confusion" between professional qualifications and ideological soundness marked the judicial-selection efforts of the American Bar Association right through to the New Deal period.[8] These efforts, ostensibly aimed toward insuring the professional quality of judges, were clear and frank attempts to gain a measure of control over the judicial decision-making process.

But although these efforts may have been at variance with the traditional "public service" concept, they underscored some of the basic and continuing motivations for lawyers' interest in controlling judicial personnel. Far from being the sole output of a tradition of public service, the bar's efforts reflected the need and desire of lawyers to exercise an effective control over the policies and practices of the judicial process. It was as much self-interest as public interest that provided the occasion and the impetus for the ABA's judicial-selection efforts.

EARLY INVOLVEMENTS IN JUDICIAL SELECTION

As opposed to its continuing *interest*, the activities of the American Bar Association in the area of judicial selection prior to 1946 fluctuated from intense effort and participation to passive comment. Its initial efforts consisted mainly of exhorting state and local bar groups to take a more active part in the selection process at their own levels.[9]

---

[7] 94 U. S. 113 (1876).
[8] See especially Benjamin Twiss, *Lawyers and the Constitution* (Princeton, N. J.: Princeton University Press, 1942). In addition to Twiss, who was basically a critic of the ABA, the conservative domination of the bar's activities has been acknowledged by Mary Louise Rutherford, *The Influence of the American Bar Association on Public Opinion and Legislation* (Philadelphia: Mary Louise Rutherford, 1937), pp. 115–130. See also John R. Schmidhauser, *The Supreme Court: Its Politics, Personalities, and Procedures* (New York: Holt, Rinehart and Winston, 1960), Ch. 4.
[9] See "Report of the Committee on Judicial Selection," 14 *ABAJ* (1928), 617.

The ABA was never without at least one committee concerned with general questions of judicial qualification and tenure, but these committees operated largely through the local bar groups. Its occasional intense participation was motivated more often than not by concern for the continued functioning of the judiciary in the manner and on the terms that the ABA believed consonant with historical American values.

As illustrations of this episodic participation, and the reasons for it, we will briefly examine three cases. Each details the ABA's response to what it called the "socialist menace," the "threatened subversion of the judiciary," or the "downgrading of property rights."

The Recall of Judges

The response of the American Bar Association to the campaign for recall of judges (1910–1920) was an intense, vituperative, almost hysterical propaganda offensive designed to alert the public to the alleged evils of such reform. Beginning with the appointment of a large "Committee to Oppose Judicial Recall," the ABA sought to enlist the aid of all local bar groups in the fight.[10] In its first year the Committee worked hard to stimulate interest and action on the part of the state and local bar associations.[11] Three years later it decided to broaden its forum from the bar to the lay public. Judicial recall was made the subject of high school and college debates and lectures. Essay contests were sponsored, with the "winning" paper receiving wide publicity and publication.[12]

As the impetus of the judicial-recall movement slackened, the Committee claimed a large share of the credit, but warned that the "menace of the judicial recall fallacy . . . still persists; and your Committee has directed its activities during the past year to combatting certain theories and measures which have for their object either direct or indirect judicial recall, as a means . . . to weaken or destroy constitutional safeguards." [13] Probably the most effective propaganda technique the Committee had at its disposal was the "socialist smear." By the simple device of labeling judicial recall as a socialist vice, the Committee was able to infect all those who supported the movement:

10 "Report of the Committee to Oppose Judicial Recall," 36 *ABA Reports* (1911), 51.
11 "Report of the Committee to Oppose Judicial Recall," 37 *ABA Reports* (1912), 574–575.
12 "Report of the Committee to Oppose Judicial Recall," 39 *ABA Reports* (1914), 607–608.
13 "Report of the Committee to Oppose Judicial Recall," 3 *ABAJ* (1917), 454.

. . . The propaganda of Socialism, which is now so widespread . . . is, from its political viewpoint, one of attack upon constitutional government. . . . It is promoted, not alone by the avowed socialist, but by numerous allies, comprising many who would disavow the name of "Socialist." . . . The socialist political platforms continuously advocate as the first necessary means of establishing socialism, the adoption of judicial recall. The ultimate object of the socialists is the confiscation of property and property rights and the turning over of all property to common ownership in the name of the state. They must first, then, eliminate that judicial function which was established in this country to safeguard the life, liberty, and property of the individual. They would abolish the United States Senate and all courts . . . and they urge the abolition of the power "usurped" by the Supreme Court of the United States to pass upon the constitutionality of legislative acts, and the revision of the Constitution (presumably on a socialist basis) of the United States. . . . The judicial function of declaring invalid any statute which contravenes constitutional safeguards to individual rights of property and liberty is, so long as it continues, a barrier to the establishment of a government of socialism.[14]

By 1918 there appeared to be little vitality left in the recall movement, but the Committee was continued as a safeguard.[15]

Although the problem of judicial recall is not identical to the problem of judicial selection, it does shed considerable light on the overall objectives of the ABA. It emphasizes the concern of the ABA that the function of judging might become too responsive to the popular will, that the role of the judge was not to be substantially different from the role of other elected officials. If judging were not to be considered as an extension of the legal process and judges as elite members of the legal profession, then the claims of the organized bar to special influence in the selection of judges would be, at best, quite vulnerable. Not to be overlooked, of course, was the ideological orientation of the bar's opposition to judicial recall. In many states the judges had become the foremost defenders against the Progressive Movement and, clearly, judges subject to popular recall were not as likely to continue in such a role.

The Brandeis Case

The response of the ABA to the 1916 nomination of Louis D. Brandeis as associate justice of the Supreme Court was also a defense of the dominant ideological values held by leaders of the American Bar

14 *Ibid.*, p. 456.
15 "Report of the Committee to Oppose Judicial Recall," 43 *ABA Reports* (1918), 85–87.

Association. Since at that time the ABA had no formal mechanism designed to evaluate specific candidates for the federal bench, its opposition to Brandeis was in the form of a signed statement by ex-President Taft and six other former presidents of the Association submitted to the Senate Judiciary Committee. Although the statement emphasized that Brandeis's "reputation, character, and professional career" made him "not a fit person to be a member of the Supreme Court," [16] it was in fact clear that it was his political and social views which the ABA leaders opposed. In light of his incredible success as a lawyer fighting in opposition to some of the most cherished and widely held values of the Association, Brandeis's legal ability could not be seriously questioned. In the words of Roscoe Pound, who was testifying at the hearings, ". . . Mr. Brandeis is in truth a very great lawyer. . . . So far as sheer legal ability is concerned, he will rank with the best who have sat upon the bench of the Supreme Court." [17] It was, of course, Brandeis's tenacious advocacy of minority causes that brought upon his head the wrath of the ABA leadership.

The Brandeis case has been extensively treated elsewhere, and the facts are too well known to require further documentation here. What interests us, however, is the type and adequacy of the response of the American Bar Association. That the opposition of the ABA to Brandeis did not come through "channels," but was articulated as the personal views of seven former presidents, should not be interpreted as something less than the accurate views of the then small membership of the ABA. At that stage in its development it was still primarily a closely knit group of successful lawyers whose views probably coincided with those expressed by the seven presidents. Yet the near success that the campaign against Brandeis had could be attributed in part to the personal prestige of the seven presidents, and their ability to mobilize other forces in support of their case. The American Bar Association had not yet developed any formal mechanism for the scrutiny of the federal judicial-selection process.

The Response to the Rejection of Judge Parker

Prior to 1932 the only formal concern of the ABA with the selection of judges, with minor exceptions, was with the state *systems*. It paid

---

[16] Quoted in Alpheus T. Mason, *Brandeis: A Free Man's Life* (New York: Viking Press, 1946), p. 489.

[17] U. S. Congress, Senate, Committee on the Judiciary, *Hearings on the Nomination of Louis D. Brandeis*, 64th Cong., 1st Sess., 1916, II, p. 251.

little attention to the particular persons chosen as judges in the states, and no attention at all to the federal judicial-selection process. Its concern with particular Supreme Court appointments was haphazard. One reason for this attitude may have been that, in the period from 1878–1937, the federal courts, especially the Supreme Court, were *generally considered* able defenders of and protagonists for the economic and social values espoused by the ABA, whereas in the same period the state courts—many with elected judges—were considered centers of radical thought. The ABA's severe condemnation of the Roosevelt Plan to increase the membership of the Supreme Court in 1937, when compared to its ambivalence toward "anti-court" measures in 1958 when the Supreme Court no longer represented conservative views, would support the hypothesis that it was not the Supreme Court per se that was being defended in 1937, but rather its making of "good" policy.[18] The ABA's disenchantment with the Supreme Court after 1937 was accompanied by a developing support of the state courts, which in the same period appeared to embrace many of the classical liberal values now rejected by the federal courts.

Among the most significant of the ABA's responses to these changes in the political position of the federal courts vis-à-vis selected conservative values was a variety of attempts to exert greater systematic influence in the selection of federal judges. As early as 1924 the Committee on Judicial Selection of the Conference of Bar Association Delegates suggested that

. . . If the principle of bar selection is right within the state, it is right within the nation—the more so, indeed, if made to serve a more exalted purpose. It is not to be countenanced, to be sure, that there be the least bit of obtrusion upon this Presidential power and prerogative, but it must be true that there lie here the possibilities for helpful suggestion which unquestionably would serve well when occasion should demand.[19]

No action was taken on this suggestion. The possibility of participation by the organized bar in the federal selection process was suggested, however, by Attorney General William D. Mitchell in 1931. Although he distrusted the results of "bar primaries," Mitchell felt that "an overwhelming sentiment by the Bar for or against a particular man makes a deep impression upon the public mind, upon the senators especially interested, and on the appointing power. This is founded on the realization that a lawyer's qualities are most clearly discerned

---

18 See Alan F. Westin, "When the Public Judges the Court," *New York Times Magazine*, May 31, 1959, pp. 16, 41.
19 "Report of the Committee on Judicial Selection," 10 *ABAJ* (1924), 824.

by the members of his own profession." [20]   Mitchell indicated that the Hoover Administration made it a practice to consult with the bar of the country on federal judgeships:

. . . In the Department, we often make up a list of lawyers of professional standing and public spirit, in the community where the appointment is to be made, and send them personal letters asking for confidential information, and in such cases, with rare exceptions, we get a frank, sincere, illuminating picture of the men under consideration.[21]

Encouraged by this receptive attitude on the part of the administration, and disturbed by the Senate's rejection of Judge John Parker's nomination to the Supreme Court in 1930, the American Bar Association made its first formal attempt to gain access to the federal selection process at the confirmation stage.   It established in 1932 a Special Committee of fifty-two lawyers, one from each state, to advise the Senate Judiciary Committee on all judicial nominations.   As is usually the case, the formation of a new Special Committee indicated the recognition of a new, important problem area:

. . . The Special Committee on Federal Appointments . . . will deal with a new aspect of the old problem of judicial selection.   Heretofore, discussion of the problem has been generally confined to the mode of selection of the state judges—whether by appointment or by election—and where the latter method prevails, to the ways in which the bar can best make its superior information as to the fitness of judicial candidates available to, and influential with, the electorate.   Genuine progress has been made in that direction.

But now the matter of confirmation, an essential part of the process of judicial selection in some states and in the Federal judicial system in particular, is seen to be of no less importance.   It does not concern the machinery, but the manner in which machinery for naming a Federal Judge is operated.[22]

With specific reference to the Parker case, the ABA expressed its concern whether ". . . the grounds urged for or against confirmation are such as may properly be considered in the choice of a judge?" [23] It stated its objection to the practice of disapproving nominees solely because of disagreement with decisions they had made as judges of other courts, "which decisions have been rendered in accordance with precedent and in the performance of that high duty which calls for fearless and impartial determination of all issues under the established

---

20 "Appointment of Federal Judges," 17 *ABAJ* (1931), 572.
21 *Ibid.*
22 "Concerning Federal Judicial Appointments," editorial, 19 *ABAJ* (1933), 28.
23 *Ibid.*

principles of law . . ." [24]   The resolution setting up the Committee called on the Senate to refuse to consider such allegations as valid evidence.

The Committee was established primarily to advise the Senate Judiciary Committee. But some attempt also was made to extend its operations to the nomination stage although the ABA did not appear to be dissatisfied with the nominations of the Hoover Administration. Due undoubtedly to the change in administrations shortly after its formation in 1932, the Committee's services were never once requested by either the new Attorney General or Senate Judiciary Committee, and at its own request the Committee was discontinued in 1934.[25]

Reviewing the activities of the American Bar Association in the area of federal judicial selection from 1878 to 1945, it is clear that they were primarily responses to the shifts in political orientation and position which began to characterize not only the federal courts but the appointing agents as well. By the time the ABA developed a concern over the decision trends in the federal courts, however, and sought to assert its influence in the federal selection process, it had come upon a period of reduced prestige. In its attempts to preserve a political philosophy on the wane, the ABA lost much of the comforts and strengths normally accruing to a nonpartisan, learned profession— strengths which, even had they been preserved, would probably have fared poorly in the wake of the liberal revival of the New Deal. Deprived—by its own actions—of its credentials as a wholly "professional" group, still representing but a fraction of the legal profession, and trying to operate in a very unfavorable political climate, the American Bar Association could only wait for the day when its own resources and a favorable political situation would make its attempts to influence the selection of federal judges more rewarding. That day was not long in coming.

THE FORMATION OF THE COMMITTEE
ON FEDERAL JUDICIARY

Responding perhaps to a more propitious climate, and also to a series of events which had cast shadows on the reputation of the United States Supreme Court, the American Bar Association in 1946 again

---

[24] Quoted in *ibid.*

[25] "Report of the Special Committee on Federal Appointments," 59 *ABA Reports* (1934), 610.

sought to create the mechanism and the mood which would enable it to "resume" its campaign for "maintaining high standards of qualification and conduct on the part of judges of the courts of the United States." [26]

Stimuli of ABA Action

The three events that could be designated as primary stimuli of the ABA's action were (1) the feud between Supreme Court Justices Black and Jackson; (2) the decision of that Court in the *Southeastern Underwriters* case; [27] and (3) the absence from the Supreme Court of Justice Jackson who was serving as Chief Allied Prosecutor at the Nuremberg War Trials. Thus, a case of deviant judicial behavior, an "upsetting" decision with alleged consequences for the continuation of a historic legal doctrine, and a case of alleged judicial maladministration triggered the ABA's action.

The Black-Jackson feud, which began quietly over Black's failure to disqualify himself from a case argued by his former law partner,[28] erupted when Jackson, in a wire from Nuremberg, accused Black of feeding anti-Jackson stories to the press and revealing the confidential proceedings of the Court in an effort to discredit Jackson's candidacy for the chief justiceship.[29] The nationwide reaction to this feud was bitter. Some newspapers sought to justify the actions of one or the other of the justices. Many suggested that both "quietly and decently . . . step down from the bench they have disgraced." [30] The *New York Times* declared editorially that "Justice Jackson has committed an error in taste and . . . Justice Black has committed the worse offense of lowering judicial standards." [31] A nationwide poll published two weeks later indicated a substantial portion of the population was disturbed by the bickering among the justices and critical of the caliber of some of the recent appointments to the high bench.[32]

---

[26] "Resolution of the House of Delegates, July 3, 1946," 71 *ABA Reports* (1946), 330.
[27] 322 U. S. 533 (1944).
[28] The case was *Jewell Ridge Coal Corporation v. United Mine Workers*, 325 U. S. 897 (1945). Good descriptions of the feud can be found in Alpheus T. Mason, *Harlan Fiske Stone: Pillar of the Law* (New York: Viking Press, 1956), pp. 642 ff.; and Eugene C. Gerhardt, *America's Advocate: Robert H. Jackson* (Indianapolis, Ind.: Bobbs-Merrill, 1958), pp. 251 ff.
[29] *New York Times*, June 11, 1946, p. 1.
[30] Quoted in Gerhardt, *op. cit.*, p. 263.
[31] "Quarrel on the High Bench," editorial, *New York Times*, June 12, 1946, p. 26.
[32] Gerhardt, *op. cit.*, p. 263.

There was a brief cry in Congress for impeachment of Justice Black and investigation of the incident, but the idea was smothered by the Democratic leadership.[33]

Regardless of the merits of the dispute, there was considerable adverse reaction to the Court, and it was a perfect opportunity for a group, such as the ABA, to begin a campaign to improve the quality of judges. This incident served to compound the smoldering dissatisfaction with the Supreme Court which had already existed for several years. This dissatisfaction had been exacerbated by the Court's 1944 decision in *United States v. Southeastern Underwriters Association.* Here, the justices, speaking through Justice Black, held that the insurance business was part of interstate commerce and subject to antitrust regulation. Though the Court did not actually do so, many critics claimed this decision limited the power of the states to regulate and tax the insurance business and reacted accordingly.[34] Congress responded by passing the McCarran-Ferguson Act, which formally authorized state regulation and taxation of the insurance business.[35] Nevertheless, the *Southeastern* decision had had, for the brief time it was in effect, an upsetting influence on the laws of insurance. More important, it came to be regarded by some lawyers as symptomatic of the disregard which the "Roosevelt" Court was showing toward traditional values and legal precedents.

Dissatisfaction with the Court had also resulted from the absence of Justice Jackson, who was appointed by President Truman to serve at Nuremberg over the protests of Chief Justice Stone. Very irritating to litigants and lawyers alike was the fact that Jackson's absence had caused a number of 4–4 decisions to be withheld pending his return. The work of the Court was obviously suffering with one less hand to share the burdens of opinion writing.

The ABA Response

Meeting in July 1946, the House of Delegates of the American Bar Association engaged in a heated debate, with the foregoing incidents the chief topics. Former ABA President William L. Ransom of New York sought to channel these expressed emotions toward more "constructive" ends:

---

[33] *Ibid.*

[34] 322 U. S. 533 (1944).

[35] 59 *U. S. Statutes* (1945), 33. The Supreme Court recognized this congressional action in *Prudential Insurance Company v. Benjamin,* 328 U. S. 408 (1946).

Respect for all our courts is the cornerstone of the American federal system. Disrespect for the courts in a republic endangers the foundations of its free institutions. Criticism of the courts is a right and function of the Bar . . . [but] mere criticism and the expression of disrespect fall short of what is expected of us. . . .

This House ought to do something constructive and remedial. . . . The profession and the public look to us for action now.[36]

Rather than adopt resolutions concerning specific situations, Ransom urged the delegates to "take such present action as will enable prompt action in behalf of the Association when needed, and assure also the remedial study of such criticisms and suggestions as have been made here this week." He successfully argued that the best course to follow would be the establishment of a committee "charged with the duty of considering and initiating action by the Association as to such situations as have developed as to some members of the Federal Judiciary. . . ."[37]

Pursuant to a motion by Ransom, the House constituted a Special Committee on the Judiciary of eleven members, one from each judicial circuit and the District of Columbia. The Committee was charged to report back to the House of Delegates its recommendations regarding the proper action to take "to promote the appointment and confirmation of competent and qualified candidates and to oppose the nomination or confirmation of unfit candidates." Furthermore, it was to recommend courses of action to be followed "whenever any judge of any federal court has . . . become disqualified or unfit to continue on the bench, or has been guilty of acts or conducts amounting to less than 'good behavior' within the meaning of the Constitution of the United States." The Committee was also directed to consider the merits of two resolutions designed to alter the existing methods of choosing Supreme Court justices, and to prevent sitting justices from accepting off-court assignments.[38]

Thus, after a twelve-year interval, the American Bar Association was to make a concerted effort to "reestablish the prerogatives" of the organized bar in the selection of federal judges. To the editors of the *American Bar Association Journal*

There were many indications that the profession and the public looked to the Association for leadership and action. It is no longer sufficient to talk about the independence and impartiality of the judiciary and its aloofness

---

[36] "Proceedings of the House of Delegates," 32 *ABAJ* (1946), 421.
[37] *Ibid.*, p. 422.
[38] "Report of the Special Committee on Judiciary," 71 *ABA Reports* (1946), 328.

from controversies extraneous to submitted cases. Those who believe in those standards for the judiciary will have to go to work to insist that they be maintained.

The resolutions . . . entrust to the new Committee a duty and responsibility which the Association has not hitherto undertaken.[39]

The Committee on Federal Judiciary (as it was later named) has become the major instrument in the postwar campaign of the American Bar Association to exert a direct influence on the selection of specific persons as federal judges. From the inception of this Committee in 1946 until the present, the American Bar Association has sought (and to a large degree achieved) public and official approval for the right of the organized bar to be consulted in the actual selection of judges. Its successful campaign to achieve this goal marks the first time in American history that the legal profession has been accorded that privilege at the federal level.

THE DEVELOPMENT OF THE COMMITTEE
ON FEDERAL JUDICIARY

The long-range goals of the Committee on Federal Judiciary were decided after considerable debate at the 1946 Annual Meeting and 1947 Winter Meeting of the American Bar Association. The first report of the Special Committee formed in 1946 recommended that, in addition to having the power to oppose or recommend nominations already made by the President and considering questions about the behavior of sitting judges, it should also be permitted to "promote" the nomination of qualified persons. The Committee felt that "the only effective method of opposing a proposed nominee not qualified for judicial office is by supporting a qualified nominee." [40] Pursuing this argument on the floor of the House of Delegates, Chairman John Buchanan of Pittsburgh argued:

. . . You cannot oppose very successfully a man with powerful political backing, who has an unimpeachable family and church record, and a modest practice in which he has been guilty of no misconduct, unless you can support, in his stead, the appointment of a real lawyer. And the Committee believes that real lawyers will be willing to signify their willingness to accept appointments to the federal bench if they can be assured of the backing of the organized Bar. . . .

---

[39] Editorial, 32 *ABAJ* (1946), 478.
[40] "Report of the Special Committee on Judiciary," 71 *ABA Reports* (1946), 236.

Without that support, real lawyers will stand little chance against the men who have supported a party ticket through thick and through thin, not without reward in appointment to minor offices, but who think that they have reached the place in political service which entitles them to recognition as judges of the federal courts.[41]

Opposition to the granting of this not inconsiderable power was strong, however, and the question was tabled by a resolution to continue the Committee "in its present form." [42]

The question of revising the Committee's charter was then submitted to the Board of Governors for consideration. At the 1947 Winter Meeting, the Board came out in opposition to the proposed grant. Instead, it suggested that the Association should urge Congress to establish, by law, qualifications of eligibility for appointment to the federal bench, including minimum requirements of legal practice and judicial experience.[43] The President of the ABA, Carl Rix, dissented from the Governors' position and urged the House of Delegates to grant the Committee the power to promote nominations. If the Committee were granted this power, it would serve to aid the state and local bar associations in influencing the nomination of judges in their own locales; otherwise, they would be forced to continue to "deal with an appointing power which, without our help, is beyond their reach." [44] By a vote of 79–52, the House overruled the recommendation of the Board of Governors. It empowered the Committee,

. . . on behalf of the Association, to promote the nomination and confirmation of competent persons for appointment as judges of courts of the United States and to oppose the nomination and confirmation of persons deemed by it to be not sufficiently qualified. It shall have power also to report to the House of Delegates or the Board of Governors on any questions relating to the behavior of judges of such courts and any matters relating to the sufficiency of the members of the federal judiciary.[45]

Pending the achievement of some results by which to evaluate the Committee's operations, it was continued as a Special Committee.

Its general goals and prerogatives settled early in its existence, the Committee was relatively free to create and develop its functions in

---

41 "Proceedings of the House of Delegates," 33 *ABAJ* (1947), 191.
42 *Ibid.*, p. 192.
43 *Ibid.*, p. 396.
44 *Ibid.*
45 Article X, Section 7 (L), 2, of the *Constitution and By-Laws of the American Bar Association.* See also "Judges of Federal Courts: Association Will Promote Qualified Nominations," editorial, 33 *ABAJ* (1947), 305–306.

accord with the objectives of the Association and the realities of the judicial-selection process. Since the seventeen-year history of the Committee is essentially one of increased prestige and prerogative, it is useful to analyze its growth in sections corresponding to three different time periods which may be characterized as (1) 1946–1952, a period of development and indifferent success; (2) 1952–1958, a period of increased public acceptance as part of the selection process; and (3) 1958–1963, a period of maximum influence within the presently constituted selection system.

1946–1952

The most noteworthy achievement of the Committee during the 1946–1952 period was the establishment of a working relationship with the Senate Judiciary Committee. Almost immediately upon its formation, the Committee was invited by the chairman of the Senate Judiciary Committee to either testify or file a recommendation on each nomination given a hearing. Thus, the collective views of the Committee would become a regular factor in the confirmation process.

The formation of the ABA Committee coincided with the election of the Eightieth Congress, the first since 1930 in which the Republican Party controlled both Houses. Senator Alexander Wiley of Wisconsin, slated to assume the chairmanship of the Judiciary Committee, announced that his Committee would try to stem the tide of "leftist" judges periodically appointed during Democratic administrations, and that at least some non-Democratic judges would have to be appointed.[46] Perhaps to emphasize his new order, Wiley announced that so long as he was chairman, "full weight will be given to the recommendation of recognized legal groups which have not been accorded the weight and respect which are their just due." [47] Wiley requested all state bar associations to assume the responsibility of giving him information on the "character, legal ability, temperament, and the political philosophy" of all nominees.[48]

Although there is no precise evidence (nor could there be), it is not unreasonable to assume that this privilege accorded the ABA and other bar groups was symbolic of the reaction to a long period of Democratic control. Would the ABA have been issued the same

---

[46] *New York Times,* December 2, 1946, p. 26.
[47] Quoted in "Report of the Special Committee on Judiciary," 72 *ABA Reports* (1947), 411.
[48] *New York Times,* February 3, 1947, p. 14.

"invitation" if the Eightieth Congress had remained in Democratic hands? As a constant critic of the actions and decisions of the post-1937 Supreme Court justices, the ABA was the perfect instrument through which Senate Republicans could attempt inroads on the nominations of a Democratic President. Since they would not normally be consulted in advance of nominations by a President of the opposite party anyway, and since by the rules (informal) of the Senate, they could not claim personal privilege to block nominations in their own state, Senate Republicans could use the adverse recommendations of the ABA and local bar groups to either justify occasional rejections of confirmation or to persuade the President to nominate "more acceptable" persons.

Consultation, however, is not the same as influence, and members of the ABA Committee who testified before the Judiciary Committee in this period found that the mere fact that they opposed a particular nominee carried little or no weight with the senators unless specific evidence of *disqualification* was presented. Then, as now, the senators on the Committee—all lawyers themselves—refused to accept as valid objections to a nomination the opinions of a few bar leaders. The mere assertion that "there were other better qualified men available" had little or no effect on the senators. Regardless of party affiliation, they had a stake in perpetuating the system which accorded the privilege of "selection" to senators of the President's party, and therefore relegated the task of the Judiciary Committee to sifting evidence of *disqualification* only.

A good illustration of the type of situation in which the ABA Committee could function most effectively was the Frieda Hennock case. In 1951 President Truman nominated Miss Hennock, a member of the Federal Communications Commission, to the Federal District Court for the Southern District of New York. In 1949 Miss Hennock's name had been submitted to the Association of the Bar of the City of New York for evaluation, and that group had reported her "not qualified." When she did receive the nomination in 1951, they again opposed her, and were now supported by the ABA Committee on Federal Judiciary.[49] She was supported by various women's bar groups and the Federal Bar Association for the Second Circuit. In this case the ABA was able to present, in secret hearings, a substantial amount of derogatory information concerning the ethics of an agreement she had entered into in 1934. The evidence was described as "so adverse that it could not be seen how further testimony could change the

---

49 *New York Times,* June 12, 1951, p. 17; and June 28, 1951, p. 16.

picture."[50]   The Senate Committee then pigeonholed the nomination and it died there with the end of the session. President Truman then offered Miss Hennock a recess appointment—as he had frequently done with other nominations opposed in the Senate—but she declined. To accept the recess appointment would have meant giving up the security of her FCC position with little assurance that she would be confirmed by the Senate. President Truman then appointed David Edelstein, an Assistant Attorney General. Edelstein was also opposed by the ABA Committee, but his nomination was confirmed with dispatch.[51]

The period of Republican control of the Senate lasted but two years, and the Democratic Committee Chairman from 1949–1953 did not hold the ABA in the same affection as had Senator Wiley. Although Senator Pat McCarran of Nevada continued the practice of formally requesting an ABA opinion on each nominee, he declared that he was "firmly resolved that the bar associations shall not choose the judiciary of the country."[52]

Thus, although the ABA Committee did contribute to the rejection of four judgeship nominations during this period,[53] it was unable to do much to promote the nomination of high-quality judges. It was not accorded the privilege of "reevaluating" the abilities of the pro- spective nominee. Its only chance of successfully blocking a nomi- nation lay in showing that the nominee had been guilty of deviant behavior. The Committee's relationship with the Senate Judiciary Committee was not, however, without its benefits to the ABA. It publicized the Association's activities, and acknowledged its role in the selection process, providing a coating of legitimacy to the Committee's efforts. It gave the Committee a public forum from which it could announce its standards and solicit support.

It was immediately clear, however, that the main thrust of the Committee's influence would have to come at the nomination stage of the selection process. This was immediately recognized by the first members of the Special Committee, and a delegation was sent to confer with Assistant Attorney General Douglas McGregor. They informed McGregor of the powers of the Committee and asked that it be consulted regarding any persons being considered for nomination to the federal bench. As reported by the delegation, ". . . McGregor

50 New York Times, September 28, 1951, p. 24.
51 New York Times, November 2, 1951, p. 1.
52 New York Times, August 5, 1951, p. 26.
53 From 1947 through 1952, the ABA Committee actively opposed ten nominations to the federal courts, four of which were subsequently rejected by the Senate.

stated that the request was a novel one, which the Chairman readily admitted."[54] McGregor promised to submit the request to the Attorney General, but even with a second plea, the Committee was not consulted in advance of appointments.[55] The Committee did try to make recommendations to the Attorney General on an ad hoc basis, but this soon proved unsatisfactory. It was at this time, however, that the Attorney General began to consult with various state and local bar groups on each nomination; this move clearly foreshadowed the entry of the ABA Committee into the process. For dealing with a multitude of groups with differing standards and methods of operation was not as useful as dealing with a single group as the representative of the organized bar.

Perhaps the most compelling cause to be assigned to the inability of the ABA Committee to establish a liaison with the Justice Department during this period was the hostility of President Truman. Reacting in characteristic fashion to the Frieda Hennock case, Truman noted that "he had appointed plenty of good judges opposed by the bar associations," and that such opposition did not upset him. He stated that he was glad to have bar association approval of his judicial appointments if forthcoming, but that failure to receive such approval would never deter him from making any appointment.[56]

In contrast to this chilly reception in the White House, the first efforts of the Committee on Federal Judiciary were warmly received in the press. Particularly in view of a long line of undistinguished Truman appointees to the federal bench,[57] there was some feeling that perhaps the "right" people were not advising on nominations. The *New York Times* took strong exception to Truman's "flippant dismissal of the opinions of bar groups." "Key members of the bar association," it said, "are the best equipped to pass upon court nominations who come from the ranks of fellow lawyers."

Since the President cannot possibly examine personally all the qualifications of all nominees to the bench, it is necessary for us to ask whose judgment he substitutes for that of bar associations. If the answer to that question is that

---

[54] "Report of the Special Committee on Judiciary," 72 *ABA Reports* (1947), 256.
[55] *Ibid.*
[56] *New York Times,* June 29, 1951, p. 23.
[57] For example, the *New York Times* said of the nomination of Fred Vinson as Chief Justice: "Secretary Vinson has been an able public servant. . . . But he is hardly the ideal appointment to the highest judicial office in the land, and he can hardly be said to measure up to the stature of his most recent predecessors in the post to which he has been named. . . ."—June 7, 1946, p. 18.

he relies on the advice of political leaders, we cannot endorse such a substitution.[58]

On balance, the record of the Committee during these formative years was promising if not entirely fruitful. It had established a cordial relationship with the Senate Judiciary Committee, had received favorable treatment in the press, and had at least in a few instances contributed to the rejection of "unqualified" individuals. Its performance satisfied the once hesitant Board of Governors of the American Bar Association, and in 1949 it was given permanent status as a *Standing* Committee, with its duties limited to matters of appointment and removal of federal judges. Peripheral subjects such as retirement and appellate judisdiction were transferred to another committee.[59]

Perhaps the most important decision that the Committee had to make regarding its objectives and style of operation was made during this formative period, and subsequent events proved it to have been the wisest of decisions. Much as any other newly formed group, the Committee had to agree on a plan of action that would both achieve the stated goals of the parent ABA, operate in a manner consistent with the expectations of the ABA leadership, and at the same time function in a way most likely to achieve positive results from the politically oriented judicial-selection process. Given the assumption that dissatisfaction with the results of the judicial-selection process stimulated the formation of the Special Committee on Judiciary in 1946, the major policy decision the Committee had to make was to answer the question, "How can the results be changed?" Clearly, the alternatives were to either work to change the system entirely—as other ABA committees were doing on the state level—or try to achieve sufficient influence within the system to make it produce more favorable results. The Committee chose to pursue the latter alternative, over the vehement and persistent objections of two of its members.

As its very first item of business in 1946, and again in each of the next three years, the Committee defeated resolutions by Loyd Wright of California and A. W. Trice of Oklahoma designed to encourage the Congress to (1) set minimum requirements of judicial experience for higher federal judges; (2) make naturalized citizens ineligible for federal judgeships; and (3) provide for minimum legal experience for lower federal judgeships.[60] The decision was made to work *within*

---

58 *New York Times,* June 30, 1951, p. 14.
59 See "Report of the Special Committee on Judiciary," 74 *ABA Reports* (1949), 385; and 72 *ABA Reports* (1947), 411.
60 "Report of the Special Committee on Judiciary," 73 *ABA Reports* (1948), 414, 275.

the prevailing system and to bank on achieving results that way. These two objectives were not incompatible at first, but they became so in late 1952 when the Committee first entered into a liaison with the Attorney General. It is entirely possible that had the Committee not devoted most of its efforts in this period to *trying* to work within the system, and had instead worked equally hard to reform it, it would not have been able to gain even the partial access which it achieved in 1952.

It should be noted that the Committee did depart from this policy in one respect. It has consistently sought bipartisan selection of judges as an intermediate step toward achieving a primary goal of the ABA—nonpartisan selection. Aside from this exception, it assumed a posture which would permit it, in the "American tradition," to seek gradual reform from within the system.

1953–1958

The first six years of the Eisenhower Administration, from 1953 through 1958, saw the Standing Committee on Federal Judiciary achieve a degree of access to the judicial-selection process not theretofore attained by any private association. Until mid-1952 the Committee had made recommendations to the Attorney General on an ad hoc basis when it learned of the existence of judicial vacancies. Very often its recommendations were submitted after the choice had already been determined or a firm commitment given. The Committee's continuous offers "to make its services available in investigating and reporting upon candidates other than those recommended by it" were never accepted.[61] Failure to reach any agreement with the Attorney General posed several problems for the Committee. First, even when the Committee could produce derogatory evidence, it was difficult for the Attorney General to take any position *other* than that of defending a nomination to which he was already committed. Second, when a nomination was publicized, it was difficult to elicit, even confidentially, candid opinions of the candidate by members of the bar. Since the expectation is that virtually every judicial nominee is confirmed by the Senate, no lawyer would want to be in a position of criticizing someone who would eventually sit in judgment on his cases.[62] Finally, if the Committee were forced to carry its whole case

---

[61] "Report of the Standing Committee on Federal Judiciary," 77 *ABA Reports* (1952), 215.
[62] *Ibid.*

to the Senate Judiciary Committee, which would consider only derogatory evidence, it would be unable to exert any creative influence in the process—that is, promoting good judges.

In the summer of 1952 a series of events occurred which permitted the Committee to gain its long-sought access to the nomination process. The Department of Justice had been rocked by several scandals uncovered by investigations of the House Judiciary Committee.[63] In the light of these disclosures, which resulted in several "vacancies" in the Justice Department hierarchy, the Committee urged Attorney General McGranery to fill the vacancies with outstanding lawyers. The Attorney General asked Stephen Mitchell, the House Committee Counsel and later National Democratic Chairman, if he could "find any lawyers meeting these specifications" and who would be "willing to come to Washington . . . at the end of an Administration that obviously is going to be replaced." McGranery is reported to have told Mitchell that if he found such lawyers, they would be appointed.[64]

Among others, Mitchell communicated with Ross Malone of New Mexico, who was a past member of the House of Delegates of the American Bar Association and then a member of the ABA's Board of Governors. After a conference with McGranery, Malone accepted the Attorney General's offer to become Deputy Attorney General, the chief agent of the Attorney General in recruiting federal judges. Recalling his tenure as Deputy Attorney General, Malone states:

Through my membership in the House of Delegates of the American Bar Association and subsequently on the Board of Governors, I was aware of the fact that the Committee on Federal Judiciary had sought for some time to make its voice heard in the selection of federal judges prior to the time that a decision had been reached in the Department and a name forwarded to the White House. I was also aware that the Committee had been wholly unsuccessful in these efforts.[65]

Malone was firmly convinced that the American Bar Association was ideally suited to furnish the administration with nonpartisan advice on prospective nominees. He therefore recommended to the Attorney General that the Department inaugurate a system of consultation with the Committee on Federal Judiciary to obtain its views before a final decision on any nomination was made. According to Malone,

---

[63] See *New York Times*, April 3, 4, 5, 1952, p. 1. In the midst of these investigations, President Truman fired Attorney General McGrath and replaced him with U. S. District Judge James P. McGranery.
[64] Letter from Ross Malone to author, March 6, 1963.
[65] *Ibid.*

McGranery agreed and directed him to make whatever arrangements were necessary.[66]

Malone "advised" Committee Chairman Howard Burns of the decision to submit names to the Committee and await its recommendations before making a final decision. He said that at the same time FBI investigations were initiated on the two or three serious contenders for each vacancy, the same names would be submitted to the Committee. Burns naturally agreed.[67]

By the time this agreement was reached, the adjournment of Congress was imminent, and the administration decided to make no interim appointments to the federal bench. Thus, there was no opportunity to put the agreement into effect. When President-elect Eisenhower designated Herbert Brownell of New York as his Attorney General, and Brownell chose William Rogers as his Deputy, the two met with McGranery and Malone to discuss the transition of administrations as it affected the Justice Department. Malone explained to them the arrangement he had made with the ABA Committee, and in his own words, "was extremely anxious to sell" this innovation to them. He reported that Brownell did not commit himself on the idea, but expressed an initially favorable reaction.[68]

Brownell and Rogers decided to continue the agreement excepting only that they requested the Committee on Federal Judiciary to discontinue suggesting names of its own in advance of being asked to evaluate a particular candidate by the Attorney General. The Committee reluctantly accepted this stipulation, noting in its next Annual Report that "your committee believes that it could be more helpful to the Department of Justice in many instances by affirmatively recommending candidates of outstanding qualifications who have been selected without any regard to political considerations." [69]

A second favorable development for the Committee was the support of its objectives by President Eisenhower. In sharp contrast to the hostile attitude of his predecessor, Eisenhower applauded the efforts of the organized bar and, in particular, the American Bar Association.

---

66 *Ibid.*

67 *Ibid.* These facts were confirmed by Committee Chairman Burns in two letters to author, dated October 8, 1962, and April 25, 1963. Burns emphasized that the liaison idea was primarily Malone's and was not opposed—but not actively supported—by Attorney General McGranery. See also "Report of the Standing Committee on Federal Judiciary," 77 *ABA Reports* (1952), 215.

68 Letter from Ross Malone to author, March 6, 1963.

69 "Report of the Standing Committee on Federal Judiciary," 78 *ABA Reports* (1953), 224.

It was through Eisenhower's influence that Supreme Court appointments were also referred to the ABA Committee for evaluation. Prior to 1953 Committee attempts to have Supreme Court nominees "checked out" by them were rebuffed. The appointment of justices of the Supreme Court had always been considered an unfettered presidential prerogative. As a result some eyebrows were raised when, upon the death of Chief Justice Fred Vinson in 1953, the chairman of the ABA Committee offered his group's "assistance" to the Attorney General in the search for a successor. Attorney General Brownell announced that any names the Committee submitted would be considered. However, before the Committee could submit a list, the recess appointment of Earl Warren was announced, and all the Committee could do was to recommend confirmation.[70]

In September 1956 the new chairman of the Committee, Bernard G. Segal of Philadelphia, met with Brownell and Rogers to review the relationship of the Committee to the Department of Justice. Segal brought up the fact that the Committee was "without function" respecting nominations of Supreme Court justices, and suggested that this be rectified. Later that same month, at a press conference, President Eisenhower said in answer to a query about possible successors to retiring Justice Minton, ". . . I believe also that we must never appoint a man who doesn't have the recognition of the American Bar Association." [71] No similar statement by a previous President has ever been recorded.

Later, at the direction of the President, the name of William Brennan was submitted to the ABA Committee. Brennan was highly recommended by the Committee and subsequently was appointed to the Supreme Court. This procedure was followed again in 1957 upon the retirement of Justice Reed. Brownell discussed with Chairman Segal a number of possibilities. When the name of Circuit Judge Charles Whittaker was given to the Committee, he was enthusiastically endorsed, and subsequently nominated.[72] The precedent of consulting with the Committee on Federal Judiciary on Supreme Court as well as lower-court nominations is still followed, although as we shall suggest subsequently, the influence of the Committee in the case of Supreme Court nominations may be more apparent than real.

---

70 "Report of the Standing Committee on Federal Judiciary," 79 *ABA Reports* (1954), 228.

71 "Report of the Standing Committee on Federal Judiciary," 82 *ABA Reports* (1957), 433.

72 *Ibid.,* p. 272. See also *New York Times,* March 3, 1957, p. 1.

At the meeting previously mentioned, Segal complained to Brownell and Rogers that in at least six instances nominations or recess appointments had been made to the lower federal courts without prior consultation of the Committee. Segal noted that this was a breech of the 1953 agreement and argued that if such omissions continued the value of the liaison to both the Committee and the Attorney General would diminish and the Committee would have to "reappraise" the nature and intensity of its efforts in behalf of the Attorney General. From that time until 1963 there was no record of an appointment to the federal bench which completely bypassed the Committee.[73]

It was during this period that the Committee's "right" to be consulted on each prospective nomination grew into a virtual veto power. From 1953–1958 there were ten nominations made over the objections of the Committee. After mid-1958, however, the Attorney General was directed by President Eisenhower to give "considerable" weight to the Committee's recommendations, and no one was nominated without Committee approval during the remainder of the Eisenhower Administration. In fact, the only nomination made contrary to the Committee's recommendation from *1956* to 1961 was a marginal case in which the candidate was opposed primarily on the ground that he was overage; and confirmation by the Senate was not opposed.[74]

In contrast to the improvement in its position at the nomination stage of the selection process, the Committee found its operations stymied by the resistance of individual senators and the Senate Judiciary Committee. Where the ABA Committee was unable to block a nomination, it was also unable to block confirmation.[75] It was readily apparent that complete effectiveness would not be achieved until an understanding, similar to that with the Attorney General, was reached with senators and the Senate Committee. Attempts were made to convince individual senators of the need for prior consultation with at least their local bar associations, if not the ABA Com-

---

[73] Interview with Bernard G. Segal, October 30, 1962. See also "Report of the Standing Committee on Federal Judiciary," 81 *ABA Reports* (1956), 440. In his report for 1963, the new chairman, Robert Meserve, noted one instance in which a "formal" report was not requested for a candidate rated low at the informal stage.— "Report of the Standing Committee on Federal Judiciary," 88 *ABA Reports* (1963), 524.

[74] This case involved J. Axel Beck, who was appointed to the District Court for the District of South Dakota in 1958. Beck was 63 years of age, and strongly supported by South Dakota's two Republican senators, Francis Case and Karl Mundt.

[75] During 1953–1961 the Committee was unable to block the confirmation of any of the candidates which it opposed.

mittee, before publicly committing themselves to nominations which they would then have to defend, even in the face of damaging and embarrassing evidence uncovered by the Committee.

It is noteworthy that in dealing with this obstacle, the Committee still followed the policy of working within the system. No attempts were made to challenge the "right" of senators to choose federal judges in their own states, although such challenges were being issued with increasing frequency in the pages of the *American Bar Association Journal*.[76]

In an attempt to at least blunt the effects of this senatorial prerogative, the Committee did resort to an extensive publicity campaign favoring nonpartisan selection of judges. It sought, without success, to have both major political parties insert pledges of nonpartisan selection in their 1952 and 1956 campaign platforms.[77]

In assessing the nature and extent of the Committee's increasing prestige during this period, the public furor surrounding the federal judiciary cannot be overlooked as a possible contributing factor. Stemming in part from its historic 1954 decision in *Brown v. Board of Education*, which alienated southerners, and a series of decisions in 1956 and 1957 that appeared to give some aid and comfort to "political" offenders, which alienated most northern conservatives, the Supreme Court was subjected to a constant and vituperative barrage of criticism.[78] Much talk and energy was given over by the Eighty-fifth Congress to ways of "curbing" the court, and of these a prominent solution was to alter the method of judicial selection. Since many of the "offending" decisions were venturesome in their departure from long-established precedents, the focus of reform centered on recruiting judges who were likely to be more conservative in their adherence to *stare decisis*.[79]

---

[76] See, among others, Ben R. Miller, "Politics and the Courts: The Struggle for Good Judges Goes On," 42 *ABAJ* (1956), 939.

[77] Quoted in "Report of the Standing Committee on Federal Judiciary," 81 *ABA Reports* (1956), 271.

[78] These "offending" decisions are well chronicled in C. Herman Pritchett, *The Political Offender and the Warren Court* (Boston: Boston University Press, 1957).

A good discussion of Congress's reaction to these decisions can be found in Walter F. Murphy, *Congress and the Court* (Chicago: University of Chicago Press, 1962).

[79] Of the numerous bills introduced in the Eighty-fifth Congress designed to "curb" the Supreme Court, at least fourteen attempted in one or another ways to alter the process of selecting federal judges. These included proposals to provide for the election of judges in the states where they serve (HJR 119), to provide for the appointment of federal judges by the state courts (HJR 438), to require judicial

Although there was much sympathy among members of the American Bar Association for this substantive criticism of the Court's work, there was no official condemnation of the Supreme Court as an institution. ABA President Charles Rhyne called on America's lawyers to fight any bills designed to subvert the Court's historic composition and prerogatives. He declared that "particular decisions may be wrong, but the independence of the judiciary connotes the power to be wrong as well as right." [80]

Nevertheless, the constant demands by critics that the method of selecting judges be changed to insure the selection of more experienced men lent strength to the ABA Committee's drive for the *informal* establishment of a similar standard. The pressures of this verbal assault may have been in part responsible for President Eisenhower's strong support of the principle of consulting the ABA on *all* judicial appointments, and for his insistence, after 1954, that all Supreme Court nominees have at least nominal judicial experience. By bringing the ABA more intimately into the selection process, the administration may have sought to stymie attacks not only on its freedom to nominate, but on the powers of the Supreme Court as well.

1958–1963

One of the complaints which the ABA Committee frequently articulated prior to mid-1958 was that it was being consulted too late in the nomination process for it to be a really effective advisor. Since the name it received for investigation was usually the name to be submitted (it rarely received the "several" names that Ross Malone had envisioned), and many political commitments had been made beforehand, the Committee could deter a nomination only by the presentation of clearly disqualifying information.[81] This procedure was also disadvantageous to the Attorney General in a number of ways, particularly in cases where there were a number of likely and apparently well-qualified candidates for the same vacancy.[82] If he were able to obtain advance information on each of several candidates spon-

---

nominees to have 5 or more years prior judicial experience (S 1184), and to require the President to make Supreme Court nominations from a list of names drawn up by the American Bar Association (HJR 406).

[80] *New York Times,* May 7, 1958, p. 27.

[81] Bernard G. Segal, "Federal Judicial Selection—Progress and the Promise of the Future," 46 *Massachusetts Law Quarterly* (1961), 143.

[82] Interview with former Deputy Attorney General Lawrence Walsh, December 22, 1962.

sored by prominent politicians, the Attorney General could more easily engineer the nomination of the best candidate, or the candidate he preferred.

With this mutual advantage in mind, Attorney General William Rogers, Deputy Attorney General Lawrence Walsh, and Bernard Segal arranged in 1958 for the institution of two new procedures. First, the Attorney General agreed to refer to the Committee for *informal* investigation and evaluation the name of *each* person being given serious consideration for a federal judgeship. This would not displace, but would rather augment the procedure already in effect whereby the Committee made a *formal* investigation and report on the candidate most likely to be selected. This new procedure was to be, in effect, a secret, preliminary screening process.

The second innovation, which apparently was initiated by the Committee, was to construct a four-point scale of evaluation to replace the general designations of "qualified" or "not qualified" theretofore used. The Committee suggested this to enable it to differentiate between "its function in seeking the best qualified candidates . . . , and its function in passing upon names submitted to it by the Justice Department." [83]   All candidates would now be rated as "not qualified," "qualified," "well qualified," or "exceptionally well qualified."

These new procedures caused a tremendous increase in the work load of the Committee. With the number of vacancies sufficiently high, the work of many Committee members became virtually a full-time job. Certainly it became one for the chairman, who would be involved in processing all informal reports, not just those in his own circuit. In 1958–1959, for example, the Committee submitted 127 formal or informal reports, compared with 72 formals for the preceding *two* years.[84] But more important, the combination of these two new procedures accorded the Committee a more significant role in the selection process. It was no longer limited simply to passing upon a choice already made and not likely to be reversed. It was now in a position not only to block unqualified candidates effectively, but also to push for candidates who were better qualified by its standards. To be sure, it still could not exert much influence at the key recruitment stage, but it had advanced substantially toward that goal. From the negativism and frustrations of a veto group, the Committee on Federal

---

[83] "Report of the Standing Committee on Federal Judiciary," 83 *ABA Reports* (1958), 350.

[84] "Report of the Standing Committee on Federal Judiciary," 84 *ABA Reports* (1959), 277.

Judiciary assumed more of a creative role in the selection process. For the first time in its twelve-year existence, the Committee was able to begin to fulfill one of the major objectives of the ABA: to *promote* the nomination of the persons it considered best qualified.[85]

In its Annual Report for 1960, the Committee was able to make the following report of progress:

[The Committee's relationship with the Administration] stands at the stage where no person is given consideration for nomination to the Federal bench without at least preliminary screening by members of your Committee, and it is reasonably assured that no appointment would be made of a person whom your Committee, for valid reasons, reports as unqualified.

In a two year period, every nomination sent to the Senate was preceded by a favorable report by the Committee.

Viewed against the background of the situation eight years ago, this represents remarkable progress. Nevertheless, the goal of this Association does not rest here.

The interplay of the various elements which go into the eventual appointment of a federal judge is such that compromises often result, and as a consequence, the appointee, though qualified, is not the most highly qualified.[86]

With that report was expressed the hope that with the inevitable transition in administrations, the function of the Committee would remain unimpaired. The Committee declared that "our gains to this date have taken root, and may before long be institutionalized as part of the political system of our country." [87] This report, adopted by the House of Delegates, urged the incoming President to continue the present working agreement *including* a pledge "not [to] nominate as a federal judge any person who, after thorough investigation and consideration is, for valid reasons, reported by the Standing Committee on Federal Judiciary as not qualified to serve as a federal judge." [88]

In addition to this plea, the Committee again sought to have a plank on judicial selection inserted in the 1960 platform of each major political party, calling for the bipartisan selection of judges. The Democratic Platform made no reference to judicial selection, but the Republicans included the following statement: "Needed federal judgeships, appointed on the basis of the highest qualifications and

---

85 "Oral Report by Bernard G. Segal to House of Delegates," Mid-year Meetings of the American Bar Association, Chicago, 1959 (mimeo).
86 "Report of the Standing Committee on Federal Judiciary," 85 *ABA Reports* (1960), 453.
87 *Ibid.*, p. 454.
88 *Ibid.*, p. 452.

without limitation to a single political party, should be created to expedite administration of justice in federal courts." [89]   This was the first known plank regarding judicial appointments in any major party platform.

Whatever fears the Committee on Federal Judiciary may have had concerning the future of its liaison with the Justice Department were directed primarily toward an incoming *Democratic* President.   If the 1960 Republican presidential candidate, Vice-President Richard M. Nixon, were elected, then almost certainly the Rogers-Walsh team would have remained and no problems of transition would have arisen.   But the views of Senator John Kennedy toward the role of the ABA Committee were not known, and the absence of a judicial-selection plank in the Democratic Platform did not alleviate this uncertainty.   Senator Kennedy did send a letter during the campaign to the President of the American Bar Association, John Randall of Iowa, advising him that he agreed with the idea of a qualified and independent judiciary, and that partisanship would not be the paramount basis for selection.[90]   But the very ambiguity of this statement may have been a chilling reminder to the Committee that its favored position depended entirely on the indulgence of the President.

Before the inauguration of President Kennedy on January 20, 1961, Attorney General Robert Kennedy and Deputy Attorney General Byron White met with Segal and ABA President Whitney North Seymour and "unequivocally" agreed to submit all names under consideration for informal screening and eventual formal evaluation. According to Segal, this commitment extended also to "appointing only those who were pronounced clearly qualified." [91]   But there seems to have been, at best, some confusion on this latter point.   Subsequent events made very clear that, unlike its predecessors, the Kennedy Administration did *not* intend to continue to extend to the ABA Committee the veto-group role it had previously occupied.   As Table 3.1 indicates, the Kennedy Administration appointed eight persons designated "not qualified" during its first two years in office.   This represented 7.3 per cent of the judicial appointments made during this two-year period, as compared with 5.7 per cent during the entire Eisenhower Administration and only 1.2 per cent during the second Eisenhower term.

---

[89] *Ibid.*, p. 455.
[90] Letter of August 30, 1960, quoted in "Midwinter Report of the Standing Committee on Federal Judiciary," 86 *ABA Reports* (1961), 118.
[91] Segal, *op. cit.*, p. 147.

TABLE 3.1

NOMINATIONS AND COMMITTEE RECOMMENDATIONS, 1953–1962

Action	Eisenhower (Per Cent)	Kennedy (Per Cent)
Nominated with Committee approval	93.7	92.7
Nominated over Committee objection	5.7	7.3
Nominated, Committee not opposed	0.6	0.0
	100.0	100.0
	(N = 175 *)	(N = 110)

* Eisenhower made a total of 181 nominations, but six were never submitted to the ABA Committee for evaluation. During the second Eisenhower term, only one nomination (or 1.2 per cent) was made over the opposition of the Committee.

Answering criticism of this record in the Committee's Annual Report for 1962, Deputy Attorney General Nicholas deB. Katzenbach "reminded" the House of Delegates "that the responsibility is the President's and the Senate's, and this Association does not have and would not wish to have a veto over the appointments to be made. "I have no doubt," Katzenbach continued,

that amidst these many appointments . . . there will be disappointments and some of the judges appointed will not come up to the standard which the Administration would wish for all judges. I would be very surprised if there were not judges appointed who will prove to have been unworthy and unqualified. I would be very surprised if this Committee were omniscient and infallible in that respect, and I do not think that they would claim that infallibility. I think that at least some of the Judges found by this Committee to be unqualified will . . . prove to have been good appointments. I think some of the Judges found to be qualified will, over a period of years, prove to have been bad appointments.[92]

Despite this apparent diminution of its influence, it cannot yet be said that over a period of time the Committee will not again approximate an informal veto group. The political-patronage pressures on any new administration are great, and it simply does not have the freedom

---

[92] "Oral Reply of Nicholas DeB. Katzenbach to House of Delegates," Annual Meeting of the American Bar Association, San Francisco, 1962 (mimeo), p. 3. It is interesting to note that the following year saw no appointment made over the Committee's opposition.—"Report of the Standing Committee on Federal Judiciary," 88 *ABA Reports* (1963), 524.

of operation which an outgoing administration with a lame-duck President can manage.[93]

One cannot disregard party affiliation and philosophy in explaining the relationship of the Committee on Federal Judiciary to the Eisenhower and Kennedy administrations. Despite its public service and nonpartisan facade, the American Bar Association is, in terms of its political orientation and policy values, much closer to the Republican than the Democratic "orbit" of supporting groups, and no Democratic administration could afford politically to overlook this factor entirely. Although there are certain political advantages which even a Democratic administration can gain from working with the ABA Committee, it could never afford a "captive" image.

THE STATUS OF THE COMMITTEE ON FEDERAL JUDICIARY, 1964

Any appraisal of the development of the Committee's formal prerogatives and functions from 1946 to 1964 would have to consider the institutionalization of its relationship with the Attorney General as its most significant achievement. Although this accomplishment and its corollary privileges may fall somewhat short of the overall goals of the ABA, they far exceed the access acquired previously by any other interest group. Barring a reversal of the ABA Committee's policy to work within the existing framework of judicial selection, its present status could probably be improved upon only by returning to the "veto-group" role it held under the Eisenhower Administration.

Whatever status and function the Committee has, of course, it has by privilege rather than by right or statute. But though its position is informal, the prospective continuity of this relationship is enhanced by the strong and favorable influence of the articulate press. Typical of the widespread acceptance of the legitimacy of the Committee's function was the following statement in the *New York Times:*

. . . President Kennedy came into office at a time of approximate political parity in the Federal Courts. This has now been thrown off balance by the appointments he has made. But there are still some forty judicial vacancies. In filling them Republicans might be favored among candidates of equal competence. But no one should be appointed who is not "well qualified"

---

93 See "Report of the Standing Committee on Federal Judiciary," 87 *ABA Reports* (1962), 606.

or "exceptionally well qualified" in the opinion of the Bar Association—and in fact.[94]

Thus, the *Times* was prepared to go even further than the ABA Committee itself and exclude appointees who were only "qualified" and no higher. Similar criticism of President Kennedy's appointment of persons rated "not qualified" appeared in newspapers throughout the country. The *Christian Science Monitor* found it "peculiar" that "of all the lawyers in the United States who are regarded as Republicans, the Administration could not find seven whose juristic abilities would warrant their appointment ahead of the seven whom a bar association considers 'not qualified.' " [95]

Although such support could not assure the stability of the Committee's position or prerogatives in the event of a dispute between it and the Attorney General, it would probably serve to prevent the eruption of minor dislocations. A more detailed description of the relationship between the Committee and the Attorney General and their mutual impact will make up the major portions of Chapter 5.

In appraising the development of the Committee's influence in the selection process, one major factor has not been mentioned. And yet it seems probable that this was the necessary, if not the sufficient, factor in giving the Committee the credentials it needed. It was not until the latter part of the New Deal that the ABA sought to represent, in theory if not in fact, the entire legal profession. To be sure, many times before the 1930s it had spoken in behalf of America's lawyers. But until it adopted, in 1936, a federated system of representation in its governing body, the House of Delegates, and actively sought to enroll the rank-and-file members of the profession on its rolls, it lacked the credentials to represent the organized bar to the Attorney General.[96]

The ABA's claim to representation is still imperfect, and still less than half of all lawyers are members. But the propriety of its assuming the role of "voice" of the American bar is much less questionable. Without these credentials, it is doubtful that it could have exerted any *systematic* influence whatever on the selection of federal judges.

---

94 March 9, 1962, p. 28.
95 February 24, 1962, p. 14.
96 See Max Radin, "The Achievements of the American Bar Association: A Sixty Year Record," 26 *ABAJ* (1940), 141, 230, 241. The ABA now has 43.7 per cent of the lawyer population on its membership rolls, as compared to only a fraction of that in 1902.

4

❧❧

THE COMMITTEE
ON FEDERAL JUDICIARY

In the preceding chapter we focused on the development of the formal prerogatives of the ABA's Committee on Federal Judiciary. Here we shall examine in detail the activities and personnel of the Committee. We will try to answer three questions: (1) Who becomes a member of the Committee? (2) What are the major judicial-selection decisions in which the Committee is involved and how does it operate internally to make these decisions? (3) What is the basis for the Committee's judgment that a candidate is or is not qualified for service on the federal bench?

THE MEMBERS OF THE COMMITTEE:
A COMPOSITE PICTURE

In describing any decision-making process, it is important to know who is making the decisions. Although any decision-maker in a democratic society finds himself limited by legal requirements or expectations and informal norms, his decisions within these limits are often products of his past environment, his personal, political, and social values, and the ways in which these factors condition his approach to the decision to be made. "Human beings perceive what goes on about them within a frame of reference determined by their total previous experiences. . . . [They] develop tendencies, called attitudes, to react in a certain way to stimuli." [1] In short, regardless

---

[1] Donald R. Matthews, *The Social Background of Political Decision-Makers* (New York: Random House Studies in Political Science, 1954), p. 3.

82

of the limitations imposed by the particular system on the decision-maker, the question of "who is making the decision?" will always affect "what" decision is made.[2]

For the same reasons that we are interested in WHO becomes a federal judge, we are concerned with who makes important decisions in behalf of the organized bar. Members of the ABA's Committee on Federal Judiciary ostensibly base their evaluations of prospective nominees primarily on "professional qualifications"—factors which they as lawyers can supposedly best discern. Yet there is the possibility that other ingredients besides professional qualifications make up the decision which formally reads: "John Doe is not qualified to be a federal judge because he lacks sufficient experience and familiarity with court procedures." One of the ways that we can obtain clues about these other ingredients is to examine the backgrounds of the men who make the decisions. The legal profession is highly stratified [3] and lawyers of different backgrounds may not similarly appraise the qualifications of a judicial candidate barring obvious instances of deviant (that is, dishonest) behavior. Which lawyers, therefore, are making these decisions, and how are they chosen? Although no causal relationship between background and decisions can be formally and specifically established, an inspection of the backgrounds of the ABA Committee members and a description of how they are selected ought to give some clues to their professional and political values—values not likely to be completely cast aside when the time for decision approaches.

Method of Selection

The manner in which the eleven members are chosen is significant not only in determining who is chosen, but also in determining the ways in which they carry out their functions. Once selected, are they relatively free to act, or must they maintain a continuing accountability to their selectors?

---

2 See David B. Truman, *The Governmental Process* (New York: Knopf, 1951), pp. 479–482, 489–493.

3 See Jack Ladinsky, "Careers of Lawyers, Law Practice, and Legal Institutions," 28 *American Sociological Review* (1963), 47–54, and "The Impact of Social Backgrounds of Lawyers on Law Practice and the Law," 16 *Journal of Legal Education* (1963), 127–144. See also Jerome Carlin, *The Lawyer as Individual Practitioner* (Ph.D. dissertation, University of Chicago, 1959), pp. 414 ff., and "Current Research in the Sociology of the Legal Profession," Bureau of Applied Social Research, Columbia University, 1962 (mimeo).

Formal responsibility for choosing the members of the Committee on Federal Judiciary rests with the president of the ABA, as does the annual designation of the chairman from among the members of the Committee. Each appointment to the Committee is for a three-year term. There is no formal restriction on the president's choice excepting only that there must be one member of the Committee from each judicial circuit and the District of Columbia.[4] Informally, the practice has been to consult the incumbent chairman on most if not all new appointments and on all reappointments. The extent to which the chairman is consulted varies, as does the weight given to his recommendation. A strong chairman normally exercises considerable influence in choosing new members. He is in a position to evaluate the work of the members, and to advise the president of the "needs" of the circuit in which a vacancy will occur. Frequently, he can suggest a number of likely candidates from which the president can choose. Where the power to advise is considerable, it is not much different, except in form, from the power to appoint, and recent chairmen of the Committee have successfully controlled appointments.[5] Clearly, therefore, the members of the Committee have to be lawyers both "visible" and "acceptable" to the upper hierarchy of the ABA leadership; in fact, as will be shown below, the Committee members themselves come almost exclusively from these same ranks.

Age as a Criterion of Selection

Who becomes a member of the Committee on Federal Judiciary? The fifty-one lawyers who served from 1946 to 1962 have all been mature if not older men at the time of their selection. As Table 4.1 shows, 43 per cent of the Committee members were over the age of 60 at the time of their appointment, and almost 90 per cent were 50 years or older. The median age at appointment was 58. This tendency to select older lawyers is intentional. It reflects the need to obtain the services of lawyers who have a wide variety of contacts in the profession and are well known in their immediate areas. One of the primary requisites for a Committee member is that he be of a caliber and type that inspires the confidence of other lawyers. Otherwise he would not be able to elicit the confidential information from other

---

[4] Article X, Section 7, (L), 1, *Constitution and By-Laws of the American Bar Association.*

[5] Interview with Bernard G. Segal, former chairman of the Committee on Federal Judiciary, October 30, 1962.

TABLE 4.1

AGE OF COMMITTEE MEMBERS AT APPOINTMENT

Age	Percentage		
40–49	9.8		
50–59		45.1	
60–63	88.2	17.6	
64–69		15.7	43.1
Over 70		9.8	
Unknown	2.0		
(Average age: 58.6)	100.0 (N = 51)		

members of the profession which is necessary to the investigation of each candidate for judicial office. The tendency toward selecting older lawyers may also reflect a desire to secure Committee members who will not themselves be candidates for judicial office. Since the Committee has set the age of 60 as the maximum optimum age of appointment, with a slight extension to 64 in unusual cases, most of its members would be "ineligible" for a federal judgeship—by the Committee's standards—upon joining the Committee or shortly thereafter.

It is interesting to note that the median age of Committee members at the time of their appointment was considerably higher than the 47–56 median age group of all lawyers in the United States in 1961.[6] In age, at least, they did not come from the most populous segment of the profession. Of course, aside from the specific reasons already stated for choosing older lawyers, there is the practical reason that lawyers of this age are likely to be more available for such "extra-curricular" activities. Their practices have been established, their reputations made, and they are likely to be less reluctant to spend considerable time away from their practices.

That the members of the Committee would come primarily from the ranks of older lawyers is not surprising, nor the cause for automatic concern. Choosing leaders from among senior members is a common and understandable practice of all sorts of groups. Senior members tend to be most experienced, to be known quantities, and perhaps less inclined to rash and thoughtless actions. But that a Committee representing the legal profession in an important phase of its activities should be so constituted is a potentially significant fact.

---

[6] *The 1961 Lawyer Statistical Report* (Chicago: American Bar Foundation, 1961), p. 25.

Law Practice and Committee Service

All the members of the Committee but one were practicing lawyers at the time of their appointment. The one exception was United States Senator Forrest Donnell of Missouri, who represented the Eighth Circuit in the early years of the Committee's existence. As indicated in Table 4.2, the majority of Committee members were, at the time of their appointment, associated with firms engaged primarily in general or trial practice. There were no Committee members who had specialized in criminal law, domestic relations, or a host of other special

TABLE 4.2

TYPE OF PRACTICE OF COMMITTEE MEMBERS AT APPOINTMENT

Type (Primarily)	Percentage of Members
General practice	60.8
Corporate and financial	3.9
Criminal	0.0
Litigation	19.6
Domestic relations	0.0
Taxation/administrative law	5.9
Not in private practice	2.0
Unknown	7.8
	100.0 (N = 51)

types of law practices. Recent data not reflected in the table indicate that the selection policy is changing to favor those primarily in trial practice. This correlates with the Committee's increasing emphasis on trial experience as *the* primary qualification for appointment to the district courts. It would appear somewhat odd for a Committee made up primarily of lawyers who spend little time in the courtroom to assess the trial abilities of other lawyers. Of the Committee members appointed since 1958, six of eleven, or 54.5 per cent, listed litigation as their specialty or predominant professional activity, whereas only three of the forty members appointed before 1958 (or 7.5 per cent) could be so identified. But this preference for trial lawyers, which has been espoused by various people involved in the Committee's operations, runs against the "requirement" that lawyers on the Committee be able to devote a considerable amount of time to Committee work. A trial lawyer's income usually depends on his work in the courtroom, whereas lawyers in other types of work "live" on retainer fees, which do not require that they follow any sort of specific work patterns.

TABLE 4.3

POSITION IN FIRM OF COMMITTEE MEMBERS AT APPOINTMENT

Position	Percentage
Senior or managing partner	25.5 } 84.3
Partner	58.8
Associate	0.0
Individual practitioner	5.9
Unknown	7.8
Not in private practice	2.0
	100.0 (N = 51)

Every member of the Committee who was associated with a law firm was, at the time of his appointment, either a partner or senior partner of that firm. As Table 4.3 shows, 84.3 per cent of all the lawyers on the Committee held such a position, whereas according to the *1961 Lawyer Statistical Report,* only 24.1 per cent of all American lawyers were partners in law firms.[7]

Complementing these figures, Table 4.4 indicates that 58.9 per cent

TABLE 4.4

SIZE OF FIRM OF COMMITTEE MEMBERS AT APPOINTMENT

Size	Percentage
Individual practice	5.9
5 members or fewer	29.4
Between 6 and 10 members	23.5
Between 11 and 20 members	11.8
21 or more	23.6
Unknown	3.9
Not in private practice	2.0
	100.0 (N = 51)

of the members of the Committee were associated with law firms containing six or more members, 29.4 per cent were members of smaller firms, and only 5.9 per cent were engaged in individual practice. By

---

[7] *Ibid.,* p. 62.

contrast, 46.1 per cent of all lawyers in 1961 were engaged in individual practice, and 61.2 per cent were engaged in individual practice in 1949 when many of the members of the Committee were first appointed.[8] Further emphasizing this contrast, only 4.7 per cent of all lawyers in 1948 were members of firms with *five* or more members.[9] Thus, the membership of the Committee substantially overrepresents the large-firm lawyer. For reasons stated earlier in the case of trial lawyers, individual practitioners and small-firm lawyers have less time to spare from their practices and are therefore less "available" for service on such as the Committee on Federal Judiciary.

The significance of the size of the firm is magnified by the fact that every lawyer who serves on the Committee on Federal Judiciary must be prepared to bear part of the costs of its operations. If he is a member of a firm which can absorb these costs, he will obviously be in a better position than if he practices alone, or with a firm which depends on his constant availability. In addition to the firm's losing the member's services, it is expected to take care of a large share of the out-of-pocket expenses involved in traveling for interviews, and so on. Until 1957 the Committee had virtually no budget. Since then it has operated on a modest allowance which does little more than provide for the secretarial aids the chairman uses in administering the Committee's operations.[10]

Bar-Association Activity as a Prerequisite

Another important indicator of the selectivity of the process of recruiting Committee members is bar-association activity. Virtually all the members of the Committee for whom information is available were very active in bar-association affairs prior to their appointment; most had achieved high bar-association office. All had attained a sufficient measure of visibility through previous work to give the president and chairman some idea of their abilities and values. These data are also a measure of high economic status; lawyers whose practice requires their full-time attention rarely have the time to participate actively—and certainly not assiduously—in extracurricular activities. Of the

---

8 *Ibid.*

9 Albert Blaustein and Charles Porter, *The American Lawyer* (Chicago: University of Chicago Press, 1954), p. 11.

10 Interview with Bernard G. Segal, former chairman of the Committee on Federal Judiciary, October 30, 1962. According to Segal, he asked the Board of Governors for a budget commensurate with the expenses of the job so that "his successor could afford to handle the job."

forty-one members of the Committee (out of fifty-one) for whom information of this sort was available, 41.2 per cent were past presidents of state bar associations and an equal number presidents of county or municipal bar groups. Virtually every member had at least one such affiliation. The figures in Table 4.5 are even more striking in view of the fact that there was no information available on ten, whose data would surely add to the percentages. These figures indicate that all

TABLE 4.5

OFFICIAL POSITIONS OF COMMITTEE MEMBERS IN BAR GROUPS
AT APPOINTMENT

Position	Percentage (of 51)
President, state bar association	41.2
President, county or municipal bar association	41.2
Executive committee or board of governors, state bar association	17.6
Executive committee or board of governors, county or municipal	9.8
Board of governors, ABA	9.8
Executive committee or board of governors, national bar group	19.6
Board of editors, bar journal	7.8
Committee chairman, state bar association	9.8
Committee chairman, county or municipal bar association	3.9
Committee chairman, ABA	5.9

these lawyers have devoted large blocs of time to bar activities. Such participation affords the opportunity to know, and to be known by, the right people.

Another index of "availability" for Committee membership appears to be prior membership in the House of Delegates of the American Bar Association. Table 4.6 indicates that twenty-eight (54.9 per cent) of the members of the Committee were delegates prior to their appointment to the Committee, many for long terms and in varying capacities. Not reflected in this table is the fact that several Committee members were selected for the House of Delegates after they were appointed to, or served on, the Committee.

As a corollary to this bar "visibility," a large number of the Committee members (41.2 per cent) were listed in *Who's Who* prior to their

TABLE 4.6

MEMBERSHIP OF COMMITTEE MEMBERS IN HOUSE OF DELEGATES
AT APPOINTMENT

Capacity		Percentage
State delegate		25.5
Bar association delegate		23.5
Chairman of House of Delegates	54.9	3.9
Section representative		2.0
Nonmember		45.1
		100.0
		(N = 51) *

* This table reflects only single memberships. Where a member served in various capacities, he was recorded only in the most prestigious. It was not infrequent to find one member serving in several capacities in succession.

selection to the Committee, and a substantial percentage (27.5 per cent) was newly listed after appointment to the Committee.

Large-City Domination

The distribution of lawyers on the Committee shows a distinct large-city flavor. Over 80 per cent of the members [11] practiced in cities with populations over 100,000. Although this percentage is not greatly out of line with the general distribution of lawyers in the country, it does indicate that large areas of the country are never represented on the Committee. Boston, New York, Philadelphia or Pittsburgh, Chicago, and either Los Angeles, San Francisco, or Sacramento receive "regular" representation on the Committee, which means that the small-town lawyers in the first, second, third, seventh, and ninth circuits are never represented and always judged by their big-city brethren. The other circuits are frequently represented by lawyers in smaller cities, though rarely by lawyers in cities of less than 50,000.[12]

---

[11] Of these, 25.5 per cent practiced in cities with populations exceeding 1,000,000 and 43.2 per cent in cities with populations of less than 1,000,000 and more than 250,000.

[12] The Committee has had but one member from a city with a population of less than 5000. Stuart Campbell of Wytheville, Virginia, was selected in 1959 by ABA President John Randall in order to give representation to a "real small community."—Interview with John Randall, September 1, 1962.

Education and Prestige

Two final items complete our composite picture of the members of the Committee on Federal Judiciary. First, what sorts of education did they receive and what sort of academic records did they compile? Virtually all members of the Committee (92.2 per cent) held law degrees and only one member had been admitted to the bar without formal legal training. Of those with law degrees, there was an almost even division among graduates of the Ivy League law schools, state university law schools, and private law schools. Most of the Ivy League graduates came from the first, second, and third circuits, which constitute the "home area" of these schools.[13] Interestingly enough, if law-review participation can be taken as an index of academic achievement, few of the Committee members were academic leaders; only 10 per cent of those who attended law schools with law reviews were members of those law review publications.[14]

Second, how were the members of the Committee rated by members of their profession? Although the Martindale-Hubbell ratings tend to reflect prestige as well as legal ability and professional accomplishment, they are the only available indices of the professional standing of lawyers. Every member of the Committee who was rated by Martindale-Hubbell was given the "a-v" or very high rating. The one lawyer rated "b-v" or high at the time of his appointment to the Committee was almost immediately advanced to "a-v." [15] These ratings tend only to confirm the proposition advanced earlier that membership on the Committee requires a minimum amount of prestige and occupational visibility.

Implications of Committee Membership Patterns

Given the relatively restricted nature of the process by which Committee members are recruited, and the clear patterns of choice which have just been shown, it can be safely predicted that the Committee

---

[13] Of the forty-seven members with law degrees, seventeen were from the Ivy League, sixteen from state university law schools, and fifteen from assorted private university law colleges.

[14] It is interesting to note that in the absence of other evidence of potential judicial ability, the Justice Department places great reliance on academic record in law school.—Interview with Assistant Deputy Attorney General Joseph Dolan, November, 2, 1962.

[15] —Which might give some clues about the genesis and basis for the Martindale-Hubbell ratings!

is not likely to include among its members many lawyers from the rank and file of the profession. Of course, that in itself is not a cause for either surprise or concern. The ABA is no different from most other groups in conferring leadership responsibilities on a select segment of its membership.[16] Certainly many lawyers from the lower echelons would have neither the inclination nor the ability to become involved in such work. But what may be of concern is the perhaps unduly narrow segment of the bar from which the members of the Committee are drawn—the large law firms, the highest salaried lawyers, the "professional" participators in bar activities.

Both the manner in which the members of the Committee are chosen and the types of lawyers who become members indicate that the Committee's views on judicial selection are likely to be the views of those lawyers constituting this segment of the profession. And the types of lawyers asked for information about prospective judicial candidates, the Committee's standards of evaluation, and the types of candidates it prefers, may reflect these views as well.

THE DECISION-MAKING PROCESS

What are the major judicial-selection decisions in which the Committee is involved and how does it operate internally to make these decisions?

The "Informal" Investigation and Report

Whenever the Attorney General receives the name of a person who appears to merit serious consideration for appointment to the federal judiciary, that name is submitted to the Committee on Federal Judiciary for a *preliminary* and *informal* investigation and evaluation. At the same time the Justice Department initiates a parallel investigation, using its vast network of United States Attorneys, Assistant United States Attorneys, lawyers in the Department's numerous field division offices, and party workers.[17] The ABA *informal* investigation is made by the Committee member in the circuit where the vacancy

---

16 See Matthews, *op. cit.*, pp. 8, 9. See also Lewis A. Froman, Jr., *People and Politics* (Englewood Cliffs, N. J.: Prentice-Hall, 1962), pp. 34 ff.

17 Similar parallel investigations were not conducted under the Eisenhower Administration. Reliance was placed primarily on the FBI field check and the report of the Committee on Federal Judiciary.—Interview with former Deputy Attorney General Lawrence Walsh, December 22, 1962.

exists. In order to preclude advance publicity, this investigation is usually limited to interviews with a few lawyers and judges who have some knowledge of the candidate's abilities and personality. Interviews with the candidate himself are rarely held at this early stage, but the candidate is required to fill out a lengthy questionnaire constructed jointly by the Committee and the Department of Justice.[18] At the conclusion of this informal investigation, a report is made to the Committee chairman, listing the salient facts and giving a tentative evaluation of the candidate—"not qualified," "qualified," "well qualified," or "exceptionally well qualified." While the circuit member is making this investigation, the chairman normally makes an independent spot check (usually by telephone) to enable him to corroborate or challenge the findings of the investigating member.

On the basis of this preliminary information, the chairman orally communicates the findings to the Deputy Attorney General or his assistant, and a tentative *prediction* as to what the ultimate formal rating—to be determined later by the full Committee—will be. With this data, that gathered from his own sources, and the political situation relevant to the case, the Attorney General decides to intensify the investigation of some names, and cease consideration of others.[19]

Given the numerous factors which influence judicial nominations, this ABA *informal* would not appear to be especially significant. But just the opposite is true. The evidence indicates that it is at this early stage that the ABA evaluation can be used to best advantage. Much of this effectiveness, however, depends on the forcefulness and persuasiveness of the Committee chairman in dealing with the Deputy Attorney General and staff. The "informal" is not a single report; rather it constitutes a series of impressions orally conveyed by the chairman to the Deputy Attorney General over a period of time. This is the period in the selection process when the choice is most likely to be "open" for discussion, and the chairman, who is in constant contact with the Deputy Attorney General, has a real opportunity to use the information he receives from the circuit member to either block the nomination of someone considered "not qualified" or enhance the chances of someone considered "well qualified." The chair-

---

[18] This questionnaire was constructed by Bernard Segal, and is distributed by the office of the Attorney General. The candidate is directed to send one completed copy to the Committee chairman, one to the circuit member, and one to the Attorney General.

[19] Approximately four informal reports are completed for each vacancy on the federal bench; from January 20, 1961, to August 13, 1962, the Committee completed 462 informals for 112 vacancies.

man is able to do more than simply file a report; he becomes, in effect, the confidante of the Attorney General. In 1959 Deputy Attorney General Lawrence Walsh told the House of Delegates that "your Chairman, Mr. Segal, has become, next to the Attorney General himself . . . my most intimate associate in Washington. I work with him and spend more time with him and talk longer with him than anybody else in the Department." [20]

Another determinant of ABA influence at this point is the timing of its report. If some commitment has already been made by the Attorney General, an evaluation of "not qualified" is of less import than the same evaluation of a candidate to whom (or to whose sponsor) no promises have been made. During the first two years of the Kennedy Administration, adverse reports on 158 nominees were made, of which eight were disregarded by the Attorney General. It is probably correct, as the ABA claims, that in the absence of these reports, a larger number of the 158 would have received appointments.[21] Where the ABA can produce substantial and verifiable derogatory information about a candidate, the Attorney General later is often able to use this information to convince a senator to withdraw his support. Even where the ABA findings are not entirely negative, but marginal, the Attorney General is in a position to use this information as a political weapon. Similarly, where the Committee has found among the candidates for a judicial vacancy one or more with outstanding qualifications, the Attorney General is often able to convince a senator to throw his support to those who are "better" qualified, even though the senator's original choice may be marginally qualified.

The great bulk of the Committee's important work is carried on at this informal stage of the process. It is done, moreover, not by the Committee as a whole, but by the circuit member and chairman, with the brunt of the initial investigation falling upon the former, and the follow-up interaction with the Department of Justice upon the latter. It is the information supplied in the informal report and the predicted rating which reflects the Committee's most important functions in the nomination process. An effective veto power rests, in any single case, with two members of the Committee—a power not easily counteracted by a reversal by the entire Committee at the next stage. No data are available showing agreement or disagreement between

---

[20] "Oral Reply of Lawrence Walsh to the House of Delegates," Mid-year Meetings of the American Bar Association, Chicago, 1959 (mimeo), p. 17.
[21] "Report of the Standing Committee on Federal Judiciary," 87 *ABA Reports* (1962), 606.

this informal evaluation and the ultimate formal rating of the Committee. But other information indicates that with the exception of marginal cases—for example, barely qualified or lacking some qualifications—such agreement would be high.

A major ingredient of this "informal" decision is the strategy of investigation by both the circuit member and the chairman of the Committee. In addition to the factual data they obtain for the Attorney General, they provide him with a cross section of opinions of members of the bench and bar. But the specific names of these informants are never divulged, and it is reasonable to assume that at least some of the inquiries are made of lawyers who share the same values as the Committee members. Thus, the degree to which each Committee member actually reaches a cross section of lawyers is a function of his own prejudices as to who can give an "informed" opinion. If the investigating member is professionally oriented, he may slight the opinions of politically active lawyers. Doing so may result in a preponderance of adverse opinion of a candidate who is politically active. As suggested in the previous section, the values of the Committee member condition his approach to investigating and evaluating candidates. The importance of this concept of strategy of investigation will be treated in full later.

The Formal Report

When the field of candidates for a judicial vacancy narrows to one or two names, the Committee on Federal Judiciary is asked to make a more thorough evaluation and investigation and submit a *formal report* to the Attorney General. At the same time, a full FBI field check is requested on the candidate(s). This investigation is again carried on by the circuit member except in the case of Supreme Court nominees, who are investigated by the chairman and, if necessary, the members of the Committee collectively. Since it is impossible for the Committee to meet more than two or three times a year, the consultation and debate is conducted by mail and long-distance telephone. The report of the investigating member plus a specific recommendation, and a summary of the relevant conversations between the chairman and the Deputy Attorney General are circulated among all the members of the Committee. Once again there are no specific data available, but interviews with present and past Committee members indicate that except in borderline cases, or where evidence is lacking, the views of the investigating member are usually adopted by the Committee as a whole. Dissent is frequent, but some deference is usually given to the only member who has not only a first-hand knowledge of the candidate, but who has in most cases interviewed the candidate personally.

Not all the members of the Committee have been, at any one time, in complete agreement on the standards of qualification. Furthermore, federal courts in different sections of the country have different personnel needs, depending on the type of cases they most frequently decide, and what constitutes adequate preparation for the District Court of Nevada may be only marginal for the Southern District of New York. The formal rating of each candidate may express a *relative* judgment, although couched in absolute terms. When saying that "John Doe is exceptionally well qualified," the Committee may really be saying that he is "exceptionally well qualified" for the particular court to which he is to be nominated, and in relation to other available candidates. (However, the recent practice of the Committee seems to be to use a national standard rather than a regional one for most cases—a practice opposed by the Deputy Attorney General.) Thus, beginning with the initial investigation and running through the formal evaluation, the Committee has considerable flexibility in reaching its major decisions.

This "formal" report by the Committee *must* be made in the light of the inevitability of appointment. Although the Committee has not hesitated to label as "not qualified" a prospective nominee, it is not in the Committee's interest to do this too often. The real influence (and service to the Attorney General) of the Committee has already come at the "informal" stage, and the formal recommendation has more public-relations value than anything else. For the Committee to retain its power and favorable public image, it must not appear to be the voice which the Attorney General "disregards at will." The "formal" decision may properly be regarded as involving not only considerations of the candidate's fitness, but the Committee's status as well. Without suggesting any Machiavellian designs on the part of the Committee, it is not unreasonable to assume that it is well aware of the limitations of its position.

Report to the Senate Judiciary Committee

When a nomination to the federal judiciary is made by the President, the Committee on Federal Judiciary is invited by the chairman of the Senate Judiciary Committee to file a recommendation or testify. In almost all cases, the Committee chairman writes a letter to the Senate

Committee, expressing the Committee's approval or disapproval of the candidate. In most instances, where the Committee approves of the nomination, the letter is perfunctory, stating simply that the Committee found the candidate "qualified" or "well qualified" for appointment and recommends confirmation. Even if the Committee feels that better candidates for a vacancy are available than the one chosen, it will always recommend confirmation of a candidate whom it rated as at least "qualified." Requirements of comity prevent it from carrying its fight for the "best" judges to the Senate Judiciary Committee; furthermore, the chances of successfully convincing the Senate Judiciary Committee to reject the nomination of the President are at best slight, and probably nonexistent where the candidate is admittedly at least nominally qualified.[22]

Thus, if the Committee wants to try to block a nomination in the Senate Judiciary Committee, it must produce clearly derogatory evidence to support its contentions. But this evidence, usually gathered from confidential sources, is often difficult to produce, and even when available, is used at the possible expense of the Committee's future use of the same sources. The Committee is limited in its participation in the confirmation process not only because of the impossibility of frequently producing acceptable evidence, but also because once the point of no return is reached, the benefits of persistent opposition decrease. Occasionally, the creation of a "spectacle" of opposition may serve to dramatize the Committee's efforts—and aspirations—and cause other pressures to be set in motion which will effectively prevent the recurrence of such nomination types.[23] But the strength and forte of the Committee lies in behind-the-scenes action, and it cannot discard this shield of anonymity without due cause. It needs publicity to generate support for its work, but anonymity to increase the effectiveness of its operations.

---

[22] From 1953–1964 the ABA Committee failed to persuade the Senate Judiciary Committee to block any nomination which the Committee opposed. In 1964, however, the exception which proves the rule occurred, and partly due to the efforts of the ABA Committee, the Senate Judiciary Committee refused to approve the nomination of David Rabinowitz (a recess appointee) to the Federal District Court in Wisconsin.

[23] Such perhaps was the reason for the Committee's all-out fight against the confirmation of Judge Irving Ben Cooper, who had been given a recess appointment by President Kennedy to the District Court of the Southern District of New York. Departing from the practices of its predecessor (see Table 3.1, *supra*), the Kennedy Administration had appointed eight federal judges over the objections of the ABA Committee during its first eighteen months in office.

The Key Role of the Chairman

As suggested earlier, it is the chairman who plays the key role in the decision-making process of the Committee. Although the formal recommendation by the Committee is made by a majority vote of all its members, the chairman exercises an informal influence in other aspects of the Committee's operations which far exceeds that of any other member. This influence is on both the internal operations of the Committee and on the work of the Attorney General and his staff.

Aside from the incidental prerogatives which accrue to any administrator, the sources of the chairman's power lie in a number of factors: the influential role which he plays in the selection and retention of Committee members; his direct and frequent communication with the Attorney General; and his active participation in *each* informal investigation made by the Committee. All these opportunities may not be utilized, but they are available for use by a strong leader such as Bernard Segal (1956–1962). Segal was able to achieve significant personal influence within the Committee, with the Attorney General, and with the public press. References in leading newspapers to "Mr. Segal's Committee" were apt characterizations of the Committee's image during his tenure.[24]

Of the sources of the chairman's power, perhaps the most important is the arrangement whereby the Committee is asked to informally evaluate all persons even remotely being considered for federal judicial office. The chairman is the only member of the Committee who is directly concerned with every case the Committee handles. He makes a spot check on the investigation results of the circuit member and is the only communications link between that member and the Attorney General. As noted earlier, the informal report is essentially a series of impressions conveyed to the Attorney General by the chairman; and these impressions (and sometimes factual data) include not only those of the circuit member, but the views of the chairman as well. Since the chairman is also responsible for a particular circuit, he is the only member of the Committee who operates free of a similar check. It is not inaccurate to consider the chairman as *a* director of the investigation, since he will frequently request the member to

---

[24] See editorial in *New York Times*, January 2, 1961: "The new Attorney General and his deputy should make clear as soon as they can . . . that they will continue working with Mr. Segal's committee to the end of appointing the best qualified men to the federal bench."

obtain additional clarifying information if he is not satisfied with the initial results.

Working as closely as he does with the Attorney General, the chairman is not restricted, as is the circuit member, to simply "filing" a report. He is an intimate partner of the Justice Department officials who work with judicial-recruitment problems, and he is often persuasive in determining which of several candidates on whom informal reports have been made will be given further consideration. Thus, he is, at least in part, influential in determining *which* names the entire Committee gets a chance to vote on in its formal recommendation. In peak periods, when the volume of business is especially great, the chairman becomes a full-time participant in the selection process, extending beyond the specific functions of the Committee.[25] He is always "on the scene" and in a position to exert a more personal and effective form of persuasion.

In every sense of the word, the chairman speaks *for* the Committee at most of the important points in the selection process. It is true that he usually speaks *in the light of* the findings of the circuit member at the informal stage, and *in the light of* the formal recommendations of the Committee at the next stage, and there is no evidence (such as intra-Committee tensions) indicating that he has not been representing at least the majority views of the Committee. Nonetheless, his public image is largely also the Committee's; his voice, the Committee's.

Largely because of his position as Committee chairman, he is often accorded prerogatives not available either to Committee members or to most public officials. His personal advice is often solicited in recruiting judges, beyond the investigation and evaluation functions of the Committee. By its agreement of 1953, the Committee refrains officially from making suggestions of its own for filling judicial vacancies.[26] But because of his frequent contacts with the Attorney General (and perhaps also because of the personal prestige of someone like Bernard Segal), the chairman is often asked to sit in on the

---

[25] During the first two years of the Kennedy Administration, the Committee investigated candidates for 115 lifetime judgeships, more than half as many as the Eisenhower Administration appointed in eight years. Committee Chairman Bernard Segal states that his law firm record showed him spending 2004 hours in one year on Committee business.—Interview with Bernard G. Segal, October 30, 1962.
[26] This stipulation was reaffirmed by the new Committee chairman, Robert W. Meserve, in his "Midyear Report of the Standing Committee on Federal Judiciary," 88 *ABA Reports* (1963), 195.

active recruiting of federal judges, particularly Circuit and Supreme Court appointments.[27]

The implications of this *ultra vires* participation by the Committee chairman in the *recruitment* of judicial candidates is of concern not only to the other participants in the process, but as well to the leaders of the American Bar Association. They realize that as soon as the label "judge-makers" is pinned on the Committee, its prestige would suffer with a probable corresponding diminution of its prerogatives. Former Deputy Attorney General Ross Malone became president of the ABA in 1958, and one of his problems was whether or not to reappoint Bernard Segal as chairman of the Committee on Federal Judiciary. Segal had already served two terms as chairman, and, according to Malone, ". . . in the minds of the lawyers of the United States, particularly the members of the House of Delegates of the American Bar Association, I was afraid that he was beginning to be regarded as the 'gate keeper' to the federal bench."[28] Malone then discussed the problem with Attorney General William Rogers and his successor as Deputy Attorney General, Lawrence Walsh, and "Neither felt that there was any problem in this regard from their point of view; both were high in their praises of the job that [Segal] was doing. . . ."[29]

Nevertheless, Malone's subsequent offer of reappointment to Segal reflected this concern:

There was never any doubt in my mind as to my desire to have you continue as Chairman of the Committee. . . . As I am sure you appreciate, the power exercised by the Chairman of this Committee is very great indeed. I think it is extremely important that no one stay in the position long enough that he comes to be regarded as a "judge-maker." Should that occur, I think that the relationship with the Department [of Justice] would suffer and that the prestige of the Committee would suffer.

After talking to a number of people about the subject, I find that you have been extremely careful to avoid any such implications in your activities,

---

[27] Former Chairman Bernard Segal, for example, played an important role in the selection of Byron White for the Supreme Court in 1962, a role which developed because of his close personal contact with the Attorney General rather than as an official duty of the Committee chairman. In fact, until persuaded to the contrary by Segal, it was the intention of the Kennedy Administration to entirely bypass the Committee in Supreme Court nominations.—Letter from Bernard G. Segal to members of the Committee on Federal Judiciary, March 31, 1962.

[28] Letter from Ross Malone to author, March 6, 1963.

[29] *Ibid.*

and I have concluded that three years is not too long a time for a Chairman of this Committee to serve in that capacity.[30]

Segal accepted Malone's offer and wrote that "Your observation concerning the danger of having anyone regarded as a 'judge-maker' is certainly a pertinent one. The problem has caused me some concern as well. . . . I have been extremely careful to avoid any such implication in my activities as Chairman. . . ."[31]

If it is true that the chairman is the most influential member of the Committee, both among the members in their operations, and of the members in relation to the entire judicial-selection process, it is also true that he has certain responsibilities which are necessary if not indispensable to the continued effectiveness of the Committee.

First, the chairman must, as Segal suggests, expedite the Committee's work to fulfill the requirements of the Attorney General. He must see to it that the reports to the Attorney General are timely and contain the information desired. This may be considered a quantitative function.

Second, the chairman must exercise a quality control over the investigations. He must be able to assure the Attorney General that the information passed on is accurate and reliable, and pertinent to the primary function of the Committee; this is to say he must be able to give reasonable assurance that the Committee's estimates of professional ability are not facades for the expression of ideological preferences.

Third, and perhaps most important for the Committee's continued effectiveness, the chairman must direct the Committee's efforts in ways most likely to prove successful, and steer it clear of certain pitfalls. He must make a major effort to provide the proper "political" guidance and orientation to the Committee's work. This is best illustrated by the chairman's role in the formal evaluation of judicial candidates. When the circuit member has completed his formal investigation and recommendation, these are sent to the chairman, who forwards copies, along with his own comments, to each member of the Committee. The chairman's remarks often reflect his conversations with the Attorney General, the latter's "case" for the candidate, and so on. Except where there is a *clear case* of conflict of standards between the Committee and the Attorney General, and the candidate does not meet the Committee's standards, the chairman is in a position to press for

30 Letter from Ross Malone to Bernard G. Segal, June 26, 1958.
31 Letter from Bernard G. Segal to Ross Malone, July 10, 1958.

at least a minimum endorsement, or a "neutral" (neither recommended nor opposed) evaluation. He may be aware of the difficulties which the Attorney General faces, particularly where the nomination is in response to strong senatorial pressure. The Attorney General may be unhappy with the nomination, but unable or unwilling to block it. If the Committee were to refuse to consider such problems in marginal cases, it would understandably cause some resentment on the part of the Attorney General. The Committee's best posture is working "with" the Attorney General. If it shows no sensitivity for the Attorney General's position and lobbies against him by refusing to assent to a reasonable number of marginal candidates, it may be on precarious ground.

The existing selection system virtually "insures" that several candidates in each batch will be only marginally qualified, if at all. The Committee is working to reduce this number, and its possibilities of doing so depend on its continued cordial relationship with the Attorney General. A chairman who is not a *two-way* communications link with the Attorney General would be doing the Committee a great disservice. The chairman must be the Committee's political advisor and strategist. However much this function may irritate members who counsel an inflexible standard, it is absolutely necessary. And it can only be done by the chairman.

How is this function reflected in an actual situation? The nomination of Byron White in 1962 affords the best example. When the Committee "met" (via conference telephone) to discuss its recommendation of White, it had already had the benefit of working with him during his fifteen-month tenure as Deputy Attorney General. All agreed that he was qualified. The question was, how well qualified was he? Segal and the other members agreed that he was well qualified, but some were hesitant about rating him "exceptionally well qualified" —the Committee's highest accolade—in view of his youth (age 44) and relative inexperience. Segal, however, managed to persuade at least a majority that an EWQ was in order.[32] He publicly explained this rating at the Senate Judiciary Committee hearings:

---

[32] As told to the author by a member of the Committee who asked not to be identified. At a subsequent bar association function, Justice White told another Committee member that he had been embarrassed by the rating and the almost eulogistic praise heaped upon him by the Committee's recommendation. As a result of its experience in the White case, the Committee decided not to rate Supreme Court candidates, but simply to state whether or not they are "professionally qualified" to serve on the high bench. The Committee decided that it was "presumptuous" of it to rate men being considered for the highest judicial

. . . At age 44, Mr. White is far from the youngest person to be appointed to the Supreme Court, but it is true, of course, that at 44 a lawyer's experience cannot be expected to have reached the level of lawyers advanced in age. This was the only phase pertaining to Mr. White which caused our Committee to hesitate momentarily in arriving at the rating to be accorded to him. But as we reflected on the abilities he had already demonstrated, the qualities of heart, mind, and temperament which we had observed and to which those of whom we made inquiry unhesitatingly attested, the largeness of his view and the depth of his understanding so vital to adjudication of the large issues to come before the Supreme Court, we concluded that he was indeed "exceptionally well qualified," an accolade we have used exceedingly sparingly in rating prospective appointees to the bench.[33]

Such a rating for one with White's experience—regardless of his capabilities—was highly unusual. It clearly reflected Segal's view that the purity of the distinction between "well qualified" and "exceptionally well qualified"—if it was indeed inviolate—was best obscured in this case.

Finally, the chairman has a responsibility for Committee public relations. Since he is usually [34] the spokesman for the Committee and consequently the focus of considerable public attention, he must conduct himself in a manner which cannot reflect unfavorably on the Committee and jeopardize its influence. He writes the Committee's Annual Report, and delivers it orally to the House of Delegates—an event which always receives extensive press coverage. An effective statement of the Committee's achievements and disappointments will usually be picked up by the wire services. Furthermore, the chairman is often in a position to exert a direct influence on editorial policy. The following excerpt of a letter from Segal to circuit member Cloyd Laporte reflects this interest:

. . . I had a long conversation by telephone with the Editor-in-Chief of the Herald Tribune before this editorial was written [of May 18, 1962]. I had a similar talk with the Editor-in-Chief of the New York Times, as a result of which I was hopeful that the Times would also write an editorial concerning

---

honor in the nation. Deputy Attorney General Nicholas deB. Katzenbach accepted the Committee's suggestion.—Interview with Nicholas deB. Katzenbach, November 7, 1962.

33 U. S. Congress, Senate, Committee on the Judiciary, *Hearings on the Nomination of Byron White*, 87th Cong., 2nd Sess., 1962, p. 7.

34 Occasionally, the circuit member who conducted the investigations which resulted in a rating of "not qualified" will himself present the Committee's case to the Senate Judiciary Committee. See U. S. Congress, Senate, Committee on the Judiciary, *Hearings on the Nomination of Irving Ben Cooper*, 87th Cong., 2nd Sess., 1962.

Mr. Tyler [appointed District Judge, Southern District of New York].   In that case, I urged that mention also be made of Mr. McClean's appointment, since it was so excellent a selection and there was certainly inadequate publicity given to it.

On May 1st, I also discussed at some length with Mr. Evans Clark, Editorial writer for the New York Times, the inexcusable delay of the Senate Judiciary Committee in acting on Judge Marshall's nomination.   He promised to get up an editorial which somehow I missed. . . .[35]

The Role of the Circuit Member

Although the chairman is clearly the dominant force in the Committee's work, the individual circuit member does possess a substantial amount of discretion, particularly in determining the scope and sources of his investigation of the nominee.   All the members of the Committee interviewed stated that they regularly solicit the views of judges before whom the candidate has practiced, some of his colleagues at the bar, plus the state ABA delegates and other ABA members in the area. But each member normally establishes a personal liaison with key members of the profession, either individually or as a group, on whose opinions he relies.   Thus, the type of evidence gathered depends in large part on the sources of the particular member.   The type of people on whom he relies may significantly determine the ultimate rating given a candidate.   Since confidential sources are respected within the Committee as well as protected from outside disclosure, the member is relatively secure in choosing his sources.[36]

The Committee as a Whole

It is the chairman and investigating member, therefore, who are the key determiners of the qualifications of any candidate.   The Committee, as a Committee, does not effectively enter the picture until a formal rating is to be decided.   That rating is determined by a majority vote of the Committee.   However, the range of choice open to the Committee at this stage is necessarily circumscribed by the decisions which have preceded.   Most of the "not qualifieds" have been eliminated.   Furthermore, in a large number of cases, the formal recommendation of the Committee does not affect the Attorney General's decision to nominate.   The informal reports which he has already

---

[35] Letter from Bernard G. Segal to Cloyd Laporte, June 6, 1962.
[36] The investigating member will normally "describe" the source of his information to his brethren.

received from the chairman, comparing the several candidates in the field, plus other necessary considerations have contributed heavily to the selection of one (or occasionally two or more) candidate as the imminent choice. By this time commitments have already been made to candidate sponsors, and the Committee's final recommendation— even if extremely poor—will probably not affect the decision unless it can produce new evidence of serious disqualifying characteristics. Much in the manner of the "bandwagon" strategy at presidential nominating conventions, the impetus in favor of a particular candidate is often irreversible by the time the Committee makes its formal recommendation.[37]

What are the alternatives, therefore, which the Committee has in voting on a formal recommendation? If on the basis of the informal and formal investigations there is little doubt that the candidate is "qualified," the only question for the whole Committee to decide is whether he is "qualified," "well qualified," or "exceptionally well qualified." At the informal stage, a predicted rating of only "qualified" might mitigate against a candidate if others are being considered who are probably "well" or "exceptionally well" qualified. But at the formal stage, the degree of qualification is not likely to have much effect on the ultimate choice of the Attorney General; on the basis of previous information—including the ABA *informal*—he has probably already made that choice. So the question of specific rating is largely an academic one insofar as the instant case is concerned. It might have an effect on future appointments—however small—since for reasons of public relations the administration would like to have as high a percentage of EWQ's as possible. But, since it cannot have much effect on the case at hand, its immediate value to the Committee is correspondingly small.

If the candidate is unquestionably "not qualified" by the Committee's standards—for example, overage, no trial experience, evidence of deviant behavior—then once again the Committee's inevitable rating is not likely to have more than a public-relations value. Via the informal report, the Attorney General is usually aware of facts which the Committee considers disqualifying, and if he has nevertheless submitted the name for a formal evaluation, the chance of its being retracted even in the light of new evidence is small. The only excep-

---

[37] These observations are predicated on the Committee being considered primarily an information source by the Attorney General, as it is presently. Where it has been accorded a virtual veto-group status, as it was from 1956–1961, the formal recommendation is of greater significance.

tions would be in those cases where the Attorney General has submitted *more than one* name, and can use an adverse Committee report to dissuade the sponsors of a particular candidate.

If the candidate's qualifications are marginal, but his nomination is imminent, the question to be decided boils down to: Can he by any circumstance be considered qualified? As noted earlier, there is no percentage in the Committee's opposing a certain nomination if it is feasible and reasonable for it to give at least qualified approval or a neutral recommendation.

If these interpretations are correct, it would appear that the influence of the noninvestigating members in each case is more apparent than real. The choices open to each member in casting his formal ballot limit the significance of that ballot insofar as the determination of the nomination is concerned. It would seem that the important acts "of the Committee" concerning the nomination of federal judges are pretty much the acts of the investigating member and the chairman.

THE COMMITTEE'S BASIS FOR JUDGMENT

Having examined so far the type of lawyers composing the Committee on Federal Judiciary and the procedures by which the important decisions of the Committee are made, let us turn to the third area of inquiry. On what basis does the Committee make its judgments? What types of people are the sources of confidential information? How do the values (that is, the definition of a "good" judge) espoused by the Committee compare with those of the rest of the legal profession?

The Rhetoric of Evaluation

It is obvious from the number of investigations which the Committee may be called upon to make in any one year that, to give some sort of rational order to what otherwise would be a confused and haphazard operation, some notion of standards must precede the investigatory process. Different Committee members undoubtedly have different ideas of what makes a good judge, and the requirements differ in the various districts and circuits. Furthermore, the Committee must operate in the light of the expectations and requirements of those involved in the nomination and confirmation process.

Thus, if it is to be able to make a plausible case for or against any candidate, the Committee must be able to state its case in acceptable terms; that is, its standards of evaluation must be clear, and relevant to generally accepted notions of the ingredients which go into the making of a "good" judge. Finally, if it is to be of substantial service to the Attorney General (the sine qua non of its existence), it must concentrate on evaluating those qualities deemed to fall within its specialized area of competence. To be sure, there can be no fine dividing line between certain characteristics which the Committee is supposed to be concerned with and those that are to be judged by other agents in the selection process. But at least a surface dichotomy must be respected.

The ostensible limits of the Committee's public function may be characterized by the term "professional qualifications." To be sure, it is a term that is easily stretched to cover a multitude of factors but it does exclude some qualifications which could not, under any system of logic, be connected to it. Thus, no case is on record where the Committee has disapproved of a candidate solely because of his (her) party affiliation. It does campaign assiduously for acceptance of the principle of nonpartisanship, but lacking success in this venture, it does not apply its standard to particular candidates. Similarly, whatever feelings the Committee has about religious or ethnic considerations must fall before the generally accepted political principle of "ethnic representation" on public bodies. Since in high "ethnic ratio" areas, the likelihood is that all serious candidates for a particular vacancy will have similar background, the Committee cannot protest that there may be better candidates available, who may lack this "peculiar" qualification.

Needless to say, the investigating member and the Committee as a whole may very well consider such "other" characteristics, but they will have to be articulated in a manner consistent with public expectations. A candidate may be labeled "not qualified" because he is overage or lacks reasonable trial experience, but not because he is an economic conservative or "one-worlder."

The problem of articulating standards is heightened by the variety of sources from which information is obtained. Bernard Segal has noted that

From the beginning, a problem with which the Committee has constantly grappled is the definition of qualified. Some standards must be applied in determining whether an individual is "qualified" to be a Federal judge. But the Committee's work is collecting the opinions of the profession—of lawyers and judges—and these opinions come to us in all varieties of expression, a whole range of informations and reflections. We dare not impose standards in advance of our canvas, we must, however, apply objective standards in collating all the data and the opinions we receive.[38]

Continuing, Segal notes that it is axiomatic that character, judgment, industry, experience, temperament, and professional ability be criteria of selection. But the difficulty comes in applying these criteria to specific cases:

All of us as lawyers have observed the metamorphosis which that thin black robe can cause in a man. But dare we count on it. The office can make, has made, its holder on occasion. On more occasions, however, the holder has reduced the office to his own level. Normally, we can rely on a lawyer's past record as a reliable guide to his future performance. We have little else to rely on; it is his past record which our canvass of professional opinion reveals.[39]

The Committee's investigation of each candidate is therefore designed to construct a composite picture of the individual's background, from which picture the Committee will attempt to predict the candidate's performance as a federal judge. This prediction, of course, will not be forthcoming from the facts alone. In appraising this information, each member, and the Committee as a whole, will rely on a whole range of personal experiences and preferences. Their backgrounds will also in part determine the type of information sought, and the proper sources of such information.

Sources of Information

The Committee seeks both factual information and opinion. As noted earlier the basic factual information is obtained from a questionnaire which the Attorney General sends—for himself and the Committee— to each person even remotely being considered for appointment. The candidate is required to return a copy of the questionnaire to the Attorney General, one to the circuit member of the Committee, and one to the chairman. If the questionnaire is answered completely and candidly, the Committee will have information on the age, birthplace, residence, education, practice, political experience, prior judicial experience, criminal record, involvement in civil suits, professional standing, health, publications, honors, and group memberships of the respondent.

---

[38] Bernard G. Segal, "Federal Judicial Selection—Progress and the Promise of the Future," 46 *Massachusetts Law Quarterly* (1961), 141.
[39] *Ibid.*

A significant number of candidates are automatically eliminated from consideration on the basis of these questionnaires by the Attorney General or opposed by the Committee for the same reasons. Using this information, including references supplied by the candidate, the Committee member will make his preliminary investigation. In addition to "working out" from the candidate (which is the way the FBI field check operates), the Committee member will normally communicate with several lawyers and judges who may have witnessed the candidate in court, or who may know of his personal life, but who are not "friends" of the candidate. The Committee seeks to sample the "informed" opinion of a *cross section* of the bench and bar in the circuit. It is felt that a legitimate candidate for a federal judgeship should have sufficient community visibility so that his probable performance as a federal judge can be assessed. But very likely there will be some conflicting views about his ability, his stability, even his honesty. In such cases, the investigating member may be faced with conflicting evidence which he must either follow-up himself or trust to one of the witnesses. Obviously, the problem of objectivity becomes at times difficult, if not insurmountable, and the determining factor in the evaluation has to be the member's (and later the Committee's) own reading of the information.

As noted earlier, all the members of the Committee on Federal Judiciary have certain "regular" contacts on whom they rely for informed opinion or leads to further information. These will normally include sitting judges in the courts in which the candidate has practiced, leading lawyers, community leaders, law school deans, and others. Since these names are confidential, there is no precise way of knowing just whom the Committee members consider bearers of "informed" opinion. And, equally, there is no way to know exactly what is meant by a "cross section" of the bar. What types of lawyers are normally relied upon? Are lawyers of all types and interest canvassed?

Responses to a sample survey of American lawyers suggest some answers to these questions.[40] What these responses suggest is that the base of the "informed opinion" on which the Committee relies is quite

---

[40] This survey of American lawyers was conducted via mail questionnaire early in 1963. A stratified random sample of 500 lawyers was chosen from the 1962 edition of the Martindale-Hubbell Directory, and the 260 valid responses constituted the sample from which the data in Tables 4.7, 4.8, and 4.9 were taken. Further details concerning the administering of these questionnaires can be found in Joel B. Grossman, *The Role of the American Bar Association in the Selection of Federal Judges* (Ph.D. dissertation, Department of Political Science, State University of Iowa, 1963), pp. 6–9, 382–401.

small. As Table 4.7 indicates, less than 8 per cent of the survey respondents had ever been contacted by a member of the Committee. Furthermore, more than 80 per cent of those responding could not even identify the member of the Committee operating in their own circuit.[41] Presumably, the vast majority of lawyers are not acquainted with the operations of the Committee.

TABLE 4.7

LAWYERS WITH WHOM COMMITTEE MEMBERS COMMUNICATED

	Percentage
Have been asked	7.7
Have never been asked	89.2
Don't recall	3.1
	100.0 (N = 260)

Even more important is the very limited scope of the legal profession represented by those lawyers who are in touch with the Committee. As indicated in Table 4.8, 85 per cent of the lawyers communicated with were members of the American Bar Association, and 70 per cent were officials of other bar groups. It would appear as if bar-association membership and office were key factors in selecting confidential sources. Although no members of the ABA Committee work through the apparatus of local bar groups, they obviously rely heavily on the opinions of individual bar leaders—a very select group. As is also shown in Table 4.8, 80 per cent of the lawyers communicated with were partners or senior partners in firms, clearly the elite of the profession.[42]

It would seem, therefore, that the Committee reaches only a very limited segment of the profession in its investigations of candidates for the federal bench. This evidence, furthermore, is supported by the experiences of the Department of Justice in the Kennedy Administration. Assistant Deputy Attorney General Joseph Dolan has

---

[41] Of the respondents, 84.3 per cent could not successfully identify any ABA Committee member who had ever served in their circuit; 8.1 per cent were uncertain; 7.7 per cent were able to supply a name. From a much smaller universe (that is, the state of Texas), Bancroft Henderson and T. C. Sinclair found a somewhat higher proportion of lawyers (20.7 per cent) who had been questioned by the ABA Committee member in Texas. *Judicial Selection in Texas: An Exploratory Study* (Houston, Tex.: University of Houston Studies in Social Science, 1964), p. 51.

[42] This is nearly four times the percentage of all lawyers who hold such positions.— *The 1961 Lawyer Statistical Report* (Chicago: American Bar Foundation, 1961), p. 62.

TABLE 4.8

TYPES OF LAWYERS WITH WHOM COMMITTEE MEMBERS COMMUNICATED

Category	Percentage
Member of the American Bar Association	85.0
Not a member	15.0
	100.0 (N = 20)
President of state bar association	5.0
President of local bar association	30.0
Chairman, state bar association committee	10.0
Chairman, local bar association committee	20.0
Official, state bar association	5.0
No bar association office	30.0
	100.0 (N = 20)
Senior partner in firm	60.0
Partner in firm	20.0
Individual practitioner	20.0
	100.0 (N = 20)

observed that in several instances members of his staff investigating candidates after the ABA investigation found that in the large cities only the "Wall Street type" lawyers were being reached initially by the Committee, although, on the prodding of supporters of a candidate whom the Committee opposed, the Committee sought other lawyers suggested by the candidate.[43]   In fact, the system of double checking the Committee's evaluation by a parallel investigation, an innovation of the Kennedy Administration, was, among other things, an effort to reach a wider range of lawyers than the Committee could be expected to reach.

The Rationale of Evaluation

Given its sources of information, on what basis does the Committee make its evaluation of prospective judicial candidates?   Although for reasons stated earlier (pp. 107–108) the Committee has never articulated specific standards of qualification, it *has* indicated certain prefer-

---

[43] Interview with Assistant Deputy Attorney General Joseph Dolan, November 2, 1962.

ences. It considers previous trial experience the most important prerequisite for service on the District Court, and political party affiliation
the least relevant for service on any court. Because of the nature of its
liaison with the Attorney General, it is unable to press for prior judicial experience as a prerequisite for Circuit and Supreme Court positions. Given these limitations, however, it would appear to follow
standards that conform closely to those generally supported by the
legal profession. As Table 4.9 indicates, lawyers who responded to the

TABLE 4.9

LAWYERS' PREFERENCES: STANDARDS OF QUALIFICATION

District Court	Rank	Circuit Court
Successful trial practice	1*	Judicial experience, state appellate court
Judicial experience, state court	2	Judicial experience, trial court
Successful corporate practice	3	Successful trial practice
Professor of law	4	Professor of law
Prior legal-political public service	5	Successful corporate practice
Stand on key political and economic issues	6	Prior legal-political public service
Political party identification	7	Stand on key political and economic issues
	8	Political party identification

* The rank order listed here does not show the actual intensity of these
preferences.

survey questionnaire ranked several items in order of preference as key
qualifications for both District and Circuit Court appointments. They
were asked to rate the characteristics in order of preference, "assuming
the equal honesty, integrity, and maturity of all candidates." The
strongest responses were for prior trial experience and judicial experience and against political party identification. All of the other factors
were fairly closely lumped together in the center of the spectrum.

By following these standards as closely as the requirements of its
liaison allow, the ABA Committee would be generally reflecting the
views of the legal profession. No data are available from which an
exact correlation could be made. But these are general standards,
which are flexible in their interpretation and application. Some of
the absolute standards which the Committee espouses—in fact, the two
it follows most closely—have been criticized by other members of

the profession. A National Conference on Judicial Selection and Court Administration, jointly sponsored by the ABA, the American Judicature Society, and the Institute of Judicial Administration, recommended in 1959 that neither maximum age nor trial experience be considered absolute prerequisites for the federal bench.[44] These recommendations were in direct opposition to the practices of the Committee, which does not consider a candidate qualified if he is over the age of 64 and does not recommend nomination to the District Court for a person without prior trial experience.[45] There is no reason to believe that the recommended policies of the National Conference are more or less representative of the views of the legal profession than are the policies of the Committee on Federal Judiciary. All that is indicated is that there are a variety of views on judicial-selection policies held by leading members of the legal profession, of which the Committee's working policy is but one. The irony of the situation, however, is that the position held by the National Conference is closer than the Committee's to that held by each of the recent Attorneys General.

---

[44] "Midyear Report of the Committee on Judicial Selection, Tenure and Compensation," 85 *ABA Reports* (1960), 172.

[45] The Committee will rate a candidate between the ages of 60 and 64 "qualified" if he is considered to be among those best qualified who are available. The Attorney General has generally agreed to this age limitation, but has refused to be bound by it absolutely. See U. S. Congress, Senate, Committee on the Judiciary, *Hearings on the Nomination of Sarah Hughes,* 87th Cong., 2nd Sess., 1962.

5

⚹⚹

THE COMMITTEE
AND THE ATTORNEY GENERAL

Earlier chapters have described the formal relationship between the
Committee on Federal Judiciary and the Attorney General—the stages
in the recruitment process where the Committee participates, the types
of investigations and evaluations it makes (and does not make), and
the differences in prerogatives which the Committee has enjoyed under
different Attorneys General. But as yet no effort has been made to
examine the dynamics of this relationship. What are the Attorney
General's implicit and explicit expectations of the Committee? What
are the Committee's expectations of the Attorney General? Under
what conditions is the Committee likely to exercise the most influence
on the Attorney General? What are the limitations of its influence?
In what ways has the Committee either limited or enhanced the power
of the Attorney General vis-à-vis the other forces in the judicial-
selection process?

THE JUDICIAL-SELECTION ROLE
OF THE ATTORNEY GENERAL

As we noted in Chapter 2, it is the Attorney General rather than the
President who controls the nomination of most federal judges below
the Supreme Court level. His power over nominations is not, however,
without limits. The process of locating prospective nominees, investigating their qualifications, and choosing among them is essentially a
staff operation. Frequently, key decisions will be made early enough
in the process to limit the alternatives which the Attorney General
will have at the later stages. And the prerogatives and influence of

other actors in the selection process—the President, the Senate, party organizations, and private groups—also limit his freedom of choice. The types of choices available to the Attorney General are particularly important to the ABA Committee, since *its* prerogatives depend to a large degree on the flexibility of the Attorney General. The ABA Committee and the Attorney General do not interact in isolation. The actions and reactions of each toward the other is necessarily conditioned by the relation of each to the other actors involved in judicial selection. An understanding of the expectations of the Attorney General held by these other actors is necessary to any analysis of the relationship between the Committee and the Attorney General. These expectations can be briefly categorized as follows: (1) the Attorney General should choose persons whom the President can nominate; (2) he should choose persons whom the Senate will confirm; and (3) he should choose persons who will not seriously offend the sensitivities or standards of any of the major interest groups on whom the administration must rely for support or who have established a legitimate claim to participate in the judicial-selection process.

Persons the President Can Nominate

There are no constitutional restrictions on the President's choice, and the only statutory restraint is that district judges must be residents of that district at the time of their *appointment*. But there are several informal norms of choice which guide, if not control, the presidential prerogative. All potential nominees must have had prior legal training, no person below the age of 35 will be given much consideration for a District Court vacancy, and few below the age of 45 will have much chance for a Circuit or Supreme Court nomination.[1] For the Supreme Court, at least, no person will be seriously considered who does not share the President's views on the "great issues" of the period. And for all courts implicit requirements of geographic, ethnic, and political (party membership) balance must be observed. But aside from these factors, the question of whom the President can nominate depends on the expectations of senators and relevant interest groups. In fact, it is these other groups in the selection process who usually set and police the norms of balance just listed.

---

[1] Only twelve out of the 410 federal judicial nominees since 1946 were under 40 years of age. Of the twelve, eleven were nominated for District Court vacancies, one to the Circuit Court. None was under 36 years of age. Including the one nominee "under 40" already mentioned, there were seven nominees to the Courts of Appeals under 45 (out of eighty-two Circuit nominations).

Persons the Senate Will Confirm

The Attorney General must also choose persons with a good chance of being confirmed by the Senate. That such a high percentage of nominees to the federal bench is confirmed does not indicate that the senators have reduced the confirmation function to a mere formality. Rather it indicates that on the whole the Attorney General is sensitive to the expectations of the Senate and considers all nominations with the senatorial role in mind.[2] Reduced to lowest terms, the senatorial expectations of the President mean at least that (1) the function and responsibility of the Senate in advising as well as consenting to nominations be acknowledged; (2) that senators from the President's party be accorded a *voice* in the selection of judges from their state which, if it is not a controlling voice, is at least a surface recognition of senatorial responsibility; and (3) that some general standards of qualification satisfactory to most senators be observed in making the selections.

The first expectation is routine and not difficult to meet. The second is more complicated, since it involves a variety of considerations. A senator may be persuaded to support a choice not originally his own, or he may be outmaneuvered and forced to "go along" with the choice of the Attorney General. But this must be done without appearing to challenge his prerogative to hold out for his own choice should he wish to do so. There would be little point in forcing a senator to block a nomination through invocation of senatorial courtesy if such a conflict could be avoided with a little tact. The Attorney General must know the senator and what *his* views on senatorial participation in judicial selection are.

A good example of this sort of situation was the controversy between the Justice Department and Senator Javits of New York over the proposed nomination of Henry Friendly to the Second Circuit Court of Appeals in 1959. There was considerable pressure in Friendly's behalf, and faced with this sort of pressure and the well-publicized fact that Friendly had been rated "exceptionally well qualified" by the ABA Committee, Senator Javits decided not to oppose the nomination. But he restated his belief in the principle that "a senator should back up his recommendation for judgeships by refusing to go along with

---

[2] Joseph Harris's *The Advice and Consent of the Senate* (Berkeley: University of California Press, 1953) still is the best description of the senatorial role prior to the assumption by the ABA Committee of its present position.

other choices." He added that he also believed a senator should be "flexible" about the principle of senatorial courtesy.[3] Clearly, a senator with stronger views on senatorial responsibility for judicial nominations would have reacted much differently. It is not unusual for a judgeship to remain vacant for a year or longer because of a deadlock between a senator and the Attorney General.

Attempting to meet the expectations of individual senators, of course, does not prevent the Attorney General from seeking to weaken the senatorial prerogative unobtrusively. One technique has been to call upon the Senate to cede as much of its prerogative to a "third force" as the Attorney General did to the ABA. Writing in 1960, Deputy Attorney General Lawrence Walsh declared that "until the organized Bar has balanced its increased influence upon the action of the President by comparable gains in its influence upon the action of the Senate, our [sic] further progress will be of secondary importance." [4]

The Attorney General has greater latitude in fulfilling the expectations of the Senate concerning qualifications since there is no general agreement among the senators themselves on just what constitutes minimum standards. The Senate could constitutionally require that, as a price of confirmation, all judicial appointees meet certain specifications. Some senators strongly favor prior judicial experience as a prerequisite for appointment to the Supreme Court, and have suggested that, under its power to "advise" as well as consent, the Senate prescribe such a limitation. Senator Stennis has urged that one of every two Supreme Court nominees be required to possess ten years' judicial experience.[5] It is interesting that no comparable standards or limitations have ever been suggested for lower-court judgeships. Possibly this is because senatorial prerogative is strongest in these cases, and nonexistent at the Supreme Court level. For the Senate as a whole to set such standards would infringe on the "right" of each individual senator to "choose" district judges in his own state. Since the decisions of district judges have relatively little effect on the constituents of other states, senators are inclined to allow each other the privilege of unfettered choice.

By way of illustration, three general standards which the present Attorney General must contend with are the senatorial opposition to

---

[3] *New York Times,* March 26, 1959, p. 17; and March 30, 1959, p. 33.

[4] "The Federal Judiciary, . . . Progress and the Road Ahead," 43 *Journal of the American Judicature Society* (1960), 157.

[5] "Federal Judicial Selection: The Letter—But the Spirit?," 44 *American Bar Association Journal* (1958), 1181.

recess appointments to the Supreme Court, the reluctance of senators from his own party to approve many appointments from the opposition party, and the informal agreement among senators whose states lie in the same judicial circuit to rotate each state's "representation" on the Court of Appeals in that circuit.

Opposition to interim appointments came as a result of the difficulties experienced by the Senate Judiciary Committee in questioning Chief Justice Earl Warren (1953), and Associate Justices William Brennan (1956) and Potter Stewart (1959). All were given appointments by President Eisenhower when Congress was not in session. Particularly in the cases of Brennan and Stewart, their status as "already sitting Justices" enabled them to evade answering questions about "the communist menace"—which they said dealt with cases which the Court was already in the process of deciding, was about to decide, or might conceivably have to decide in the near future. In 1960 a bipartisan coalition of senators pushed through a resolution telling the President that

It is the sense of the Senate that the making of recess appointments to the Supreme Court may not be wholly consistent with the best interests of the Supreme Court, the nominee who may be involved, the litigants before the Court, nor indeed the people of the United States, and that such appointments, therefore, should not be made except under unusual circumstances, and for the purpose of preventing a demonstrable breakdown in the Administration of the Court's business.[6]

Although support for the resolution was not overwhelming, and the debates on the floor clearly indicated that the power to make interim appointments was a constitutional prerogative which the Senate could not legally curb, the sponsor of the resolution, Senator Philip Hart of Michigan, suggested that it might operate to caution a President intent upon making an interim appointment. There was no suggestion that the Senate refuse to confirm such appointments if made.[7]

How binding is this "sense of the Senate" resolution on the Attorney General? When the Senate Judiciary Committee held hearings on the nomination of Robert Kennedy as Attorney General, Senator Hart stated the essence of the resolution and told Kennedy: "I shall not ask for your comment on the wisdom of it, but I do hope that you will give thought to this expression which is reflected in Senate Resolution

---

6 Senate Resolution 334, 86th Cong., 2nd Sess., 1960.

7 U. S. *Congressional Record*, 86th Cong., 2nd Sess., 1960, CVI, Part 14, pp. 18130–18145. The vote was 48–37.

334." [8]   Given the present Democratic majority in the Senate, it is highly unlikely that any Supreme Court nominee of the President, interim or otherwise, would be rejected. But that the Senate troubled to express itself so clearly on the issue would probably serve as a cautionary factor if an interim appointment was contemplated. Both of the two Kennedy appointments to the Supreme Court in 1962 occurred while Congress was in session. The President did make seventeen recess appointments to the federal bench in 1961, but all were to the lower federal courts. [9]

The second illustration of the "type" of senatorial standard with which the Attorney General must contend is party-label consistency. This is primarily a requirement for lower-court judgeships, and does not really apply to Supreme Court nominations. How much of a requirement this is depends on a number of factors, including the number and distribution of senators from the President's party, the state in which the "out-party" appointment is contemplated, and the electoral status of the President. If the President is a "lame duck," either by choice or law, and nearing the end of his final term, he is likely to have (and transfer to his Attorney General) a greater degree of freedom with judicial (as well as other) appointments. The smaller the number of senators of his own party that have to be considered on patronage matters, the greater his freedom to appoint federal judges of the other party. "Out-party" appointments are likely to be made anyway in states where there are no senators of the President's party, or in multiple-judge states, where the senator who is of the President's party might accept one or more such nominations. The possibility of appointing an "out-party" judge in a small state, with few judgeships, and one or both senators belonging to the same party as the President, is very small indeed. Patronage for the senator in such a state is likely to be limited anyway, and the "giving away" of a choice plum would not be acceptable.

Since every President in the twentieth century has appointed at least a few judges from the opposition party to each level of the federal courts, the question is always "Where can such appointments be made with the least chance of repercussion from senators?" In addition to the factors already listed, the degree of political activity of the pro-

---

[8] U. S. Congress, Senate, Committee on the Judiciary, *Hearings on the Nomination of Robert Kennedy*, 87th Cong., 1st Sess., 1961, p. 27.
[9] Vacancies that occur more than thirty days before Congress adjourns may be filled by recess appointments only if the appointee is willing to serve without pay. This congressional rule is an effective prohibition on many such appointments.

spective "out-party" candidate is always a factor, particularly if the appointment is to be made in a state where there is at least one "in-party" senator to be persuaded.[10] It is also very likely that such nominations will produce better-than-average judges. With an eye toward bipartisan support at the next election, the senator can justify his assent to an "out-party" appointment by declaring that "he would not block a worthy appointment simply on the basis of party considerations."

A third illustration of senatorial standards which the Attorney General must consider is the feeling shared by many senators that every state in a circuit should be represented, in rotation if necessary, on the Court of Appeals for the circuit to which the state belongs. Such a question was raised in 1956, when Solicitor General Simon Sobeloff was nominated for the Fourth Circuit Court of Appeals. Senators Sam Ervin of North Carolina and Olin Johnston of South Carolina argued that this vacancy ought to go to South Carolina and not Maryland where Sobeloff was a resident. Of course, the main objection to Sobeloff was not his residence, but his participation in the government's successful argument in the *Brown* case. Nevertheless, the residence argument was taken off the shelf to support the opposition. Although neither senator from South Carolina could block the confirmation because they were not of the President's party, they might have done so if eligible.[11]

It is clear that none of these requirements is a mandate to the Attorney General. Rather they are standards which are flexible within a certain limit of tolerance, and which the Attorney General cannot entirely ignore.

Persons Satisfactory to Major Interest Groups

The Attorney General must choose persons for federal judgeships who will not seriously offend the sensitivities of any of the major interest groups on whom the administration must rely for political support or who have established a legitimate claim to participate in the judicial-selection process. Groups that have a substantial interest in the outcome of the judicial process will have a keen interest also in the

---

[10] Senator McNamara of Michigan blocked the nomination of Republican State Chairman John Feikens, who had been originally given a recess appointment by President Eisenhower, and who was reappointed by President Kennedy. Feikens was not only active in Republican politics, but was a personal foe of McNamara.

[11] U. S. Congress, Senate, Committee on the Judiciary, *Hearings on the Nomination of Simon Sobeloff*, 84th Cong., 2nd Sess., 1956, pp. 115 ff., 232.

selection of judges. Some groups, particularly minority groups that have a limited influence—if any at all—in other decision-making processes of government, find a *direct* interest in judicial selection as a prerequisite to their continued "success."

Other groups, less well formed and organized, and perhaps even "potential" groups, have a different type of interest in judicial selection. Their interest is to "be represented" by one of their own kind or persuasion serving on a particular tribunal. There is no particular reason, for example, why all Jewish people in the United States should have a common, direct interest in the selection of any particular judge. There is no evidence that "Jewish" judges have exhibited common decision-making propensities. What some Jewish people do share in common—politically—is an interest in being "represented" at least on the Supreme Court and on every District Court which encompasses a significant Jewish community. In recruiting federal judges, this is an expectation the Attorney General must take into account—not only for Jewish communities, but for other minority groups as well. Furthermore, he must take care not to offend any or all of these groups by appointing, in nearby communities, judges completely hostile to their beliefs. (The appointment of segregationist judges in some southern states is a conspicuous exception.) Although the concepts of ethnic and geographic balance may have little to do with the efficient administration of justice,[12] they are well-established norms of selection for many public bodies in this country. Very often, of course, the senator of a state will take these interests into account, and will press for the "proper" distribution of judges in his state.

Taking account of the interests of groups that have asserted—and have been accorded—a proprietary claim to participation in the judicial-selection process presents a different problem altogether for the Attorney General. The groups involved here are the various bar organizations, especially the American Bar Association. There is no real problem of representation here, in the sense in which that term was just used, since it may be assumed that all persons appointed to the federal bench will have had legal training, and a large number will be practicing lawyers. The organized bar, of course, is very interested in having selected as judges persons who share its general views on the proper roles of courts and judges and in increasing the

---

[12] Of course, where an ethnic group has been systematically excluded from political office, as has been the Negro in the deep South, the ascension of a member of that group to a judgeship—or any other office—is likely to bring about some change in the decision-making habits and results of the court.

number of "practicing" lawyers appointed and decreasing the number of "political" lawyers selected. But unlike other interest groups which prefer to operate outside of the selection process, bar groups have long shown an interest in being included in that process. They *claim* the "right" to be consulted on the basis of expert knowledge of the products of the selection process: the judges.

The Attorney General depends on those two units which limit his freedom of choice in the selection of judges—the Senate and the Committee on Federal Judiciary. Along with the FBI and the network of attorneys associated with the Department of Justice, senators and the ABA Committee are the prime resources on which the Attorney General must depend for information on prospective candidates. In a sense, each gives him a type of information inaccessible to the others. Since with the exception of the senators, the services of each of these groups could be dispensed with, their continued service is at least a sign of minimal dependence by the Attorney General. Thus, the groups that limit some of his alternatives create others.

This brief exposition on the role of the Attorney General in the judicial-selection process has emphasized that, in carrying out this function delegated by the President, he must operate in a complicated and often bewildering array of converging and diverging political forces and impulses. To talk of his "selecting" federal judges is to talk of his ability to shape these forces in a manner which insures at least that the balance of power will rest on the executive side of the ledger.

Under the pressures generated in the last three decades by the organized bar's campaigns to improve the quality of judges at all levels, the Attorney General's role in the selection process has become an increasingly positive one. The ultimate responsibility for judicial selection is his, and, if for no other reason than the desire to avoid the public criticism of the bar, he is not likely to accept a passive role. Although he does not have complete freedom of choice for most judicial nominations, he has sufficient resources at his command to occupy a controlling position. He may not be able to engineer a nomination over the adamant opposition of an "in-party" senator, but through strategic delay or the recruitment of alternate candidates, he can generate sufficient pressure on a senator to achieve a workable compromise in most instances. He may occasionally have to pay a high price for such a compromise; and sometimes the price will be prohibitive and he will have to approve a nomination that he dislikes. But he cannot afford to have such instances be more than exceptions.

THE COMMITTEE AND THE ATTORNEY
GENERAL: MUTUAL EXPECTATIONS

Within the formal structure of their liaison, the Committee and the Attorney General interact in ways which generally are functions of their mutual expectations. Each has certain objectives to be gained by the relationship; thus each expects certain types of actions by the other. And beyond this, each has certain *minimal requirements* which have to be satisfied by the relationship; the nonfulfillment of these requirements, for whatever reason, would jeopardize the liaison. What follows is a *theory* of the liaison between the Attorney General and the Committee drawn from the available data.[13]

The Attorney General's Expectations

The Attorney General uses the Committee on Federal Judiciary primarily as an information source and as a counterforce against the other political forces operating in the selection process. He expects the Committee to supply him with reliable information about prospective judicial candidates which he could not, under ordinary circumstances, obtain through his own resources. This information is primarily evaluative: the interpreted opinions of the capabilities of the candidate held by other members of the legal profession. The Committee claims, and there is no evidence to the contrary, that because of its official position and the fact that all of its members are successful and well-known lawyers, it is able to elicit, in confidence, the candid view of members of the profession which would not be given to "outsiders"—for example, FBI investigators or Justice Department lawyers. Furthermore, the FBI information is unevaluated and often difficult to interpret; [14] the Committee can fill this gap by gathering the opinions of lawyers and judges who know the candidate, and also through its own evaluation. Finally, the Committee can

---

13 Although illustrations for this theory come from the ten-year period, 1953–1963, the theory itself is based on the relationship between the Committee and the Attorney General since 1961—that is, a relationship in which the Committee occupies a consultative rather than a veto-group role.

14 See Harold Chase, "Federal Judges: The Appointing Process," paper delivered at the 1964 annual meeting of the American Political Science Association, Chicago, Illinois, pp. 16–18. Any statement made about the candidate is included in the FBI report. In the final analysis, the Deputy Attorney General must decide the merits of each statement.

provide some of this information at a very early stage in the selection process; early enough to give the Attorney General a head start in heading off the forces supporting undesirable candidates. The Committee can do this in relative secrecy, whereas to initiate the FBI check at this very early stage would serve to publicize the Justice Department's interest in the candidate and possibly stimulate the activation of forces in his behalf, or in opposition.

The fulfillment of this expectation is perhaps the most important of the Committee's services to the Attorney General. *In and of themselves,* none of the other services that the Committee provides would justify its present status. But these other services are important and cannot be discounted.

The Committee is also expected to provide for the Attorney General a reasoned evaluation of the qualification of prospective candidates, and a formal recommendation for those likely to receive a nomination. Although the Committee's sources are never disclosed by name to the Attorney General, the reasons for its recommendations must be sufficiently explicit to be plausible. Furthermore, the evaluations must be reasonably verifiable by recourse to other sources. Prior to 1961 the Attorney General did not conduct full-scale parallel investigations, and the information of the Committee was accepted at face value. Since that time there has been a fundamental disagreement between the Committee and the new administration over the value of previous trial experience, and its recommendations, when based on that factor, are discounted accordingly.[15] Thus, although absolute agreement on standards is *not* a prerequisite as far as the Attorney General is concerned, he does expect that, in all cases, and particularly in controversial areas, the Committee's standards will be discernible. Furthermore, as suggested earlier, the Attorney General expects the Committee to be reasonably flexible in its application of standards, to understand the cross pressures from other sources to which the administration is subjected, and to try to find a candidate at least minimally qualified on the urging of the Attorney General where the latter feels impelled to make the nomination.[16]

The Committee is expected to produce information and make recommendations that are sufficiently persuasive to permit their use by the Attorney General to convince senators and other political sponsors to withdraw their support of competing candidates. The Committee

---

[15] Interview with Assistant Deputy Attorney General Joseph Dolan, November 2, 1962.
[16] *Ibid.*

can be an invaluable political resource to the Attorney General in this way. It is also politically helpful when it endorses a candidate in that such action gives the "Attorney General's candidate" the popular image of also being the "choice" of the legal profession.

As differentiated from what he expects from the Committee and what uses he can put it to, the Attorney General has some minimal requirements and prohibitions which constitute the limits of the Committee's status. *First,* there is the requirement of limited function. This can cover a wide variety of factors, but as used here it has particular reference to the scope of the Committee's investigations and recommendations. By agreement with the Attorney General, the Committee ostensibly limits its inquiries to those factors that have a bearing on the professional qualifications of prospective candidates. It is with respect to just such factors that the Committee claims specialized knowledge and the "right" to be consulted. If it were to recognizably deal with political factors such as party affiliation and the views of the candidates on contemporary social issues, it would almost certainly lose the coating of legitimacy which now supports its operations. And the benefits of its work to the Attorney General would be seriously diluted. Furthermore, any evidence of a particular political orientation influencing the Committee's recommendations would completely destroy its usefulness to the Attorney General, and the relationship would be shattered. The pre-Committee history of the American Bar Association's involvement in the judicial-selection process in behalf of very conservative interests, and the present ideological orientation of the Association, are prejudices from which the Committee must dissociate itself. Although the Committee has always had among its ranks men who shared this conservative view, it has had a goodly share of moderate liberals, and in fact has been led by men of such views since 1956.[17]

Although officials in the Justice Department today state that they have seen no evidence of any attempt by the Committee to use the facade of judicial reform to insure ideological conformity of a particular type on the federal bench, the fact remains that even to those who work closest with the Committee, such attempts, unless very crudely executed, would be hard to perceive.[18] It is very easy to translate

---

[17] Both Bernard Segal and Robert Meserve have long been associated with various philanthropic and political groups which are ordinarily classed as "liberal." Meserve is a member of the "Brandeis" law firm in Boston.

[18] Interview with Assistant Deputy Attorney General Joseph Dolan, November 2, 1962.

political values into "judicial characteristics." For example, the Committee's insistence on previous trial experience as a prerequisite for service on the District Courts may operate against the lawyer active in politics and the professor of law, and favor the practicing lawyer who is more likely, by the very nature of his profession, to be more conservative in his judicial ways, if not in his political views.

The Committee, if it wished, could also use its recommendation system to upgrade candidates considered more conservative and downgrade those with opposite views. Although the specific degree of qualification, as we have seen, may not have too great an influence on the Attorney General, the chances of someone receiving an "exceptionally well qualified" rating being nominated are far greater than those of one receiving either a "well qualified" or "qualified." So subtle is the distinction between any two of these that the reasons for the difference are often unclear. Such a system is clearly susceptible to misuse.

That despite this requirement the Committee does in fact consider factors other than professional characteristics was revealed, perhaps unwittingly, by Chairman Bernard Segal. In an address at the induction of Abraham L. Freedman as Federal District Judge for Eastern Pennsylvania, Segal commented:

Your honors may ask whether it is the function of our Committee to go beyond the legal and professional attainments of a prospective appointee. *We believe it is.* [Emphasis mine.] For while professional attainments are prerequisites, the extracurricular activities of a lawyer's life are of the utmost importance in fitting him for the bench. They provide him with those special, private insights which mark the great judge.

[Judge Walter Schaefer has noted that] "the main ingredients of his decisions must be drawn from his own mind and heart to bear upon the facts and the legal doctrine that counsel put before him."

Of course, a man's philosophy and his activities are reciprocal; each is shaped by and influences the other. A man's whole being and all his activities determine what he thinks and what he is. An informed view on the issues of our time and a sympathetic understanding of the problems of all the citizens of the community relate directly to the work of a judge in each small case, each issue. The judge derives his principles from many sources, for he is fashioning morality in action.[19]

The inevitable intermingling between professional qualifications and the *weltanschauung* of the prospective judge, and the virtual impossibility of considering the one completely independently of the other,

---

[19] Quoted in *The Legal Intelligencer,* October 3, 1961.

is recognized and apparently accepted by the Attorney General, as it is by the Committee. The requirement is apparently satisfied if the candid consideration of such factors does not result in automatic opposition to persons of a particular political persuasion, and so long as the public image of the Committee contains the more limited view of its function.

The Committee is keenly aware of public criticism of the possibilities of misuse of its influence, and Committee spokesmen miss no opportunity to restate its recognition of the "rules of the game":

. . . We must realize the extremely delicate position the Committee occupies. The Committee is not an agency of government. It has no official status. Its position and its influence can be maintained only so long as the government officials with whom it works continue to have complete confidence in the complete objectivity, the scrupulous fairness, and the painstaking thoroughness of the Committee's investigations and reports.[20]

Furthermore, in what seems to be an implicit subrequirement, the Annual Report of the Committee continually restates the policy that it "has made it clear, both to the appointing power and to the Judiciary Committee of the United States Senate, that it does not deal with what may broadly be called 'political factors.' . . . This Committee does not think it a part of its task to try to pass upon the desirability of nominating for a given vacancy a person whose economic ideas or ideas as to governmental policy may accord with, or differ from, those of its members."

We would except . . . an instance where the expressed views of the nominee are such as to indicate to the Committee a basic lack of judgment or a lack of respect for the law of the land, or an instance where the prospective nominee demonstrated a probable lack of ability to deal fairly with persons whose views differed from his.[21]

It would seem that the Committee can give weight to nonprofessional considerations provided that they do not arouse partisan conflict and confine themselves to those considerations on which members of both parties agree in principle.

The *second* minimal requirement for continued liaison is that the Committee must continue to work within the system, and not use its prestige to encourage major reforms. (This does not preclude, of

---

[20] Bernard G. Segal, "Federal Judicial Selection—Progress and the Promise of the Future," 46 *Massachusetts Law Quarterly* (1961), 141.
[21] "Midyear Report of the Standing Committee on Federal Judiciary," 88 *ABA Reports* (1963), 195–196.

course, working for greater influence within the system, as evidenced by the informal report agreement of 1958.) The Committee made this same decision early in its life, and has rigorously supported it in the intervening years, despite the contrary efforts of several individual members. In order to work effectively with the Attorney General, the Committee must recognize his problems, and, even when it disagrees with his decisions, it must not often yield to the temptation to carry the fight to different decision levels. Furthermore, it must not be a party to organized efforts to alter the system, particularly such efforts which seek to eliminate the Attorney General from the judicial-selection process. This latter requirement is not "hard to take," since it also operates in the interests of the preservation of the Committee.

Two illustrations of the Committee's responses to possible breakdowns in its rapport with the Attorney General will suffice. In 1957 Committee member Ben R. Miller of Louisiana sponsored a resolution which, among other things, opposed the continued participation of the Attorney General in the selection process. The resolution was debated by the House of Delegates in 1958 after receiving an unfavorable report from the Committee on Judicial Selection, Tenure, and Compensation. Committee members Cloyd Laporte and Roy Willy argued that the resolution could only be construed as a slap at the Attorney General and would jeopardize the Committee's liaison. Said Willy:

It is true that we have not yet reached the stage where we have the opportunity to name the man best qualified in the states from which the appointments are to be made. There is still politics which enter into it. . . . But we have a responsibility to maintain a friendly relationship with the Attorney General's office. . . .

Why should we antagonize that source with which we are now working on such friendly terms by impugning the motives? [22]

Miller agreed to a suggestion that specific mention of the Attorney General be deleted from the resolution, and it was passed by a voice vote,[23] but its criticism of the role of the Justice Department and of

[22] "Proceedings of the House of Delegates," 44 *American Bar Association Journal* (1958), 1110.
[23] *Ibid.*, p. 1111. Bernard Segal claims that if he had not been called away from the meetings on personal business he would have been able to block the resolution, instead of merely being influential in toning it down.—Interview with Bernard G. Segal, October 30, 1962.
The key provisions of the resolution, as finally passed, were:
"Judicial appointments should be completely removed from the area of political patronage and made only from those lawyers and judges, irrespective of

the existing selection system was nonetheless clear. At the very least it implied that the selection of federal judges should be removed from party politics; that the organized bar should be given fuller responsibility for judicial recruitment, instead of being relegated solely to a consultative position. Not to be overlooked is the fact that, even as amended, the resolution was an implicit criticism of the policy of the Committee on Federal Judiciary that the best results were to be obtained by working within the existing system.

Voicing its strong opposition to the resolution, the *New York Times* stated that ". . . Once the organized bar has candidates of its own, its views will be suspect." [24] Miller responded by claiming that the editorial misconstrued the resolution:

> Your editorial erroneously assumed the resolution represents an attempted usurpation by lawyers of control over judicial nominations. To the contrary, it does not suggest whom the Commission should comprise and it should of course be composed of nationally respected citizens, to receive suggestions from all segments of our society. . . . We have had many fine judges—but this is despite the system and not because of it. . . .
>
> Thinking people should realize that our judges cannot retain the respect they must have unless the system of their selection is drastically changed. That method must be such that the public accepts them as highly qualified, impartial, and non-partisan arbiters and interpreters of the law.[25]

Miller also challenged the effectiveness of the Committee's work with the Attorney General, claiming that the bar's objectives could not be obtained by working within the existing system.

---

party affiliation and political consideration, who possess the highest qualifications.

"Suggestions for nominations should originate in an independent commission established as an agency of the President, to advise with the President on appointments, and to receive from outside sources and from all segments of the organized bar, suggestions of names and persons deemed highly qualified for appointment as judges in their respective jurisdictions.

"The 'nominations' of all persons to serve as members of the federal judiciary should rest solely in the President of the United States; and the United States senators in a spirit of unselfish public service should restrict themselves to their constitutional duty of conducting thorough investigations, and expressing their considered judgment, on the qualifications of the nominees.

"To avoid any suggestion of partisanship and to make the courts truly non-partisan or bipartisan, it is desirable that there should be some recognition of a general principle that a substantial percentage of the members of any federal court should be from the ranks of a party other than that of the President who is to make the appointment."

[24] *New York Times*, August 29, 1958, p. 22.
[25] *New York Times*, September 29, 1958, p. 26.

The Miller resolution, compounded by his letter to the *Times*, may have alerted the Committee to possible tensions with the office of the Attorney General, for it was followed closely by a caustic reply by Committee Chairman Bernard Segal. Writing to the *New York Times*, Segal strongly reaffirmed the Committee's support of the Attorney General's role in the selection of judges:

On September 29th, a letter was published from Ben R. Miller on "Choosing the Federal Judiciary," which referred, in part, "to the procedure and effectiveness of the liaison between the Attorney General of the United States and the Standing Committee on Federal Judiciary. . . ."

Since the writer is not now a member of the Standing Committee and has not been for more than a year, I feel constrained to present the current status of the relationship between the Attorney General and the Standing Committee.

The present liaison . . . is excellent. Indeed, it has reached an all-time high. . . .

During the time I have been chairman . . . there has been only one occasion when the President made a nomination . . . without reference to the committee.

. . . Both Attorney General Rogers and Deputy Attorney General Walsh have granted every request for conference or consultation which I have made of them in behalf of the Committee. They have been, at all times, receptive to suggestions and proposals for improving the administration of justice, including the procedure employed in the nomination of judges.

There is, of course, work still to be done, new ground to be broken. With this in mind, the committee observed [in its Annual Report for 1958] that the total objectives have not yet been attained. "That will not be," the report concludes, "until the best qualified lawyers or judges available without regard to their political affiliations are appointed to the Federal judiciary." [26]

Deputy Attorney General Lawrence Walsh has commented that the 1958 resolution did not have, and could not have had, much effect on the Committee's status. "Segal's position," he said, "depended on his personal integrity. Nothing the ABA could do could affect it." [27] Nonetheless, Segal had found it necessary to disavow the Miller letter and the ABA resolution publicly, and it is difficult to believe that without his disavowal *some* fences would not have been broken.

Contrary to the aims of the Committee on Federal Judiciary, the 1958 resolution sought to extend the "Missouri Plan" concept to the federal level; it sought to extend the role of the organized bar from mere consulting at the nomination stage to an active participation in

---

26 *New York Times*, October 14, 1958, p. 36.
27 Interview with former Deputy Attorney General Lawrence Walsh, December 22, 1962.

the initial recruitment of judges. Following the passage of the resolution, the House of Delegates appointed a five-man Special Committee on Nonpartisan Selection of Federal Judiciary. This Committee, which included Ben Miller and was chaired by Harold Gallagher of New York, a cosponsor, met with Attorney General Rogers and Deputy Attorney General Walsh to seek support for the objectives of the resolution. However, both Rogers and Walsh declared that the appointment of a nominating commission "would be neither desirable nor practical, particularly at this time." The Committee then prepared a brief explaining the resolution and submitted it to President Eisenhower and other governmental figures. Noting that the federal bench was now "in balance" (see p. 140 ff.), it urged the President to establish a bipartisan nominating policy, and to establish an advisory commission on nominations by executive order. Interestingly enough, the brief "contemplated that the President will have the assistance of the Department of Justice in investigating the qualifications and fitness of persons under consideration for judicial appointment." [28] Such wording would indicate that the Special Committee was at least conscious of the effects of its actions on the role of the Standing Committee on Federal Judiciary.

Although President Eisenhower did accept the suggestion that some sort of bipartisan principle be introduced into judicial appointments, and used the promise of bipartisanship in an attempt to force passage of an omnibus judgeship bill, no further action was taken on the "Commission" idea. The formation of this Special Committee to implement the Miller resolution was clearly a challenge to the policies of the Committee on Federal Judiciary and a potential source of difficulty between the Committee and the Attorney General.

A second breakdown in the Committee's relationship with the Attorney General became possible in 1962, when, for the first time, the Attorney General disregarded the Committee's objections to candidates in "wholesale" numbers. Yet Chairman Segal's response in the Committee's Annual Report played down that fact and instead commended the Attorney General on the generally high quality of his other appointments, and discussed at length the political pressures which would prevent even an Attorney General bent on making quality nominations from achieving that goal entirely:

. . . Your Committee is not unmindful of the fact that the objectives of the President, the Attorney General, and the Deputy Attorney General as to the

---

28 See "Report of the Special Committee on Nonpartisan Selection of Federal Judiciary," 84 *ABA Reports* (1959), 434. The brief is reprinted in *ibid.*, p. 436.

quality of judicial appointments do not differ essentially from those of the Committee. We are fully aware that political pressures are great on any President, especially at the start of a new Administration marked by a change from one party to another, and that the need for confirmation by the Senate is a major consideration in the making of nominations. Inevitably, the cumulative pressures resulting from the unprecedentedly large number of appointments in so short a period have been greater than ever before; . . .[29]

Segal's statement was obviously designed to also counteract the inevitable "I told you so's" from those in the American Bar Association who doubted the effectiveness of the Committee's liaison with the Attorney General. Segal's words were undoubtedly directed as much toward the Attorney General as they were toward dissidents in the American Bar Association. The press usually reports the proceedings of the ABA annual meetings by quoting excerpts from the major addresses and reports, and Segal's "soothing" words were duly headlined along with his criticisms. The *Washington Post* for August 8, 1962, ran the following headline: "ABA Praises Kennedy Bench Choices Despite 8 Regarded as Unqualified." The lead paragraphs of the article stated:

The American Bar Association's Committee on the Federal Judiciary reported today that, despite the appointment of eight persons it believes unqualified, the Kennedy Administration has done a good job in selecting federal judges.

Bernard G. Segal of Philadelphia, chairman of the Committee, said that his group rated 72 of 113 selections by the President as being exceptionally well qualified or well qualified.[30]

Thus, Segal was able to praise the Attorney General, criticize eight judgeships, and shift the onus for these eight from the Attorney General to "other political pressures."

The *third* minimal basic requirement for continued liaison which the Committee has to meet is to refrain from suggesting candidates of its own and thus acquiring the image of "judge-maker." This was an initial requirement of Attorney General Brownell in 1953, which the Committee accepted reluctantly.[31] However, as the Committee's influence has increased, it has accepted this limitation and turned its attention toward stimulating the state and local bar associations to

---

[29] "Report of the Standing Committee on Federal Judiciary," 87 *ABA Reports* (1962), 606.

[30] Segal went on to say that "his group hopes that in the future the Administration will make no more such appointments."

[31] "Report of the Standing Committee on Federal Judiciary," 78 *ABA Reports* (1953), 224.

undertake this initial function in the recruitment of federal judges. If the latter can do this successfully, the Committee is unlikely to seek that prerogative for itself. But if the state and local groups are unable or unwilling to do the job, the Committee will probably have to reappraise its acceptance of the Attorney General's requirement. Given the access which the Committee has achieved to the Attorney General, the next goal of the organized bar must be the achievement of comparable influence with the Senate, and the only way this can be done is "to exert local pressures on the United States Senators and on the political powers in the states and local communities who customarily provide the initial sponsorship for candidates and bring them to the attention of the President and the Attorney General." [32]

The Committee's Expectations

The converse of the expectations and requirements which the Attorney General holds for the Committee on Federal Judiciary is that the Committee also expects certain results from the liaison and certain types of responses on the part of the Attorney General. Its expectations are of a different order than those of the Attorney General, for the Committee is more dependent on his indulgence than he is on its services. In fact, in light of the Committee's delicate and informal position, any talk of "requirements" might be fatuous indeed. Failure of the Attorney General to meet any of the Committee's expectations would probably not result in a breakdown of the liaison; but it might result in changed patterns of behavior on the part of the Committee. If the liaison were to fail to produce at least a partial achievement of the Committee's goals, a major reassessment of its policies would be in order.

First, the minimum expectation of the Committee is that it will be *consulted* by the Attorney General on all nominations. This also means (since 1958) that it will be asked to investigate and informally assess the qualifications of every person considered for nomination to any federal court. Prior to 1956 the Attorney General had occasionally made a nomination without reference to the Committee, usually in instances where the nominee was already associated with the Department of Justice, and it was felt that his qualifications were well-enough known to permit dispensing with the ABA investigation. But Bernard Segal was able to persuade Attorney General Brownell that

---

[32] "Report of the Standing Committee on Federal Judiciary," 87 *ABA Reports* (1962) , 607.

of all candidates, those from the Justice Department were *most* in need of outside appraisal. Since that time consultation has been regular with but two exceptions.[33]

Keeping the bargain did produce, however, certain tensions which aptly illustrate how significant "being regularly consulted" is to the Committee. Activities leading to the nomination of Byron White as Associate Justice of the Supreme Court are a good example. Chairman Segal had been called into personal consultation with Assistant Deputy Attorney General Joseph Dolan when the resignation of Justice Whittaker became known, and, during the course of those consultations, other members of the Committee were called for information regarding specific names being considered. Segal learned, however, that the President did not intend to consult with the Committee beyond these informal discussions.[34] He spoke to the Attorney General, who claimed that, when he had assured ABA President Whitney North Seymour that the administration would continue the relationship of its predecessors with the Committee, Supreme Court nominations were excluded. Seymour denied that any such exception had been made. Attorney General Kennedy claimed the decision not to consult the Committee formally had been the President's.

Shortly thereafter, Attorney General Kennedy called Segal to say that the President had decided on Byron White, "and hoped that (he) would issue a statement following the nomination." Segal refused, saying that the Committee had not yet acted and he could not speak in their behalf, although he was personally gratified by the nomination. Segal told Kennedy that newspapers would probably ask whether the Committee had been consulted, and that, if so, he "could only reply in the negative."

Segal tried to persuade the Attorney General that failure to formally consult the Committee would be a step backward, and probably would have adverse effects both upon the Committee's work and upon the general acceptance of the appointment. He urged Kennedy to try to change the President's mind.

The Attorney General then talked with the President and imme-

---

[33] In the 1962 Report, Segal acknowledged the cooperation of the "new team" in the Justice Department. *Ibid.*, pp. 602–603. But in the 1963 Report another such instance was recorded. See Note 73, Ch. 3, p. 73.

[34] All the information on the White appointment "crisis" in this and subsequent paragraphs comes from a letter from Bernard Segal to all members of the Committee in which Segal tried to recount the events preceding the nomination.—Letter of March 31, 1962. All the important facts have either checked with other existing information, or have been corroborated by other sources.

diately advised Segal that the latter was agreeable to having the name submitted, and would delay his announcement accordingly. Two hours before the President's statement, the Committee "met" via conference phone call, and decided—as described earlier—that White was "exceptionally well qualified" to be an Associate Justice.

Segal reported the action to the Attorney General, who then asked "quizzically, whether (he) would 'now' be ready to issue a statement after the President announced the appointment?" Segal agreed and wrote a laudatory recommendation, part of which the President incorporated into his announcement.[35]

A *second* expectation which the Committee has of the Attorney General is that the latter will give serious consideration to the Committee's recommendations, if not always follow them. Prior to the advent of the Democratic Administration, the Committee might have expected that no candidate opposed by it would receive a nomination. But subsequent events (described in Chapter 3) have made such an expectation impossible. Nonetheless, the Committee would have to seriously reexamine its policies if it became apparent that its views were being lightly regarded. The Committee does not believe this to be the case. In his Annual Report for 1962, Segal noted that were it not for the Committee's efforts an even greater number of potential "not qualifieds" would have received nominations. Furthermore, he noted that "approximately 60%" of the judges appointed during the preceding year had been either "well" or "exceptionally well" qualified,[36] the inference being that this was due, at least in part, to the Committee's influence.

Giving serious consideration to the Committee's recommendations could not preclude, of course, the Attorney General from setting his own standards and making his own evaluations, using the Committee's recommendations as evidence to be considered. No Attorney General has ever actually conceded the power to veto nominations to the Committee, although Attorney General Rogers did infer that nomination without the approval of the Committee would occur only in unusual circumstances.[37] Where the standards of the Attorney General and those of the Committee tend to converge, as they did during the Eisenhower Administration, and the Attorney General relies heavily on the

35 *New York Times*, March 31, 1962, p. 1.
36 "Report of the Standing Committee on Federal Judiciary," 87 *ABA Reports* (1962), 606.
37 William P. Rogers, "Judicial Appointments in the Eisenhower Administration," 41 *Journal of the American Judicature Society* (1957), 40.

Committee's word, it is not far from having achieved a veto power in practice if not in theory.

However, where there exists a substantial conflict over standards, as is the case now, the Committee could not reasonably claim that less serious consideration was being given to its recommendations. Less weight is being given to them in cases where a disputed standard, such as trial experience, is involved. But, failing to convince the Attorney General to adopt its own standards, the Committee could not feasibly claim that its views were being taken lightly. The Committee does campaign for adoption of those standards that it prefers. But if its opinions are respected, the "requirement" is satisfied.

Third, the Committee expects the Attorney General to work through it exclusively as the voice of the legal profession. The American Bar Association has received a considerable boost in prestige—reflected in tremendous membership increases—from the work of the Committee. As the claimed national agent of the organized bar, the ABA gains credence through the work of the Committee. Such a favorable image would be substantially diluted if other bar groups received "equal billing." Deputy Attorney General Byron White stated in 1962 that

the converse of our submitting names to the Judiciary Committee of the American Bar Association is that we do not submit names for judgment to any local bar association. We do not do that in any case. While we do receive recommendations from them and while the members of the local bar associations are contacted a great deal by our own representatives and by the American Bar Association, we do not submit names to local bar associations. We feel that we cannot do this because it would be impossible to deal with the very large number of associations that there are around the country. . . . It would be extremely difficult for us to give any real feeling or judgment for the standard that might be applied by the local bars in judging men or any feeling for how much time or how much care they might put into their work.

We feel that it is feasible, however, to get the opinions of the organized bar through the Judiciary Committee, whose people we know and with whose standards we are quite familiar.[38]

The Committee on Federal Judiciary does have considerable use for the local bar groups in its total strategy for increasing the influence of the organized bar in the selection of federal judges, and this will be described in Chapter 7. But it would not look kindly on any competition from those groups for its favored position with the Attorney General.

Fourth, the Committee expects the Attorney General to acknowledge

---

[38] Byron White, "Role of State and Local Bar Associations in Selection of Federal Judges," Address before the National Conference of Bar Presidents, Chicago, February 17, 1962 (mimeo), p. 3.

its contributions to the judicial-selection process. The Committee, as we have seen, has not convinced all the leaders of the American Bar Association of the effectiveness of its liaison, and occasional good words from the Attorney General or his staff give the Committee support in its own organization. In response to this expectation, such words as the following are often spoken:

> Mr. Chairman, Distinguished Members of the House of Delegates: My remarks this morning will be brief, and the first thing I want to do, . . . [is to express] the gratitude which this Administration has, and the gratitude which you as members of the Bar should have, and the gratitude of all of the people of the United States, to Bernie Segal for the dedicated work that he has done as Chairman of this Committee. He, over the past years, has devoted . . . full time to this important responsibility. He has given of himself and of his wisdom and of his judgment unsparingly, and I think that the results of that effort and work . . . will be with us for years to come with respect to the judges who have been appointed to the bench during his period of tenure. . . .[39]

Aside from its obvious public-relations function, this sort of rhetoric by the Attorney General and similar statements by the chairman of the Committee make it possible for the participants in the liaison to disagree without being disagreeable. It fulfills the same sort of need expressed by the prohibition of derogatory remarks by one member of the United States Senate of another member.[40]

We have tried to suggest in this section some of the expectations which define the relationship between the Attorney General and the Committee on Federal Judiciary. Some are fulfilled, others modified to account for possible tensions which might be detrimental to either or both parties concerned. Some are resolved only by the greater authority of the Attorney General. The ultimate decision to nominate is his, and has never been openly challenged by the Committee.

THE COMMITTEE AND THE ATTORNEY
GENERAL: AREAS OF CONFLICT

In the previous section we listed one expectation of each participant which was not completely fulfilled: of the Attorney General that the

---

[39] "Oral Reply of Nicholas deB. Katzenbach to House of Delegates," Annual Meetings of the American Bar Association, San Francisco, 1962 (mimeo), p. 1.

[40] Commenting upon the Segal-Katzenbach interchange at the 1962 ABA meetings, Assistant Deputy Attorney General Joseph Dolan declared that "Segal said what he had to say, we said what we had to say, and then we got back to work."—Interview with Joseph Dolan, November 2, 1962.

Committee provide him with plausible evaluations of all prospective candidates, particularly of persons considered "not qualified"; and of the Committee that the Attorney General give serious consideration to all recommendations of the Committee if not follow them entirely. Each of these expectations was listed in modified form, since neither had been fulfilled. The Committee would prefer, of course, that the Attorney General *never* nominate over its objections. The Attorney General would prefer that the Committee would always base its recommendations on standards to which he could assent. Clearly, there would be a mutual value if each of these expectations were more likely to be fulfilled.

Mutual fulfillment was approached prior to 1961, but, with the advent of the Kennedy Administration, certain obvious conflicts on minimum requirements for the federal bench have developed. Understanding of these basic conflicts, as they appear in recent controversial nominations, will give us more insight into the impact of the Committee on the judicial-selection process.

The basic conflict between the Committee and the present Attorney General is over standards of minimum qualification and eligibility for the federal bench. In this group there are three main areas of contention: (1) amount of legal and judicial experience required; (2) degree of importance attached to party label; and (3) maximum age of eligibility and physical capacity of the nominee to serve as a federal judge. These are listed in order of the seriousness of the conflict.

Conflict over Trial Experience

The most fundamental difference between the Attorney General and the Committee on Federal Judiciary is their respective attitudes toward the importance of trial experience as a qualification for appointment to the District Courts. With the ABA Committee it is a *sine qua non* for the rating of "qualified" or higher; with the Attorney General it is simply another relevant factor to be considered.[41] The Committee feels that in order to preside in a trial court, a judge must have an "easy" familiarity with court procedures which could *only* be gained by a reasonable amount of previous trial experience, preferably some of it in the federal courts.[42] Since the trial judge sits alone and must make many important decisions "on the spot," it is felt that this is "no spot to train." Such is not the case on an appellate court, where the key decisions come after long intervals, and at least three judges

[41] *Ibid.*
[42] Segal, *op. cit.*, p. 143.

hear every case. The present administration operates on the assumption that a person "could be" qualified with little or no trial experience, providing other capabilities are present. It is believed that a deficiency in trial experience can be made up, whereas deficiencies in ability are more likely to be "permanent." What the Attorney General is looking for in all cases is a "sensitivity" to litigation practice, which does not—in his opinion—necessarily correlate with trial practice. He notes that some of the best recognized lawyers in metropolitan communities have had little or no trial experience, but would still be assets to any federal court.[43]

The Committee's view was shared by the Eisenhower Administration. Former Deputy Attorney General (and former federal district judge) Lawrence Walsh felt that a good lawyer without trial experience may very well become a good judge, but that it would take a considerable number of years on the bench, and his education would be at the possible expense of the litigants.[44]

The Committee does not rate trial experience as high for either Court of Appeals or Supreme Court positions. Given the different types of functions which these courts perform, the Committee agrees with the Attorney General that formal experience is secondary to legal ability, intellectual horizons, familiarity and understanding of broad public-policy issues, and so on. The Committee does believe, however, that a certain balance should exist on multiple-judge appellate courts: some trial lawyers, some "political" lawyers, even a professor of law now and then.[45] It is interesting to note that neither the Attorney General nor a majority of members of the Committee [46] subscribe to the notion that prior *judicial* experience is the most important prerequisite for service on an appellate court, although neither thinks that such experience is without merit entirely.[47]

---

[43] Interview with Deputy Attorney General Nicholas deB. Katzenbach, November 7, 1962.
[44] Interview with former Deputy Attorney General Lawrence Walsh, December 22, 1962.
[45] Interview with Bernard G. Segal, October 30, 1962.
[46] Several members of the Committee stated privately that, as far as they were concerned, college professors ought never to be considered for the federal bench. But the majority of the Committee does not hold to this view excepting only that college professors without trial experience would not be rated qualified for a District Court vacancy. Most of the members apparently feel that appellate courts should contain a sprinkling of law professors, "political" lawyers, men with prior judicial experience, and men with trial experience.
[47] See Felix Frankfurter, "The Supreme Court in the Mirror of the Justices," 105 *University of Pennsylvania Law Review* (1956–1957), 791–793.

Conflict over Partisanship

The question of partisanship is one on which the Committee and the Attorney General are at odds, and, paradoxically, because the contrast in their positions is so great and potentially incendiary, the conflict over this standard has been reduced largely to the level of rhetoric. For reasons stated earlier, the Attorney General is required by the necessities of politics to appoint mostly from the ranks of his own party, whatever his own views on the matter. The Committee believes that appointments should be made on merit irrespective of party affiliation; but in the absence of a completely nonpartisan approach, the Committee feels that a bipartisan policy is acceptable. At the very least it would hope to prevent one party from dominating the federal bench, as the Democrats did in 1953 when they held 80 per cent of all federal judgeships.

Since the Committee does not suggest candidates of its own, it is confined to rating candidates who for the most part are of the President's party. It could not *refuse* to rate Democrats unless some Republicans were also appointed. Thus, the Committee is forced to cooperate in a partisan system which it opposes. Although this cooperation is a price of its continued participation *at all,* it causes considerable consternation with "the folks back home" and provides ammunition for the Committee's critics in the American Bar Association.

In 1957 Attorney General Rogers noted that the preponderance of Democrats on the federal bench had dwindled to 60 per cent and the division would likely reach 50 per cent before the completion of Eisenhower's second term (since he had appointed almost all Republicans). Rogers declared that

. . . it would seem desirable as a matter of national policy to prevent a gross imbalance from occurring. Probably no fixed formula is practicable. However, I believe the public interest would be well served if the two major parties gave consideration to arranging some appropriate safeguards to prevent a gross imbalance from occurring in the federal courts regardless of how long either party is in office.[48]

When Congress began considering a bill to provide new judgeships in 1959, Rogers was authorized by the President to state that half of any

---

[48] Address at the Denver Regional Meeting of the American Bar Association, 1957, quoted in "Report of the Standing Committee on Federal Judiciary," 82 *ABA Reports* (1957), 278.

new judgeships provided by Congress would be filled with Democrats.[49] This was calculated to dissolve the opposition of the Democrat-controlled Congress toward providing a large patronage plum for an outgoing Republican President. Even when assured that the Democratic appointees would be real Democrats, and not the "Eisenhower Democrat" variety, and would be subject to approval by the Democratic leadership, the Democratic leaders in Congress decided to gamble—successfully as it turned out—on winning the presidency in 1960 and thus having *all* the judgeships for themselves.[50] This offer, incidentally, may have been the first time in American history that a President has offered to share his appointment power with senators of the opposite political party.

The Eighty-seventh Congress, working under a Democratic President, finally passed an omnibus judgeship bill calling for seventy-three new positions.[51] These, combined with the normal number of vacancies which occur each year, gave President Kennedy the unprecedented opportunity of appointing over a hundred federal judges in his first year in office.

Presidential candidate Kennedy had told the ABA that he "would hope that the paramount consideration in the appointment of a judge would not be his political party, but his qualifications for office." [52] However, in testimony before the House Judiciary Committee which initially considered the omnibus bill, Attorney General Kennedy refused to commit the administration to a policy of bipartisan appointments, saying only that "the best qualified individuals should be selected." [53] In response to criticism of the Democratic position, House Judiciary Committee Chairman Emanual Celler denied that only Democrats would be appointed. "But," he added, "being a realist, candor compels me to say: Being a Democrat will not hurt. It may help." [54] When he signed the judgeship bill, President Kennedy omitted any mention of partisanship—or bipartisanship.

When Kennedy was inaugurated as President, there was almost exactly the same number of Republicans as Democrats on the federal bench. Yet, with the exception of three recess appointments made by President Eisenhower which Kennedy resubmitted, each of the first

---

[49] *New York Times,* May 31, 1960, p. 24.
[50] *Congressional Quarterly Weekly Report,* November 3, 1961, p. 1813.
[51] *Public Law* 87-136, May 4, 1961.
[52] Letter to ABA President John Randall, August 30, 1960.
[53] U. S. Congress, House of Representatives, *Hearings, Federal Courts and Judges,* 87th Cong., 1st Sess., 1961, p. 402.
[54] *New York Times,* May 5, 1961, p. 17.

eighty-five new appointments went to a Democrat, and, in the Committee's words, "a great opportunity had been lost." [55]   Although the administration did make several Republican appointments toward the end of 1962, it never accepted the principle of bipartisanship.[56]

Having lost the battle, and with no prospect to fight it again in the near future, the Committee will have to continue working, as it has, in a partisan framework.   Party affiliation may not be a relevant factor in determining who is qualified for the federal judiciary, but it is the primary factor in determining who is eligible for consideration, and this choice the Attorney General has reserved for himself.

Conflict over Age

Both the Attorney General and the Committee on Federal Judiciary agree that a qualification for appointment should be expectation of reasonable length of service as a federal judge.   During the Eisenhower Administration, the Committee and the Attorney General agreed (upon the urging of the Committee), that no person 60 years of age or over should be appointed to a lifetime judgeship, unless that person were among the best qualified available for the position.   The rule was not applied to judges already sitting who might be elevated to a higher court.   But *no* person was to be appointed to any court if he or she had passed the sixty-fourth birthday.[57]   Attorney General Kennedy generally agreed with the policy expressed by the rule, but did not consider it an absolute prohibition on his freedom of selection; it was just one of several factors to be considered.   In 1961, the Attorney General submitted the name of Thomas Michie for the Federal District Court for the Western District of Virginia.   Michie was rated exceptionally well qualified by the Committee despite the fact that he was 65 years old at the time.   But, in a letter to Assistant Deputy Attorney General Joseph Dolan, Bernard Segal asserted that in the future, the Committee would hold to the original age rule:

---

[55] "Report of the Standing Committee on Federal Judiciary," 87 *ABA Reports* (1962), 609.

[56] The Committee had called upon the Kennedy Administration to "unequivocally break the bonds of partisanship" and "assured" it that the public support which would inevitably follow such action would compensate for any party discontent. *Ibid.*, p. 610.

[57] The Committee voted to include this rule in its standards in 1957. —"Report of the Standing Committee on Federal Judiciary," 82 *ABA Reports* (1957), p. 278. According to Bernard G. Segal, Attorney General Rogers attended the Committee meeting and agreed to the rule.—Interview with Bernard G. Segal, October 30, 1962.

In various conversations pertaining to Mr. Michie, I told you of the serious concern our Committee has lest Mr. Michie's appointment set a precedent which would impair the rule, followed for some years, that a lawyer 60 years or over should not receive an *initial* appointment to a life-time judgeship in a federal court, unless he merits a rating of well qualified or exceptionally well qualified and is in excellent health; and in no event, should he be eligible for such appointment if he has reached his 64th birthday. It is unfortunate that a misunderstanding has arisen as to whether the rule has been applied to age 64 or age 65. I wish to confirm to you the unanimous vote of our committee that, hereafter, we will not render a favorable report in any such case where the person under consideration is 64 years of age or over.[58]

Since well-qualified judges are often hard to recruit, given the low salaries paid, both the Attorney General and the Committee were willing to stretch the rule. However, the former considers good health as a compensating factor if the nominee is over the age of 64, whereas the latter now would permit no exception. The standard of good health is one accepted by both the Attorney General and the Committee. Unlike the question of age, however, which is easily definable, the matter of health lends itself to no such easy categorization. The conflicts between the Attorney General and the Committee over this variable have been essentially matters of judgment.

Conflicts over Ratings

There is no real conflict between the Attorney General and the Committee over the different degrees of qualification, although there may be a considerable difference of opinion. This is because the Attorney General rarely has the opportunity to search for the "ideal" candidate, and his decision is influenced by a number of factors—such as political sponsorship—which the Committee need not consider in determining the specific rating to be accorded. In fact, since the introduction of the informal-report system, the actual formal rating is of greater value to the Committee as an index of the success of its operations than it is to the Attorney General, who in most cases has decided upon nomination before submitting a name to the Committee for formal evaluation. Furthermore, the greatest gap between ratings is between "qualified" and "not qualified" and it is this distinction which concerns the Attorney General most. There is much less of a difference between "qualified" and "well qualified."

---

[58] Letter of March 5, 1961.

Conflicts over Goals

Although it has been mentioned before, no theory of the relationship between the Attorney General and the Committee could be complete without referring to the conflict inherent in the merging of both the idealist and pragmatic approaches to a problem. Each is seeking the best possible judge for each vacancy, but each defines "best possible" in ways which are sometimes mutually exclusive. The Committee's definition contains several characteristics which, either by empirical analysis or impression, are said to be necessary qualifications in the making of a good judge. The Committee's definition of "best possible" judge excludes the major ingredients of the Attorney General's definition, although it recognizes the reasons for the difference. The Attorney General's definition conceives of the selection of a federal judge as the result of a variety of political impulses, some persistent, others occasional.

In a way this basic definitional conflict is responsible for the conflicts in standards previously outlined. With the assumptions under which he must operate, the Attorney General is simply not free to adopt the more rigorous and inflexible standards of the Committee, even if he were to agree with them.

Ten Cases of Conflict and Their Resolution

At this juncture it will be useful to examine some recent cases of conflict between the Attorney General and the Committee over the standards described. In each case the conflict was resolved in favor of the Attorney General. No comparable information is available for those conflicts resolved in favor of the Committee, but subsequently we shall consider the possibilities of such action. In evaluating each of these cases, it is important to keep in mind certain key questions. (1) What was the conflict involved? (2) What caused it to be resolved as it was? (3) What, hypothetically, could have caused it to be resolved in favor of the Committee? [59]

CASE "A": Judge, United States Court of Appeals. "A" was appointed to the Court at the age of 42. He was rated "not qualified" by the

---

[59] Except where otherwise noted, all of the information for these case studies has come from conversations with members of the Attorney General's staff and from the printed or recorded Senate Judiciary Committee hearings. None of the ABA Committee members interviewed would discuss any individual case in detail. Names have been excluded only where the data relied upon is not already a matter of public record. Minor details have been altered to further conceal identities.

ABA Committee in its formal report, although in his informal report to Assistant Deputy Attorney General Joseph Dolan, Chairman Segal thought he would be rated "qualified." "A" graduated first in his class at the state university law school, where he was editor of the law review. After his graduation, he began working with the Justice Department in its various divisions. Within a few years he had moved to an administrative office in the Antitrust Division and held various other posts within that division. Subsequently, he held other administrative positions in the Department of Justice, including a period as an assistant to the Attorney General. "A" then switched to private law practice in Washington as a partner in a "New Deal" law firm. He also lectured on federal antitrust law at several law schools. Finally he was appointed to a high administrative post in the court system, a post which he held until he was appointed to the Court of Appeals.

"A" was primarily the candidate of Senator _____. Under an arrangement between _____ and the other senator from that state, each made alternate appointments, with the other in support, so "A" was ostensibly backed by both senators. "A's" name was first on a list of three submitted to the Attorney General. "A" was also supported enthusiastically by three Supreme Court justices. All the people in Washington questioned by the Justice Department gave good reports.

Virtually all the adverse reports on "A" came from lawyers in his home state who, according to Dolan, did not know him and did not like him. They considered him a "carpetbagger candidate," since he had never engaged in private practice in his home state, and had worked for the federal government most of his life. Another man under consideration for the position was rated "exceptionally well qualified" by the Committee on Federal Judiciary. Its opposition to "A" was primarily on the basis of these adverse reports in his home state, plus the fact that, except for a short period, most of his experience had been administrative. The Attorney General, on the other hand, gave more credence to his uncontested intellectual ability, his good record in the Justice Department, and most important, to the fact that he was supported by two important Democratic senators. The Attorney General's parallel investigation caused him to completely discount most of the derogatory information which the ABA Committee had uncovered in the candidate's state.

CASE "B": Judge, United States District Court. "B" was appointed to the Court at the age of 45. He was the State Attorney General when appointed, and was rated "not qualified" by the ABA Committee in its formal report. "B" was the candidate of a Democratic senator who recommended him very highly. The other senator from that state thought "B" a good but not outstanding lawyer.

The ABA informal report on "B" was very unenthusiastic although Segal thought it inconclusive as to whether he would eventually be rated "qualified." The ABA informal investigation indicated that "B" had initially failed the bar examination, that members of his home bar "were almost uniform" in their disapproval, and that "B" was reported to have fought with a state investigating commission over its tactics in uncovering vice. Although he had a Martindale-Hubbell ability rating of "very high," the ABA noted that he had little actual trial practice, his partners having done most of the trial work when he was in private practice, and his Assistant Attorneys General having handled state litigation. The report also stated that newspapers had speculated that the Democratic Governor wanted "B" made a federal judge to remove him as a competitor, and also that one senator thought that if "B" ran for governor, the incumbent Governor would run against the senator in the senatorial primary. The ABA member investigating was disturbed by what he regarded as a considerable amount of "puffing" in "B's" responses to requests for personal data. He claimed to be chief counsel in more cases than he was directly involved in. Finally, the ABA had serious reservations about his health. He was reported to have had cancer of the lip, abdomen, and back, several years before, and the report suggested that for these reasons alone the Committee would probably report him as unqualified. Finally, the ABA Committee did an informal on another candidate for the position, a State Supreme Court judge, and found him "exceptionally well qualified." But the latter refused to be considered for the judgeship for financial reasons.

The staff report compiled by various Justice Department investigators tended to contradict many of the negative findings of the ABA. On the suggestion of the two senators, a check was made of some twenty lawyers in the state, all rated "very high" by Martindale-Hubbell. The response was mixed. Some claimed that "B" was pugnacious and had a low "boiling point," others simply that he was minimally qualified, but not the best available. Of six state judges interviewed, four said he was qualified, but not outstanding. They reiterated that he was "inclined to be opinionated and tactless." One judge said that "B" did not have sufficient trial experience, but was temperamentally suited; another that he was not temperamentally suited, but had sufficient legal background. Other lawyers suggested that "B" was "growing" as a lawyer and was potentially a good judge. Three federal judges questioned all made favorable comments. The report stated that, although he flunked the bar exam the first time, he passed it the second with "flying colors" and attributed his first failure to "jitteriness" upon returning from the war.

Much of the derogatory information about "B" and certain allegations about his underworld connections turned out to be the result of a confusion with his brother. "B's" brother, a District Attorney, was alleged to have been involved in some payoffs over enforcement of prostitution laws, but no evidence connecting "B" was discovered. The question of his health also proved groundless.

Clearly, the appointment "was not all roses." From the Justice Department's standpoint, "B" was a lawyer of average ability. But there was no substantiated derogatory evidence against him, despite all the rumors. He appeared to meet the minimum standards of the Justice Department. Thus, despite the fact that he was unanimously voted "not qualified" by the Committee on Federal Judiciary, "B" received the nomination. It is doubtful that he would have received it were it not for the insistence of the two senators.

CASE "C": Judge, United States District Court. "C" was appointed to the Court at the age of 56. He was rated not qualified by the ABA Committee in its formal report. "C" was the candidate of the state political boss, who reportedly was given this patronage as a reward for his support of a successful presidential aspirant. In a letter to a member of the White House staff, "C" stated:

At the time that . . . and I visited with the President last February, I informed the President that I would be a candidate for Federal District Judge at the time the next opening occurred in the Northern District of _____.

I understand that Congress will create two new judgeships for the Northern District of _____, and I will be a candidate for one of these positions. I appreciate the President's consideration for appointment.

I am 56 years of age, married, and have one daughter. I am a graduate of _____ University, . . . cum laude, and a graduate of _____ Law School, with the Order of the Coif. I was admitted to the . . . Bar in 1930 and have been in the practice of law since that date.

I have been Treasurer of the Democratic Party of . . . for the past twelve years, and I have likewise served as Treasurer of the Democratic Steer Roasts which we hold each year. I am chairman of the . . . County Board of Elections. . . .

The ABA informal report indicated that although recommended by the city bar association (first on the list of qualified nominees), "C" was practically unknown as a lawyer, and had little experience trying cases. His integrity was never questioned. "C" was supported by one senator and an influential congressman.

Aside from his "strong" political sponsorship, which probably assured his nomination in the absence of strongly derogatory information, "C's" excellent intellectual record in law school convinced the Attorney General that he was qualified. Assistant Deputy Attorney General Dolan has since noted that law-school achievement and intellectual ability had become an increasingly important factor in the Attorney General's evaluation where other factors such as trial experience were lacking.

CASE "D": Judge, United States District Court. "D" was appointed to the Court at the age of 45. He was rated "not qualified" by the ABA Committee in its initial report, then "neither recommended nor opposed" on the formal evaluation sent to the Senate Judiciary Committee. "D" was a former administrative assistant to a prominent senator and for two years a state circuit judge. He was strongly recommended by that senator. In fact, the senator had publicly announced that "D" was his choice at the same time he communicated his preference to the Attorney General.

The only question appeared to be his lack of substantial experience, and when the nomination became imminent, the ABA Committee undoubtedly felt that it could not substantiate a "not qualified" and instead registered its dissent in ambiguous fashion. Given the lack of derogatory information, and the strong senatorial sponsorship of two administration stalwarts, the Attorney General did not have very much latitude in making this appointment. It is interesting that the ABA was much less unhappy with "D," who only had a "high" (b-v) rating from Martindale-Hubbell, than it was with "B," who was "very high" (a-v).

CASE "E": Judge, United States District Court. "E" was appointed to the Court at the age of 59. He was considered "doubtful" by the ABA Committee's informal report, "not qualified" in its final recommendation. "E" was recommended by a leading Democratic senator, and supported by the other Democratic senator from that state. He was reported to have contributed $5,000 to the senator's campaign fund. Whether or not this was true, it is known that the senator was adamant in his insistence that "E" receive the appointment.

Newspapers in that state reported that the senator was asking the appointment of "E" as his price for continued (unusual in some areas) support of the administration program.

The "E" case produced an unusually large number of unsolicited letters to the Attorney General, most of them favorable. However, the bar of the state was split wide open, with about a third declaring that "E" was not competent at all, and an equal number praising the nomination as outstanding. The ABA thought that "E" had a limited vocabulary, and difficulty in comprehending legal problems, and predicted that he could not write an acceptable opinion. It contended that many of the lawyers who had publicly supported "E" privately admitted that they did not believe he was qualified, but were afraid to say so. But they admitted that he had considerable support.

The Attorney General's staff report noted that he had been endorsed by four members of the state supreme court, and two federal Circuit judges. It found that "numerous" lawyers and state judges considered "E" above average. The report, plus the data gathered by the FBI, appeared to the Attorney General to dispel the image of "E" as a lawyer more interested in making money from the profession than anything else. An Assistant Attorney General admitted that this was a "difficult" case, and it was resolved in favor of "E" ultimately because of the insistence of the senator.

CASE "F": Judge, United States District Court. "F" was appointed to the Court at the age of 63. He was rated "not qualified" by the ABA Committee "in any event," but also because of his advanced age. In a letter to Senator Eastland, Chairman Segal stated:

I regret to advise you that the members of our Committee are unanimously of the view that ["F"] is not qualified for this appointment in any event.

I have been instructed by the Committee to add a further comment, since [he] is 63 years of age. Our Committee has steadfastly adhered to the position that if any lawyer is to be tendered appointment of a lifetime judgeship at this age, then certainly it should only be a lawyer who is among the best qualified of the judges and lawyers available for the appointment.

"F" was endorsed by the Governor and "in-party" senator of his state. Prior to accepting a recess appointment, he had been Police Commissioner for a large city. The ABA objected to the fact that he was not even a member of the federal court bar and had had little litigation practice. He was not among the top names recommended by the county bar association.

"F" was also opposed by the local chapter of a veterans' group and the city chapter of the Americans for Democratic Action, which opposed his aggressive use of the City Police in alleged violation of free speech and press guarantees:

. . . Throughout his tenure as Safety Director, ["F's"] aggressive police actions have been matched by an aggressive temperament which refuses to admit mistakes. Even when compelled to retreat from one course of conduct he has not admitted fault but has merely moved on to another police campaign equally unconstitutional.

Nevertheless, the Attorney General felt that he had met minimum standards for a federal judgeship.

CASE "G": SARAH T. HUGHES, Judge, United States District Court for the Northern District of Texas. Judge Hughes was appointed to the Court in March 1962 at the age of 65. She was rated "not qualified" by the Committee on Federal Judiciary solely on account of age, although there were also some misgivings about her active involvement in politics.

The Attorney General was looking for a female judge, and Judge Hughes was one of the few women available with the requisite qualifications. She was endorsed by Vice-President Johnson and Senator Ralph Yarborough of Texas, and was highly recommended. She had consistently been supported in bar primaries in Dallas, where she had been a state circuit judge for twenty-six years, despite the fact that, being a liberal, she held views incompatible with those predominant in the area. In the last judicial election, she had received nearly 70 per cent of the vote in a predominantly Republican county. In view of these facts, and considering that she was in robust health, had almost a perfect attendance record in twenty-six years on the state bench, and that the life expectancy of women is a few years longer than for men of comparable age, the Attorney General decided to ignore his usual policy of not appointing anyone who had reached the age of 64. Her active involvement in politics and enthusiastic methods of campaigning were written off as simply prerequisites of staying in office in the state of Texas.

As we shall see in the next chapter, the ABA decided to carry its fight against Judge Hughes to the Senate Judiciary Committee, where it was soundly repudiated. It was not prepared to see its "rule" on age turned into simply an admonition, as it had on previous occasions such as the Michie case.

CASE "H": J. AXEL BECK, Judge, United States District Court, South Dakota. Beck was appointed to the Court in March 1958 at the age of 63. He was originally opposed by the ABA Committee as being overage and not outstandingly qualified. However, in its formal report, the Committee decided "neither to recommend nor oppose" his confirmation. The Committee felt that Beck had had inadequate experience for a person his age. He had never been in a federal courtroom in his life and was opposed by the State Bar Association. His main qualification seemed to be that he was a successful politician; he was the Republican National Committeeman from South Dakota. Beck was strongly backed by Senators Francis Case and Karl Mundt; in fact, according to the *New York Times:*

A Judgeship was . . . created for Mr. Beck. Congress last year passed a bill authorizing a second permanent Federal Judge in South Dakota, although neither the Bar Association nor the judicial system itself had found any need for more judges.[60]

When the two senators refused to back down, the case was handled "through the office of Sherman Adams" as a party matter, and Beck received the nomination.

In each of these eight cases, the conflict between the Attorney General and the Committee was ultimately resolved by a decision of the former to disregard the recommendation of the latter. In these and other doubtful cases, there is usually considerable bargaining between the Attorney General and the Committee before a final decision is made. Frequently, the Attorney General can force the Committee to reassess its evaluation by presenting new evidence which contradicts the Committee's findings. Or the Attorney General can try to persuade the Committee (through its chairman) that a judgment of "qualified" would not really be out of line with the Committee's standards or that a "not qualified" would not be justified by the evidence.

As noted earlier, the influence of the Attorney General in the determination of the Committee's final evaluation is likely to be considerable in some cases, negligible in others. Where the Committee decides not to oppose confirmation after opposing nomination, as it did in the "D" and Beck cases, the resolution in favor of the Attorney General has been made partly by his success in persuading the Committee not to pursue its opposition—thus conceding at least part of the Attorney General's argument. In some instances, the Attorney General resolves the conflict by persuading the Committee to come through with a "qualified" where it was not originally of a mind to do so. This frequently happens on judgment cases: does the candidate have *sufficient* trial experience, or is he in *adequately* good health. The experience

---

60 February 25, 1958, p. 20.

question is often resolved by having the candidate acquire the extra time in court "required" by the Committee as a price for its assent. Nominations are frequently held up as much as a year—although ostensibly for other reasons—to build up the candidate to meet the Committee's "requirements." The question of health does not lend itself, of course, to the same sort of procedure. But over a period of time and numerous medical examinations and opinions, the Attorney General can often persuade the Committee to "go along." Such was the situation in each of the following two cases.

CASE "J": former Judge, United States District Court. "J," a leader of his state delegation for Eisenhower, was appointed to the Court at the age of 62. His nomination was originally opposed by the ABA Committee because of a history of heart trouble. However, Attorney General Rogers explained to Segal that he could not ask President Eisenhower to refuse to nominate a judge because of a previous heart attack, and the ABA withdrew its opposition. "J" got the job, suffered a stroke, and resigned three years later on a disability pension. This case alerted the ABA investigators more than ever to health factors, and doubtful cases began to be referred to prominent cardiologists, radiologists, and other specialists.

CASE "K": Judge, United States District Court. "K" was appointed to the Court at the age of 52. The ABA Committee thought that he was "well qualified" except that he had suffered two heart attacks. The Attorney General negotiated with Segal and the Committee for six months, during which time "K" underwent a series of tests and retests from different specialists. Finally, the ABA consented to rate him as "qualified" and the appointment was made. As with "J," "K" was supported by the two senators from his state, both of the President's party, and it is reasonable to assume that he would have eventually been nominated regardless of the ABA Committee's recommendation. It is important to note that the Committee *was* able to delay the nomination until a more adequate check-up had been performed.

Thus, we have seen that the Attorney General can favorably resolve his conflicts with the Committee by (1) unilateral disregard of its recommendations; (2) attempting to "fit the candidate" to suit the ABA's standards; or (3) persuading the Committee to support his own determined course of action. Regardless of which method of persuasion is used, the Attorney General is most likely to insist on resolving a conflict in his favor where there is strong senatorial sponsorship or some other commitment to the candidate has already been made. If the Attorney General has "no way out," he will try to invoke (2) or (3), but if necessary invoke (1). In any case, by this time, the decision is his to make. The Committee has no sanctions to support its position other than its own persuasiveness or the threat of an ex post facto appeal to public opinion (that is, a fight against confirmation).

All conflicts, of course, are not resolved in favor of the Attorney General. Where he is *free* to be persuaded, that is, where no prior commitment has been made, the Attorney General will accord a higher value to the Committee's evaluation. Although no exact figures are available, it is probable that a large number of the Committee's negative recommendations are made in cases where appointment would have been unlikely anyway. In such cases, the Attorney General is likely to enthusiastically accept the Committee's ratings to stifle the aspirations of such contenders and their supporters. The lesser the conflict between the Committee and the Attorney General, the greater the likelihood that it will be "persuasive."

The Committee is likely to be almost as persuasive where the Attorney General agrees with its negative rating of a prospective candidate and is able to use it to defeat an otherwise "promising" but weakly sponsored candidate. In situations where the administration feels that a certain appointment would be politically disadvantageous (such as a minority-group appointment of low caliber) a negative ABA rating is likely to "come in handy." Finally, not to overlook the positive side of the ledger, where the Attorney General has a free hand, a strong recommendation by the ABA Committee of one candidate accompanied by weak ratings for his competitors is likely to be significantly influential.

It becomes clear, therefore, that conflicts over standards can usually be resolved in favor of the Committee only in situations where the more basic conflict over goals is first eased. Where the Attorney General does not have to satisfy certain dominant political requirements, he is more likely to find himself accepting the recommendations of the Committee.

IMPACT OF THE COMMITTEE ON THE ATTORNEY GENERAL

Any assessment of the impact of the work of the Committee on the role of the Attorney General in the judicial-selection process must acknowledge that differing degrees of receptivity to the Committee's work by different Attorneys General makes a general conclusion vulnerable. However, since we have already noted the differences in receptivity between Attorneys General Rogers and Kennedy, the obvious reservations in the generalizations set forth will be apparent to the reader and will not be reiterated.

It is useful to consider the impact of the Committee on the Attorney General in terms of (1) the limitations it has imposed on his function, and (2) the opportunities it has created for him. Both of these criteria deal with the *process* of judicial selection. The impact of the Committee on the *results* of the process of judicial selection will be considered in Chapter 7, after similar considerations are given to the impact of the Committee on the role of the Senate in Chapter 6.

Limitations on the Attorney General

The access which the Committee has been accorded to the process of judicial selection at the federal level has resulted in several limitations on the freedom of action of the Attorney General. The Attorney General is expected to formally consult with the Committee on every name being considered for a vacancy. By consulting with the Committee, he is exposing himself to arguments which if made by an outside group he would be freer to ignore, but which he must now at least consider. Although the Committee has no device analogous to senatorial courtesy to compel compliance with its views or even consideration of them—and is itself strictly limited to considering names suggested by the Attorney General—the views that it espouses and the standards it creates generate a certain amount of effective pressure on the Attorney General.

The Committee's thorough investigations of each candidate have forced the Attorney General to conduct parallel investigations to combat the Committee's evaluations if negative, or confirm them if positive. The Committee's persistent efforts are probably responsible for the "age rule" and "health check" becoming important factors in each case, and although the present Attorney General does not agree with the Committee's "trial experience" standard, its insistence on that point has not been without effect. The Committee's concern with both the "trial experience" and "partisanship" factors has at least caused the Attorney General to devote more time and energy to justify his own treatment of the same. In short, the Committee has limited the freedom of the Attorney General by assuming a watch-dog role, and by annexing a position that provides an unparalleled opportunity for a private group to scrutinize the selection process and express its views.

Opportunities Created for the Attorney General

The creative impact of the Committee on the role of the Attorney General probably exceeds that of the limitations imposed. The information that the Committee is able to obtain on each prospective candidate, and the weight of its evaluations, has given the Attorney General greater latitude in balancing the various forces operative in the recruitment process. It has given the Attorney General the rationale and evidence necessary to successfully bargain with a senator intent on a particular nomination or a state party organization decrying the loss of any patronage opportunities. It has created sufficient popular interest in and concern for federal judicial selection to cause even the most powerful senator to hesitate before "pushing" through a disputed nomination. Its ratings have acquired a "legitimating" function to the extent at least that a President who consents to the nomination of a "not qualified" candidate will often be publicly criticized for breaking the "rules" of the game. To be sure, the Kennedy-Johnson Administration agreed to no such rules—as did its predecessor—but it is still held accountable for a breach of these rules.

Finally, and perhaps most important, the Committee on Federal Judiciary has had a nationalizing influence on the federal judicial-selection process. Such national responsibility was always operative with respect to Supreme Court appointments, but not before the liaison of 1952 had it been openly extended to the inferior federal courts as well. Although the Committee's evaluations and recommendations are not very explicit and are always relative to the situation and available candidates in each judicial district, they have operated to lay the foundation for a minimum national standard of qualification discernible to the general public. By doing this, the Committee has in reality reinforced the role of the Attorney General. By combatting the inherent decentralization of the selection process, it has, in effect, extended the freedom of the Attorney General to actively recruit judges instead of simply processing those recruited by others.

6

※

THE COMMITTEE

AND THE SENATE

The ABA Committee's success with the Attorney General has not been matched by the attainment of similar influence either with individual senators or with the Senate Judiciary Committee. Yet its relationship with some senators and with the Senate Judiciary Committee has not been without benefits, nor without the promise of some future attainments.

This chapter will explore the ABA Committee's relationship with individual senators and with the Senate Judiciary Committee. Particular emphasis will be placed on those aspects that are likely to determine or control the future development of the ABA Committee's influence over the selection of federal judges.

THE INDIVIDUAL SENATOR AND JUDICIAL SELECTION

Elaborating briefly on the description of the Senate's role in the selection of federal judges contained in Chapters 2 and 5, it is fairly clear that with most senators, the tradition of senatorial responsibility for lower-court appointments is deeply ingrained. For a variety of reasons, including the practical impossibility of the Senate as a whole considering each nomination in depth and the very real need for high-status patronage positions, individual senators of the President's party have been accorded vast deference in the choice of judges from their own states. Although recognizing the special position of the federal judge in our political system, most senators have not been willing to consider judgeships in a manner apart from other executive appointments.[1]

---

[1] See quotation on p. 31.

They generally have not conceded the need for deference to individuals or groups who claim to have specialized knowledge of and ability to discern desirable judicial "types."

The present role of senators in the judicial-selection process seems to be determined by a set of assumptions which can be summarized as follows: (1) a perceived need for judicial patronage; (2) a claim to specialized competence in choosing all officials residing in a senator's home state; (3) an interpretation of senatorial responsibility which extends, wherever consistent with the Constitution, to all areas where competence is also perceived; and (4) a lack of feasible alternatives to the existing methods by which senatorial responsibility is carried out. These assumptions support the expectations of a senator that he will play a significant role in choosing all lower federal judges from his state to be appointed by a President of his own party and, that his discretionary choices will be supported and reinforced under the rule of senatorial courtesy. The actual role that each individual senator chooses to play will, of course, vary. Some will insist on the uninhibited exercise of this prerogative; others will seek only a voice in the selection process. But even when the senator plays an active role, it is usually not a solo performance. Rather the senatorial role may more accurately be viewed as one of moderator of the relevant political forces in his state and in his party.

Challenges to these expectations by the Attorney General or President, or by an outside group such as the ABA Committee on Federal Judiciary, are likely to be met by rejection (increased internal solidarity in the Senate), absorption of some of the techniques and standards of the threatening group to blunt its criticisms while rejecting its overtures, or, in extreme cases, granting the group certain procedural concessions such as formalized consultation. The particular response, or combination of responses, to such challenges depends on the type of group issuing the challenge, its grass-roots support, and the perceived need of the senator to respond to such a challenge.

THE COMMITTEE AND THE INDIVIDUAL SENATOR

The Senator as Obstacle to Committee Influence

The Committee on Federal Judiciary sees the prerogatives of the individual United States senator, as already described, as the major obstacle to its increased influence in the selection of federal judges.[2]

---

2 See quotation leading to note 4, Chapter 5.

The role of the individual senator makes it almost impossible for the Committee to crack the partisan habit of nomination, and until it does the ultimate achievement of its goals is in serious doubt. No matter how cooperative the Attorney General is, or what his acceptance of the Committee's standards, as long as he is bound by the political commitment to partisan appointments, his hand is stayed. If the partisan element were eliminated from consideration as a relevant standard of qualification, the Committee would have a golden opportunity to fill the void by urging substitution of its own standards.

Eliminating considerations of partisanship would have a detrimental effect on the continued prerogatives of the individual senator generally. For as soon as the appointment of a federal judge is no longer a party matter, the claim of the senator to special competence fades.

The individual senator who claims the right to *choose* federal judges in his state makes it impossible for the Committee to have substantial influence with the Attorney General even if the senator's candidate is considered "not qualified" by the Committee. For in such a case, as we saw in the previous chapter, the Attorney General is not often even open to persuasion by the Committee of the merits of its recommendation. When a senator publicly commits himself to a single candidate, only the most deviant sort of behavior uncovered would suffice to thwart the nomination at that stage.

The power accorded each individual senator to control judicial nominations makes the confirmation process something of a formality, excepting only in those instances where a particular appointment may prove to be a source of acute embarrassment to the Senate as a whole. In most other instances, however, confirmation merely reinforces the earlier decision of the individual senator, and is not an "open" decision-making process on which the Committee may exert meaningful influence. As we shall illustrate below in the Irving Ben Cooper case study, even when the Committee compiles what appears to be a substantial amount of derogatory evidence against the candidate, its chances of blocking confirmation are slim. Thus, that part of the federal judicial-selection process controlled by the individual senators remains effectively barred to substantial Committee influence.

Breaking the Senatorial Hold

The ultimate success of the Committee's efforts to overcome this senatorial obstacle will depend on its ability to persuade some or most senators that (1) judicial appointments *are* substantially different from other executive appointments, requiring the participation and advice of outside groups possessing special knowledge; (2) that the Committee on Federal Judiciary and local bar groups are the logical groups to perform this service; (3) that senators can have confidence in the accuracy of the Committee's reports and in its objectivity; and (4) that a senator who publicly commits himself to supporting only qualified men as federal judges, regardless of party affiliation, will vitiate pressures to consider judgeships as patronage.

The Committee's activities in furtherance of these objectives reflect its decision to work within the existing system. As with its relationship with the Attorney General, the Committee feels that no good would be presently served by attacking the senatorial prerogative as such. It does not seek, at least openly, to exclude the senator from the judicial-selection process. Rather it seeks to have him recognize that it too should be an intimate participant. Thus, the most significant measure of the Committee's success in pursuing these objectives would be (1) the willingness of individual senators to withhold the public announcement of their recommendations until they consult with local bar groups, and the Department of Justice and the Committee have had an opportunity to make a preliminary study of other available candidates; and (2) the willingness of individual senators to suggest a number of names for each vacancy instead of just one, with the final determination made by the Attorney General.

How has the Committee sought to achieve these goals? *First,* it has relied on the Attorney General to initially convey to individual senators the Committee's evaluation of suggested candidates, thus establishing a confidence in the Committee's work. As noted previously, the Attorney General can use the Committee's adverse recommendation to persuade a senator to withdraw his support of a particular candidate. But even to the extent that the Committee is successful in this endeavor, it is still exercising a primarily negative or reviewing function. It is not "getting to" the problem at its source: the initial selection of several names for further intensive consideration.

Second, it has worked hard to establish intimate contact with at least a few senators who are counted on to pass the word of the Committee's good service. Several senators have sought the Committee's recommendations through the Attorney General, and a few have communicated directly with the Committee.[3] Lawrence Walsh, former Deputy Attorney General, has described the "conversion process" this way:

---

[3] Bernard G. Segal, "Federal Judicial Selection—Progress and the Promise of the Future," 46 *Massachusetts Law Quarterly* (1961), 150.

. . . Sometimes a senator is somewhat cynical when he is told that the Bar Association doesn't think his man is qualified, is impressed when you tell him why it is the man isn't qualified, and if he himself doesn't know and goes back to the persons who suggested the name to him and gets from them a concession that regardless of the conclusion of qualification or lack of qualification, the underlying facts as reported by your Committee were right to the heart of the target, that Senator is not simply ready to acquiesce in working with your Committee, he is anxious to do so. . . .[4]

Senators are often as much the captive of political pressures as the Attorney General, and very often they must force through a nomination that is not personally to their liking, but required by the dictates of their political situation. The Committee has sought to demonstrate to various senators that it can help to extricate them from this predicament. Bernard Segal recalls the case of a senator who confessed privately to Segal that unless he nominated his state party chairman for a District Court vacancy, his chances of getting reelected were slim. The senator said that he knew the man was not qualified, but that he could not see any alternative choice for him to make. Segal recalls that, through a series of phone calls and letters, he was able to find another candidate for the senator to nominate whom the Committee rated "exceptionally well qualified." When the Committee, as expected, rated the state chairman "not qualified," the senator was then able to withdraw his support in favor of "Segal's" candidate. The senator was reelected.[5] This recognition by the Committee of the nuances of the selection process is a key to the success which it has had in persuading some senators to call upon its services. It would get nowhere in its efforts by turning its collective nose up at the "seamier" sides of the selection process.

Third, the Committee has intensified its campaign of several years duration to establish a legitimate role for the local bar groups in the selection process. Because of its agreement with the Attorney General, the Committee itself cannot actively or formally recruit candidates for federal judgeships, although it has occasionally breached the spirit if not the form of the agreement. But if local bar groups become active participants in the process in their own areas, they can at the same time enlarge the scope of the Committee's influence by trying to weed out the nonacceptable candidates at an early stage. This would enable the Committee to concentrate its efforts on choosing between people

---

[4] Statement of Lawrence Walsh, "Proceedings of the House of Delegates," 45 *American Bar Association Journal* (1959), 364.
[5] Interview with Bernard G. Segal, October 30, 1962.

with different degrees of qualification (but all at least minimally qualified) rather than simply acting as the guardian of minimum standards. Furthermore, it is the local bar groups which stand the best chance of entering into the recruitment efforts of individual senators at an early stage. Bernard Segal has commented that

. . . state and local bar associations . . . have not even scratched the surface of their potential influence in this area. Local units of the Organized Bar simply must do more than they have done up to now, to bring the tremendous force of their political leaders to assure the sponsorship, at the very beginning of the appointment process, of qualified individuals only. For if the first candidates publicly named by any responsible person were all individuals on whom a favorable report could be given, then the ultimate choice would necessarily be made from among a much higher-qualified group.[6]

In August 1961 the House of Delegates of the ABA urged all state and local bar associations to undertake the functions of recruiting and persuading the best-qualified judges and lawyers to accept nomination if tendered (always a major problem), and to establish a liaison with senators and party officials who participate in the recruitment process.[7] This resolution was supported by the Department of Justice, which also stands to gain some freedom of action by the weakening of the senatorial prerogative.

This dependence by the ABA Committee on the efforts of local bar groups is all the more interesting in the light of the admission by members of the Committee that, generally speaking, positive recommendations of prospective judges by local groups are worth little because of the political motives behind such actions. Were these local bar groups to set up their own rating systems, and set the stage for disagreements with the ABA Committee, the purposes of the latter might very well be defeated.

Fourth, the Committee on Federal Judiciary has sought to further its objectives through a widespread use of publicity and political pressures. Of course, there is already widespread sentiment among the leadership of the organized bar for major reforms in the present system, and the Committee need do nothing to foster the dissemination of information by the several bar groups already active in that field. Most of the literature produced by such groups calls for more radical departures from the existing system than the Committee is willing to countenance or be associated with. But as long as the Committee does

---

[6] Segal, *op. cit.,* p. 150.
[7] "Proceedings of the House of Delegates," 46 *American Bar Association Journal* (1961), 1044.

not support them, such demands do not subvert the Committee's position, but instead tend to create popular dissatisfaction with the senatorial role, leaving individual senators more vulnerable to the Committee's influence.[8]

Sometimes the Committee *is* embarrassed by the strong language of such demands, but it has not yet suffered any permanent adverse effects. For example, the 1958 resolution of the House of Delegates, to which we have already made reference in a different connection, also contained an explicit criticism of the senatorial role which apparently caused considerable antagonism toward the Committee:

. . . The nominations of all persons to serve as members of the Federal Judiciary should rest solely with the President of the United States; and the United States Senators, in a spirit of unselfish public service, should restrict themselves to their constitutional duty of conducting thorough investigations and expressing their considered judgment on the qualifications of the nominees.[9]

The Committee, of course, refused to endorse the resolution, and there is no evidence that obvious embarrassment was not the worst result.

Several influential newspapers have endorsed the Committee's work. These newspapers have generally supported the suggestion that senators privately consult with bar groups and the Attorney General on the qualifications of prospective candidates. Illustrative of this, in 1961, the *St. Louis Post-Dispatch* criticized Missouri Senators Stuart Symington and Edward Long for publicly announcing their choice of James Meredith to be a Federal District Judge. They "injected a new element into what should be a choice based on a candidate's merits by forcing the Attorney General and the President to decide whether they should embarrass Senators Symington and Long by rejecting Mr. Meredith."[10] Meredith was eventually rated as "qualified" by the Committee and received the appointment.

Publicity is also very effective in extracting promises from senatorial candidates to consult with the bar on all judicial appointments. At the request of the President of the Oklahoma Bar Association, both incumbent Senator Mike Monroney and challenger Hayden Crawford gave assurances that they would consult with the Association regarding all such appointments. Said Monroney:

---

[8] See Glenn R. Winters, "The Bar Association and the Selection of Judges," 21 *Idaho State Bar Journal* (1947), 14.
[9] See notes 22 and 23 in Chapter 5, p. 128.
[10] *St. Louis Post-Dispatch*, editorial, November 29, 1961.

I would, of course, make no initial recommendation to the Attorney General without first seeking the advice of Oklahoma lawyers. Nor would I recommend any person who was not highly recommended to me by the members of the bar. The formal consultation with the organized bar is on the part of the Attorney General, and he has given great weight to its findings in making his own recommendations to the President. I completely approve of this policy and would under no circumstances urge the appointment of a person not found qualified.[11]

Crawford noted that "he would welcome the opinion of the Bar Association in all matters pertaining to legislation and the administration of justice." [12] Of course, neither candidate promised to formally consult with the Oklahoma Bar Association. Their commitments were solely to seeking advice and welcoming "opinion." Nor did either candidate renounce the senatorial prerogative to suggest names to the Attorney General. But Monroney did say that he would abide by the ABA's recommendation to the Attorney General, which in effect was a repudiation of the position taken earlier in the year by Senator Robert Kerr, who had insisted on an appointment to the judiciary despite an adverse ABA Committee rating. Furthermore, both candidates recognized the legitimate interest of the bar association in the selection process.

A Measure of the Committee's Success

How well has the Committee on Federal Judiciary succeeded in achieving these goals? What has been the response of individual senators to the Committee's efforts? Although several senators have stated for the record their support of the Committee's efforts,[13] such statements are not reliable indicators of the degree of support the Committee is actually getting. In at least one instance (and there are undoubtedly others), a senator who has consistently spoken in favor of some of the procedures advocated by the Committee, and who was listed by members of the Committee as "one of their best friends in Congress," publicly announced the names of several persons he had chosen to fill an equal number of judicial vacancies without any ostensible prior consultation.

To test the support of individual senators for the Committee's ob-

---

[11] Telegram to Jack N. Hays, president of the Oklahoma Bar Association, October 30, 1962.

[12] *Ibid.*

[13] See speech by Senator Kefauver, U. S. *Congressional Record,* 87th Cong., 2nd Sess., 1962, CVIII, p. 4195.

jectives, and to avoid the risk of having a senator give a "politically necessary" answer, questionnaires to be returned anonymously were sent to each senator in the Eighty-eighth Congress. Each senator was asked:

1. Do you AGREE or DISAGREE with the idea that senators ought not to publicly announce their recommendations for judgeships until they have consulted with the Department of Justice or the ABA Committee? 1a. Do you presently follow this procedure? 1b. Do you plan to follow this procedure?

2. Do you AGREE or DISAGREE with the idea that senators ought to submit a *list* of names to the Department of Justice instead of just one? 2a. Do you presently follow this procedure? 2b. Do you plan to follow this procedure?

Of the one hundred senators polled, forty valid responses were returned. As Table 6.1 indicates, 55 per cent of the responding senators

TABLE 6.1

SENATORS WHO SUBMIT NAMES

	Proposition 1			Proposition 2		
	Dem.	*Rep.*	*Total*	*Dem.*	*Rep.*	*Total*
Agree	57%	50%	55%	11%	33%	18%
Disagree	43	50	45	89	67	82
	100	100	100	100	100	100
	(N = 28)	(N = 12)	(N = 40)	(N = 28)	(N = 12)	(N = 40)

agreed that they ought to consult with the Department of Justice or the ABA Committee before announcing their recommendations for judgeships. But only 18 per cent thought that they ought to submit a *list* of names from which the Attorney General could choose the best qualified for the senator to "recommend." For the senator to consult on only one name, however, is of little effect to the Committee, although it is certainly an indication of sentiment. Consulting on only one name does not provide the Attorney General with the flexibility on nominations which the ABA seeks for him—and for itself. The responses to propositions 1a, 1b, 2a, and 2b were almost identical to the answers to the major questions. Twenty-one of the senators who agreed with proposition 1 stated that they either followed the procedure or planned to do so. Eight senators stated that they either submitted lists of names to the Attorney General or planned on doing so. Apparently one senator followed this procedure while disagreeing with it in principle.

Unfortunately, there are no data on the attitudes of senators during the early years of the Committee's operations, and there is no way of knowing whether these attitudes are significantly different from those a decade earlier. In the absence of such information, it is still fair to suggest that the Committee has either achieved or cultivated some support for its objectives. At least 20 per cent of the *present* members of the Senate are willing to consult with the Department of Justice before committting themselves to a particular nomination. If these responses can be projected to cover the entire membership, as much as 50 per cent of the entire membership might do the same. Judging from the earlier quoted statements of members of the Attorney General's staff that "more and more senators were adopting this procedure," it is a fair hypothesis that the work of the Committee has been at least partially responsible.

The small percentage of senators who are willing to submit a list of names does indicate, however, that even if senators can be persuaded to call upon the resources of the Justice Department in the selection process, they are generally unwilling to cede the power of even limited choice to any other agency. Whatever small progress the Committee may have made in this regard, it still has a large task ahead of it.

THE JUDICIAL-SELECTION ROLE OF THE SENATE JUDICIARY COMMITTEE

The Functions of the Committee

Understanding the role of the Senate Judiciary Committee in the judicial-selection process is central to our analysis of the work of the ABA Committee on Federal Judiciary. We must explore the types of judicial-selection decisions which the Senate Committee makes and its perceived role in the overall recruitment process if we are to understand its relationship to the ABA Committee.

The formal role of the Senate Committee consists of advising the Senate whether or not to confirm the nomination of a federal judge made by the President of the United States. But its importance in the selection process is not grounded entirely in the series of discrete and isolated decisions which constitute the approval of a judicial nomination. The importance of the Committee lies as well in its ability to condition the entire selection process which culminates in the decision to grant or refuse confirmation.

Upon receipt of a nomination from the Senate, the clerk of the

Senate Judiciary Committee sends a "blue slip" to each senator from the state in which the nominee resides,[14] with the stipulation that approval will be assumed if the slip is not returned within a week. Notification is also sent to the Committee on Federal Judiciary of the American Bar Association and frequently as well to the state bar group(s), giving each the opportunity to either file a recommendation or produce evidence for or against the nominee. When the blue slips are returned, a public hearing is scheduled at least a week following the insertion of a notice in the *Congressional Record*. These procedures are routine and virtually automatic and are handled primarily by the clerk.

The first important decision concerning the handling of the nomination is the choice of a subcommittee by the Committee chairman. If the nomination is not controversial, that is, the blue slips are favorable and there is no announced or predicted public opposition, the Chairman's decision is also routine. Virtually all noncontroversial nominations to the District and Circuit Courts are considered by subcommittees of three, with Supreme Court nominations usually considered by the entire Judiciary Committee.[15] The question of which senators actually sit on the subcommittee is not always important. But if there *is* evidence of opposition—either by a senator, a bar group, or representatives of some other major interest—the choice of members of the subcommittee could be crucial, and it is a choice that rests almost entirely with the chairman of the Committee.

From the Eighty-second through the Eighty-seventh Congresses, public hearings were held on most nominations to the federal judiciary. In that period 9.2 per cent of the Circuit nominations and 7.9 per cent of the District Court nominations were not considered at public hearings—in most cases because the nominations were submitted to the Senate late in the year and processed quickly in the hectic last days of a session.[16]

---

[14] This includes senators who are not of the party of the President. If the nominee resides in the District of Columbia, there is, of course, no senator to query. Although the blue slip provides space for comment, it is most often returned with simply a note of approval over the signature of the senator.

[15] Over 98 per cent of the lower-court hearings from 1951–1962 were before a subcommittee of three (276 out of 282). Of the remaining six, five were heard by a subcommittee of five, one by the full Judiciary Committee. A three-man subcommittee is the general rule, with exceptions only in controversial cases or when another senator sits with the subcommittee at his own request.

[16] Of the twenty-four nominations not subjected to subcommittee hearings, fifteen (or 63 per cent) were "end of session" rush jobs, three (or 12 per cent) were withdrawn in the face of senatorial objections, and the remaining six (25 per cent) were

Although all hearings on judicial nominations share certain common characteristics, they do vary both with the nature of the decision to be made and with the intended direction—if any—which the hearing is supposed to take. Consideration of a Supreme Court nomination is quite different in both substance and form from consideration of a lower-court nomination. In reviewing a Supreme Court nomination, the Committee is not only passing upon what is frequently a President's personal decision, but a decision of great public significance and interest. Supreme Court nominations occur infrequently—on the average of one every twenty-two months—and thus represent something of an "occasion." The public expects that the entire process of recruiting, nominating, and confirming a justice of the Supreme Court will be conducted in a manner commensurate with the importance—if not the dignity—of that office.

Hearings on Supreme Court nominations are subjected to close public scrutiny. In newspaper talk, they are always front-page news. They are also frequently the focus of interest-group conflict, and seem to be a particularly fertile ground for the expression of ideological fringe-group sentiments. Illustrative of this type of testimony was the opposition to John M. Harlan in 1955 because of his previous association with the Atlantic Union, a group alleged to favor federated world government.[17] The senators from the home state of the nominee will customarily testify in his favor and, a recent practice, the candidate himself will frequently also make himself available for questioning. Hearings on Supreme Court nominations frequently focus on the candidates' political ideologies most relevant to contemporary issues before the Court. Thus, each of the last four Eisenhower appointees had to reiterate for the Committee that he did not believe judges should "make law" or be guided by anything other than "the law."

The grandiloquence of Supreme Court hearings conforms to public expectations. It also effectively conceals the fact that the hearings are essentially a pro-forma part of the decision process. Despite such events as the adverse questioning of Justice Brennan by the late Senator McCarthy,[18] none of the Supreme Court nominees since 1951 was

considered by the Committee itself without the benefit of hearings—for reasons which are not known. Before 1947 the Committee held hearings only on controversial nominations. See Section 133 of Legislative Reorganization Act of 1946.

[17] See U. S. Congress, Senate, Committee on the Judiciary, *Hearings on the Nomination of John Marshall Harlan*, 84th Cong., 2nd Sess., 1956.

[18] See U. S. Congress, Senate, Committee on the Judiciary, *Hearings on the Nomination of William J. Brennan*, 84th Cong., 2nd Sess., 1956.

seriously endangered.   And given the fact that the Senate as a whole has seen fit to reject but one Supreme Court nominee since 1893, it is difficult to support the proposition that the function of the Senate Judiciary Committee is to objectively investigate the qualifications of Supreme Court nominees and decide to recommend confirmation accordingly.

The Senate Judiciary Committee's consideration of most District and Circuit Court nominations is, on the surface, largely perfunctory. (In all but a few cases, no transcript of the hearing is ever published.) Except where serious objections to the nomination have been raised by major groups, where a senator is invoking the personal privilege of senatorial courtesy, or a bloc of senators finds the nomination symbolically objectionable, the entire process of consideration is likely to cause little stir.   And cases involving controversies of this sort are relatively scarce.   As Table 6.2 clearly shows, in an eight-year period the large

TABLE 6.2

ACTIVE * OPPOSITION TO LOWER-COURT NOMINATIONS, 1951–1958

	Congress			
Type of Opposition	82nd	83rd	84th	85th
Primarily bar organizations	20%	6%	2%	0%
Primarily nonbar groups or individuals	8	19	20	11
Senatorial courtesy invoked	8	0	0	0
No serious opposition	64	75	78	89
	100%	100%	100%	100%
	(N = 25)	(N = 53)	(N = 41)	(N = 38)

* This table does not reflect mere statements of opposition by bar groups, but only those instances where there was actual testimony given.

majority of lower-court nominations were entirely noncontroversial. Although comparable data on the Eighty-sixth and Eighty-seventh Congresses were not available, other information does indicate that the situation was similar.

The figures in Table 6.2 represent the *outside* limit of active opposition to lower-court nominations.   They do not reflect the intensity of the opposition or the seriousness with which it was considered by the members of the Committee.   Figures that better indicate the extent of hard-core opposition are the percentages of hearings lasting beyond one session and the length of time elapsing between the first hearing of the subcommittee and the subcommittee's approval of the nomination.

Table 6.3 reflects these percentages and shows the close association between the tendency to extend the number and length of the hearings and the development of opposition to the nomination. Equally interesting and characteristic of the operations of the Committee is

TABLE 6.3

LENGTH AND NUMBER OF HEARINGS AS A FUNCTION
OF OPPOSITION, 1951–1962

Type of Opposition

	No Serious Opposition	Mostly Bar Opposition	Primarily Non-bar Opposition	Senatorial Courtesy	Nomination Withdrawn
Time elapsed from first hearing to committee action:					
1–14 days (N = 276)	91%	94%	81%	67%	0%
15–28 days (N = 1)	0	6	0	0	0
1– 6 mos. (N = 6)	1	0	19	0	50
No hearing (N = 24)	8	0	0	33	50
	100%	100%	100%	100%	100%
Number of hearings:					
1 (N = 269)	90%	81%	71%	67%	0%
2 (N = 6)	1	6	14	0	0
3 or more (N = 8)	1	13	10	0	50
No hearing (N = 24)	8	0	5	33	50
	100%	100%	100%	100%	100%
	(N = 265)	(N = 16)	(N = 21)	(N = 3)	(N = 2)

that most hearings, regardless of the controversiality of the nomination, are dispatched in short order. It is only those few hearings that carry over for an extended time which may be accurately labeled controversial. Delay is the most frequently used weapon of the Committee. Ironically, the most effective opposition to a nomination—that is, the invocation of senatorial courtesy—frequently results in no hearing at all or in a short hearing in which the position of the objecting senator is publicly stated and the nomination is then summarily rejected. In fact, excepting only those few cases where senatorial courtesy has been invoked, there is no necessary relationship between opposition and senatorial support.

Two other important characteristics of the Senate Judiciary Committee's consideration of lower-court nominations are suggested though not reflected by Table 6.3. The first of these is the almost complete lack of *independent* investigation of the qualifications of the nominee, or even of whatever charges have been made against him. The second is that with only few exceptions, the subcommittee does not conduct a *de novo* investigation.

Compared to the information usually brought to light in a Supreme Court hearing, the informational basis of the Committee's consideration of lower-court nominations is very sketchy. As with Supreme Court nominations it has a summary of the FBI report made on the nominee and a brief sketch of his qualifications submitted by the Justice Department. But in the absence of organized opposition, the Committee has little information on which to evaluate the qualifications of the candidate, especially since the FBI report is primarily concerned with conduct rather than qualifications. The decision as to whether to recommend confirmation is treated not as an independent decision, but rather as ancillary. The frame of reference in which the Committee considers a nomination places the burden of proof of *disqualification* on those who challenge the nomination. It is not enough to argue that the selection was not the best possible one, or even that it was not a good one at all. In order to block confirmation, it is almost always necessary to prove that the nominee has been guilty of conduct which contravenes accepted norms of legal or personal conduct.

Placing the burden of proof on those who oppose confirmation has insured that virtually all nominations to the lower federal judiciary will be confirmed. In the period under study, the Judiciary Committee recommended the approval of 301 (or 98 per cent) of the 307 nominations it received for consideration. Although anyone can oppose confirmation, those who are seriously concerned with a particular nomination may find it expedient to withhold their fire except when the chances of success are better than average.

Opposition to a nomination by the ABA Committee, by another respected group, or by an individual senator serves to alert the Senate Judiciary Committee to possible "flaws" in the nomination. But in the absence of these cues, there is no attempt by the Committee to actually evaluate the qualifications of the nominee; and even with the presence of such cues, there is no certainty that the nomination will be considered in more than a perfunctory fashion.

There is no case on record of a rejection on the basis of political belief; in fact, almost without exception, there is no attempt by the

Senate Committee to even inquire into the political beliefs of the nominee. Of the variables tested for possible influence on the ultimate decision of the Senate Judiciary Committee—including ABA opposition, blue-slip votes, party affiliation, interest-group opposition, and alleged prior misconduct—the only ones that seem to be consistently influential are adverse blue-slip votes or *proven* allegations of deviant behavior. Each of the six nominations rejected or "deterred" by the Judiciary Committee since 1951 tested positively for one or both of these variables. None of the nominees rejected or forced to withdraw had strong senatorial support. And, by way of contrast, *no* nominee approved by both senators from his state—regardless of party— was rejected.

Much of the character of the Senate Committee's role in the selection of federal judges comes from the fact that it is the last essential participant in the process. To be sure, the decision by the Committee to report favorably or unfavorably must be followed by Senate approval and then by the actual appointment by the President. But neither of these subsequent actions is more than a formality; they can, in fact, be considered automatic upon approval of a nomination by the Committee.[19]

Coming as it does at the end of a sequence of decisions which make up the recruitment process, the Committee is uniquely limited. It is reviewing rather than innovating, and although its decisions may have effects on future selection policies, they cannot positively alter the policy responsible for the selection at hand. And unlike the opportunity afforded a committee considering a bill, the question of confirmation is not subject to amendment or modification. The nominee must be either accepted or rejected (officially or unofficially); and though these limited alternatives leave the Committee considerable room for discretion, it has rarely exercised that discretion.

For purposes of analysis it is useful to compare the work of the Judiciary Committee with three hypotheses about Senate Committee behavior generated by other research efforts.[20] Although these other hypotheses were developed with reference to committees considering

---

[19] Over 97 per cent of all lower-court nominations were unanimously approved by the Senate without debate (299 of 307). No nomination approved by the Committee was rejected by the Senate. Of the seven Supreme Court nominations during this period—all of which were favorably reported by the Committee—five were approved by voice votes, two (Harlan and Stewart) were confirmed by 71–11 and 70–17 votes, respectively.

[20] These are similar to the hypotheses tested by Ralph Huitt, "The Congressional Committee, A Case Study," 48 *American Political Science Review* (1954), 340–365.

prospective legislation, rather than exercising a consent function, they do—with only a few modifications—have great relevance for this inquiry as well.

The first hypothesis would define the Committee's role essentially as that of an impartial arbiter, evaluating the merits of a presidential nominee to the federal judiciary. The second pictures the Committee as providing a public forum for a clash of competing interests at a crucial stage in the selection process, with the Committee functioning as the objective judge of the interests in conflict. The third places the Committee right in the struggle, a participant instead of a detached observer, using its power to exert strong influence on the types of persons chosen for the federal bench.

The first hypothesis, of course, is based initially on the constitutional description of the recruitment process, as it was understood by the framers. As interpreted by Hamilton, the Senate's function was not to choose judges, but rather to consent to their selection by the President.[21] Yet the Senate has never been content with such a role, and, with the exception of Supreme Court nominations in the twentieth century, individual senators of the same party as the President have considered *influencing* the choice of—if not actually selecting—federal judges in their states as a senatorial prerogative. This means that many of the judges whom the Committee is theoretically supposed to be evaluating are not chosen by the President exclusively; if the Committee were to sit in judgment on the *merits* of each candidate, it would, in effect, be sitting in judgment on its fellow senators.

Implicit in this first hypothesis is the function of setting standards of fitness. If the Committee were to objectively evaluate judicial nominations, it would have to do so with reference to some predetermined standards of judicial fitness—standards more specific than the maxims of honesty, a "clean" record, and no adverse blue-slip reports which seem to be the present guidelines of Committee action. And it would also have to investigate each nominee to a degree it does not now do. Yet once again, for the Committee to adopt such a posture would put it in the position of not only judging, but actually curbing the prerogatives of individual senators to choose judges for their own reasons. Although lower federal judges are formally chosen by the President, they are frequently chosen for reasons of local politics and for reasons which could not bear public scrutiny. For the Committee to attempt to objectively consider the merits of each nominee would

---

21 *The Federalist* (New York: New American Library, Mentor, 1961), p. 405. Professor Harris supports Hamilton's interpretation on this point, *op. cit.*, pp. 28–38.

inevitably involve an attempt to alter an existing and delicate political balance.

It is interesting to note that there have been several recent attempts to impose standards of judicial fitness on the President, standards such as a minimum amount of prior judicial experience.[22] But it is revealing that not only have they been unsuccessful, but with few exceptions such attempts have been concerned primarily with Supreme Court nominations over which individual senators have little influence. The Senate as a whole has been wary of attempting to limit the prerogative of the individual senator regarding judicial appointments, and the Judiciary Committee could do no less.

Clearly, this first hypothesis, as it stands, cannot adequately explain the work of the Senate Judiciary Committee. With two slight modifications, however, it gains considerable vitality. If the Committee's role as an arbiter is applied not to the merits of the individual judicial candidates, but rather to the senatorial role in the selection process, it explains much more. For the Committee, in fact, does seem to be policing the form, if not the substance, of the decisions of individual senators. Its role is essentially to make sure that all the rules of the game regarding judicial selection have been complied with, that the "eligible" senators have been consulted to the extent they desire. The approval of the Committee is a conference of legitimacy on the way in which any particular judge has been chosen. That the Committee rarely has to express its disapproval—that is, withdraw legitimacy—is an indication only that the norms of behavior which the Committee is charged with protecting are widely accepted and not often violated.

This hypothesis, however, is also subject to a possibly significant reservation. For only about 68 per cent of the total nominations considered by the Committee during this period were from states in which at least one senator was of the same party as the President. This means that at least one-third of all the nominations considered by the Committee were probably not senatorial selections. Yet there is no substantial difference in the treatment accorded nominations of either type. They seem to be processed in about the same way and are approved at an equivalent rate. In such cases there is no attempt by the Committee to take over the role that an individual senator would

---

[22] Senator John Stennis of Mississippi has recently proposed that the Senate use its prerogative of "advice" as well as its prerogative of "consent" to require that every other Supreme Court nominee have at least ten years of judicial experience. —"Federal Judicial Selection: The Letter—But the Spirit?," 44 *American Bar Association Journal* (1958), 1181.

play if he was of the President's party. About the only explanation of this phenomenon possible at this point is that the function of policing and protecting the senatorial prerogative seems to require that *all* nominations be considered under the same conditions, and that the Committee could not act substantially differently toward different types of nominations. In either case the operations of the Committee seem to reinforce the decentralized nature of the federal judicial-selection process.

The second hypothesis under consideration, that the Committee provides a public forum for the clash of competing interests and in turn judges that conflict, is quite plausible only in two distinct and limited spheres of its activities. The hearings on a Supreme Court nomination frequently become the focus for ideological group conflict —conflict which usually centers around types of decisions which that Court has recently made and is likely to have to consider again in the near future.

Much more frequently, however, the hearings on lower-court nominations provide the opportunity for individuals with a grievance against the courts, or against a particular decision in another court by the nominee, to express their protests. In most cases such complaints are not given much weight and pose no serious threat to the nominee; many are so patently neurotic in origin that the Committee does not bother to investigate them further. In a very few, the alleged grievance is sufficiently plausible to provoke further inquiry by the Committee. The Committee seems to be disposed to permit such persons to "have their day in court"—which undoubtedly performs some function in the political system, but has little relevance for the selection process. There is no evidence that the Committee seriously considers such charges in deciding on approval or disapproval of a nomination.

In a very real sense, however, the conflicting interests which the Senate Judiciary Committee is called upon to judge are those among the executive, individual senators, and local party organizations. And they are interests that relate primarily to the role that each will play in the recruitment process rather than to any dispute over the qualifications of a particular candidate. Furthermore, it is difficult to argue that the Committee is an impartial judge of such conflicts, since, as we have already suggested, one of its main tasks is to reinforce the norms of individual senatorial participation in the selection process. It would seem, therefore, that the third hypothesis, that the Committee is itself a part of the struggle, is more adequate to our purposes. It seems to capture the essence of much of what the Senate Judiciary Committee does. And it does so not only with respect to the Committee's defense of the individual senatorial prerogative, but also with respect to the Committee's infrequent ventures into the problems of qualifications for judicial office.

An illustration of this latter role variation was an attempt by the Committee during the Eighty-fifth Congress to bring pressure to bear on the administration to appoint judges committed to the principle that judges were not supposed to "make law."

During the period 1954–1957 the Supreme Court had made a series of important and controversial decisions in the areas of race relations and civil liberties, and the Court's critics had charged that such "deplorable" decisions were the inevitable results of appointing as judges men not firmly wedded to the principles of *stare decisis*. Among others the Committee devised an oath which each prospective appointee to the federal bench had to take before being confirmed. By taking the oath the nominee was presumably sworn to "not knowingly make any decision designed to alter the meaning of the Constitution. . . ." [23] There is no evidence that the taking of this oath influenced the behavior of judges after they were confirmed, or even the actions of judges already sitting, but it was certainly an effort by the Committee to exert such influence.

Although this action by the Committee proved abortive, it was clearly an attempt to use the confirmation function to pursue a purposeful interest apart from the limited question of granting approval to confirmation. That it failed gives some indication of the limitations to the Committee's role—limitations that seem to stem from the fact that the Committee is essentially a caretaker rather than an innovator.

Summarizing our consideration of these hypotheses, it would seem as if the Senate Judiciary Committee's major function in the selection process is to reinforce and protect the prerogative of individual senators to control lower judicial nominations in their own states or, alternatively, to insure that presidential nominations do not violate any of the rules of the game. If the senator of the President's party is satisfied with a nomination in his state, and if the nominee has been guilty of no known deviant behavior, then it is unlikely that consideration of the nomination will be more than perfunctory. But if the nominee does not have the approval of the senator from his own state (indicating that a conflict between the senator and the executive has been resolved in favor of the latter), then the Committee provides a means for that

---

[23] See speech by Senator Stennis, U. S. *Congressional Record*, 84th Cong., 2nd Sess., 1956, CII, Part 6, p. 7277. The oath was suggested by Senator O'Mahoney of Wyoming. *New York Times*, March 27, 1958, p. 17.

senator to reverse the decision if he wishes to do so. The work of the Committee further reinforces the mediate role of the political party, and by so doing reinforces as well the essentially partisan nature of the selection process.

With Supreme Court nominations, where individual senators possess no comparable veto power, the Committee's role is somewhat different. The confirmation of a Supreme Court nominee is more of a "public" issue, and the relevant forces bearing on the decision of the Committee are somewhat more numerous. Much more than any lower-court nomination, a Supreme Court selection is the focus of ideological conflict which stimulates the concern of most major interests in the society; and although there is no evidence in the period under study that the Committee's decision has been influenced by ideological considerations, it does at least provide a forum for the expression of opposition to the existing and possibly future patterns of Supreme Court decisions.

Furthermore, the choice of a Supreme Court justice is almost always a *presidential* choice, and although the Committee is reviewing a selection of the leader (usually) of the majority party, it is still not a *senatorial* decision and an appropriately greater degree of detachment on the part of the Committee is called for. Supreme Court hearings are not *de novo* inquiries, but they are nevertheless much fuller explorations of the qualifications of the nominees than investigations in the vast majority of lower-court nominations.

THE ABA COMMITTEE AND THE
SENATE JUDICIARY COMMITTEE

The Influence of the ABA Committee

It has already been noted that since 1947 the ABA Committee has been asked to comment formally—by letter or direct testimony—on each judicial nomination before the Senate Committee. But because of the nature of the Senate Committee's role, the ABA has not been able to exercise substantial influence. The ABA Committee has found that the burden of producing credible testimony against a nominee is very great; and furthermore it has found that even when it has been able to produce what appeared to be a preponderance of adverse evidence, it was unable to break the momentum toward confirmation which each nomination carries with it. As long as the Senate Committee is concerned primarily with reinforcing the "procedural" rules of the game rather than with actually investigating and evaluating the qualifications of each nominee, there is little that the ABA Committee can do at this stage of the selection process.

As shown in Table 6.4, the Senate Committee recommended confirmation of most of the nominations that the ABA Committee had opposed. And of the three nominations opposed by the ABA Committee *and* either tabled or rejected by the Senate Judiciary Committee, only one rejection—that of Frieda Hennock in 1951—could be attributed even in part to the efforts of the ABA.

TABLE 6.4

ABA RECOMMENDATIONS AND ACTIONS OF THE SENATE COMMITTEE,
1951–1962

	ABA Rating			
Senate Action	*Recommended*	*Opposed*	*Neither Recommended nor Opposed*	*Not Rated*
Approved (N = 301)	99%	82%	100%	67%
No action (killed) (N = 4)	1	6	0	33
Rejected (N = 2)	0	12	0	0
	100%	100%	100%	100%
	(N = 282)	(N = 17)	(N = 5)	(N = 3)

This underlying incompatibility between the objectives of the Senate and ABA Committee should surprise no one. For they are essentially interested in different things, although both are nominally concerned with choosing federal judges. Not only has the Senate Judiciary Committee consistently refused to be bound by ABA opposition to a particular candidate, but it has discouraged efforts by the ABA Committee to impose upon *it* the task of judging the merits of individual candidates. It has been hostile to any attempts to change its focus from disqualification to qualification.

Benefits of Liaison to ABA Committee

In the absence of the opportunity to exert meaningful influence with regard to specific nominations, the ABA Committee can still make good use of its relationship with the Senate Judiciary Committee. The ABA Committee can derive considerable prestige from this relationship.   As far as the public is concerned, the Committee is a "consultant" of the Senate Committee; its views are regularly solicited:

> Except on rare occasions when special circumstances, such as the pending adjournment of the Congress, necessitate the dispensing with public hearings, the Senate Judiciary Committee, through Senator Eastland, its Chairman, has continued during the past year to afford your Committee the opportunity to appear or otherwise express its views on the qualifications of all nominees for judicial office, for incorporation into the record at the public hearings of its Subcommittees.   We appreciate the statements made from time to time by Chairmen of such Subcommittees and certain other members of the Senate Judiciary Committee, commending your Committee for its helpfulness in connection with the important responsibilities of the Senate Committee.[24]

Most important, however, is that the ABA Committee can use its relationship with the Senate Judiciary Committee to win public support, if not vindication, for such standards of qualification which it supports and which the Attorney General may not accept.   The Committee's relationship with the Attorney General is primarily a private one, shielded from public view.   Failing to "win" its point at that stage, it must transfer the battle to another setting.   Of course, this is not done with the primary intention of defeating the nomination in contention.   It is intended to have a deterrent effect on similar nominations in the future by embarrassing the Attorney General or, alternatively, by creating pressures favoring the Committee's position which will eventually be brought to bear on the Attorney General. The Committee's decision to oppose a nomination beyond the filing of a formal letter of recommendation will usually indicate that some issue beyond the specific nomination—such as a standard of qualification—is at stake.   But even then this sort of operation must be handled very delicately for two reasons: first, the Committee might jeopardize its liaison with the Attorney General by appearing to undermine *his* prerogatives; and second, the great publicity given to such a fight would tend to limit the ability of the ABA Committee to obtain confidential information in future cases and thus lessen its usefulness to the Attorney General.

Finally, the Committee can use these hearings as a means of educating the senators to the Committee's procedures and, hopefully, as a means of instilling confidence in the work of the Committee.   If successful, such education would presumably have the beneficial effect of convincing individual senators to consult with the Committee at an earlier stage in the process.

---

[24] "Report of the Standing Committee on Federal Judiciary," 87 *ABA Reports* (1962), 603.

The Fight against Sarah Hughes

The Committee's opposition to Judge Sarah Hughes well illustrates these hypotheses. As noted in Chapter 5, the Committee voted to rate Judge Hughes as "not qualified" because of age; she was in her sixty-fifth year at the time of the nomination and had reached her sixty-fifth birthday at the time of the Senate hearings. The reader will recall that the Hughes appointment was the second which the Kennedy Administration had made which violated the age limit of the Committee—a rule with which the Attorney General had expressed general agreement. In the first such case, the ABA Committee had overlooked the age factor and rated Thomas Michie "exceptionally well qualified." But it had warned the Attorney General that it would not compromise its position the next time; when the Attorney General decided to nominate Sarah Hughes, the Committee formally opposed the nomination.

In order to further emphasize its point, the Committee decided to continue its opposition in the Senate Judiciary Committee hearings. There was no problem of producing credible evidence since the facts were not in dispute. Sarah Hughes was admittedly 65 years of age and, according to the Committee, otherwise qualified. The Committee was clearly fighting for a principle. It lost.

Judge Hughes was supported by Senator Yarborough of Texas and Vice-President Johnson. She was not opposed by Senator Tower. With Senator Long of Missouri, who presided at the hearings, Senator Yarborough and the Vice-President sought to belittle the significance of the ABA's contention. Yarborough argued that the congressionally stipulated ages of retirement were meant to be qualifying and not limiting ages:

. . . Their interpretation is wholly without merit, and as a member of the American Bar, I am a little bit embarrassed that my bar association should have such an erroneous view of the law.

. . . It will be recalled that Congress has at least once clearly rejected any mandatory retirement provisions on the basis of age.

. . . I think that the American Bar Association makes a grave mistake in placing the emphasis upon age rather than the qualifications of the person, upon number of years passed in life, rather than on mental alertness.[25]

Senator Long, noting that the "nominee looks more like 45 than 65," declared that "it might be well if [the ABA Committee] would read

---

25 U. S. Congress, Senate, Committee on the Judiciary, *Hearings on the Nomination of Sarah Hughes* (recorded), 87th Cong., 2nd Sess., 1962, pp. 6–8.

the law occasionally and confine themselves perhaps to the purpose
for which they were created instead of attempting to influence appointments of this kind . . . as they have attempted to do in many cases
over the country." [26]

In sum, what is the present status of the relationship between the
Committee on Federal Judiciary and the Senate Judiciary Committee?
Although the ABA Committee is formally invited to comment and
produce testimony on every nomination, it does not play an essential
role in the deliberations of the Senate Committee. Although the
senators on the Committee have differing opinions on the weight to be
given to the advice of the ABA Committee, none of those queried [27]
would say more than that the ABA's role was a useful one, and that
the weight given to its testimony depended on the credibility of the
opinions expressed. At the other end of the spectrum, several of the
senators, who were clearly hostile to the American Bar Association
as a whole, felt it was not representative of the legal profession and
were generally suspicious of its "very conservative" orientation.[28] But
even these senators said that they "welcomed" the views of the Committee, as well as those of any other group. But the private opinions
of these senators confirm what has already been suggested, namely
that only where the ABA Committee can produce credible adverse
testimony can it be influential in the decision-making process of the
Senate Judiciary Committee.

Benefits to the Senate Judiciary Committee

Of what value is this liaison to the Senate Judiciary Committee? As we
have seen, the decisions of the Senate Committee on nominations are
largely made apart from the results of the hearings. If the ABA
Committee were able to present valid evidence of disqualification, it
might be able to pierce this armor. But since it is usually unable to
do so, the senators on the Committee are understandably reluctant
to be persuaded to block a nomination merely on the basis of hearsay

---

[26] *Ibid.*, pp. 2, 10.
[27] Senators Hart, Johnston, Hruska, Dirksen, and Long were reached either by
mail or in person. The views of several other members of the Committee, such as
Senators Kefauver, McClellan, and Keating, had been recorded for other occasions.
  Findings contradictory to those in this study are reported in Bancroft Henderson
and T. C. Sinclair, *Judicial Selection in Texas: An Exploratory Study* (Houston, Tex.:
University of Houston Studies in Social Science, 1964), pp. 57–59.
[28] Those who might be considered "hostile" to the aims and views of the ABA
Committee are Senators McClellan, Long, and Johnston.

evidence. The liaison with the Committee on Federal Judiciary may be considered a political asset to the Senate Judiciary Committee, a protective covering for its deliberative process, rather than a significant contribution to these deliberations.

IMPACT OF THE ABA COMMITTEE ON SENATORIAL CONFIRMATION: THE CASE OF IRVING BEN COOPER

Since confirmation concludes the process of selecting a federal judge,[29] it would be appropriate here to consider the impact of the Committee on Federal Judiciary not only at the senatorial stage, but on the preceding aspects of the process which lead to confirmation. To do this most effectively, we will use a recent controversial case as an illustration for the hypotheses previously stated.

The Irving Ben Cooper case is unusual. Being so, it produced an inordinate amount of copy which enables the viewer to get an intimate view of the various stages of the selection process. Since it was, in effect, a test of the ABA Committee's influence, it provides the perfect study of the limits of the Committee's goals and influence, a bird's-eye view of the Committee in action.

The Nomination of Irving Ben Cooper

Upon taking office in 1961, President Kennedy asked Democratic Congressman and House Judiciary Chairman Emanuel Celler to suggest some names for federal judgeships in New York. There were no Democratic senators from that state, and the President refused to deal with the feuding Regular Democratic Organization and Reform Democrats until a cessation of hostilities had been achieved. He asked Celler to suggest, among others, "an independent Democrat . . . who had fought for good causes, men of unquestionable integrity and with judicial sensibility." [30] Celler submitted a list of names, one of which was Irving Ben Cooper, a former judge of the Court of Special Sessions of New York City. Celler wrote, "I submit this name to you because I believe him to be the best qualified for one of the Federal District

---

[29] Of course, following confirmation, the President can still choose not to make the appointment. But this alternative is an improbable occurrence.

[30] U. S. Congress, Senate, Committee on the Judiciary, *Hearings on the Nomination of Irving Ben Cooper,* 87th Cong., 2nd Sess., 1962, p. 3. (Hereinafter referred to as *Cooper Hearings.*)

Judgeships for the Southern District of New York. . . . I would be less than frank if I did not tell you that I would be greatly disappointed were he not nominated." [31]

Despite early unfavorable reports from the Committee on Federal Judiciary, the Attorney General decided to recommend Cooper's name to the President for nomination. The investigations of Cooper conducted by the Attorney General's staff produced very mixed results. There was some indication of a "temperament" problem, but his ability and integrity were unquestioned.[32]   Cooper had resigned from his city-court judgeship in 1960 because of ill health, but apparently was in good health again in 1961.   Cooper's nomination was also supported by numerous state and federal judges, and such political dignitaries as Eleanor Roosevelt, Mayor Robert Wagner, former Senator Herbert Lehman, and Robert Moses. He was opposed by the two leading bar groups in New York City, the Association of the Bar of the City of New York, and the New York County Lawyers Association.

Brushing aside a last-minute plea from the president of the Association of the Bar to hold off making the nomination until Congress reconvened in 1962, President Kennedy nominated Cooper shortly before Congress adjourned. When that nomination lapsed, he gave Cooper a recess appointment on October 6, 1961, and renominated him for the lifetime judgeship at the beginning of the second session of the Eighty-seventh Congress.[33]

Response of the ABA

Following the recess appointment, the Association of the Bar employed independent counsel and made a thorough investigation of Judge Cooper, which was to become the basis of the case made against him in the Senate Judiciary Committee hearings. This investigation did turn up some derogatory information not previously known; the information indicated at least that Congressman Celler did not know Judge Cooper as well as he claimed. Whether or not this information, if known, would have prevented the nomination initially is speculation. But having already committed itself to Cooper, the administra-

---

[31] Letter from Emanuel Celler to Attorney General Robert Kennedy, May 24, 1961.
[32] Interview with Assistant Deputy Attorney General Joseph F. Dolan, November 2, 1962.
[33] *Cooper Hearings,* p. 291.

tion could not easily withdraw its support, however much it may have wished for a "second chance."

The American Bar Association's Board of Governors voted to oppose Judge Cooper in the Senate beyond the filing of a formal recommendation for rejection.[34] Since the Association of the Bar of the City of New York had already made the same decision,[35] the ABA decided that, except for the testimony of Committee member Cloyd Laporte, it would let the Association of the Bar handle the presentation of evidence against Judge Cooper at the hearings.[36]

Thus, there is some question as to whether the ABA Committee would have been able to pursue the case against Judge Cooper without the aid of the New York City bar. It was the latter who produced virtually all the credible witnesses to support the case and whose counsel conducted the case. Even if it had so desired, the ABA Committee could hardly have refrained from participation.

Since this case was the first since the establishment of the Committee's liaison with the Attorney General in which it had gone *all out* to reverse the latter's decision to nominate, an examination of the reasons for the Committee's decision is in order. *First,* this was the only "not qualified" of the eight Kennedy nominees so rated by the Committee who was not sponsored by a Democratic senator. Thus, strategically speaking, Cooper's nomination was most vulnerable. Although both New York senators supported the nomination, Cooper was not their man. *Second,* this was clearly a case in which the Attorney General was unhappy with the nomination, based on information received after the recess appointment had been made. Presumably he would not look with too much disfavor on the Committee's efforts to carry the battle to another level of decision. *Third,* this was one of those infrequent instances in which enough witnesses could be produced to make a credible case. *Fourth,* the issue at stake—the temperament and emotional stability of a judge—was primarily a factual issue. The Committee believed, and rightly so, that most senators accepted emotional instability as a disqualifying characteristic. Therefore, all it had to prove was the fact, and not undertake the much more difficult assignment (as it had done unsuccessfully in the Sarah Hughes case) of persuading the senators to accept a different *standard* of qualification. *Finally,* given all these favorable factors, the Committee

---

[34] *Ibid.,* pp. 29, 30.
[35] *Ibid.,* pp. 44, 45.
[36] *Ibid.,* pp. 45 ff.

undoubtedly saw an opportunity to vindicate its opposition not only to Judge Cooper, but to the other "not qualifieds" nominated by the Kennedy Administration, and this appeared to be a good chance to recoup its fortunes. Unlike several of the other "not qualifieds" nominated by President Kennedy, Judge Cooper was also opposed by both of the major local bar groups in the New York City area, and the Committee was in a sense protected from the oft-repeated charge that it was not "close enough" to the situation to obtain an accurate view of the candidate.

In view of the great publicity accorded the opposition to the Cooper nomination, and the prospect of a "big fight," the chairman of the Senate Judiciary Committee appointed a subcommittee of five to hear the case. Senator Eastland himself served as chairman of the subcommittee, joined by Senators McClellan, Johnston, Hruska, and Keating. The hearings began on March 19, 1962, and dragged on at periodic intervals through early August.

The Case against Judge Cooper

The case against Judge Cooper was based on the allegations that (1) he lacked the kind of judicial temperament necessary to the proper administration of justice, and (2) he lacked sufficient general legal experience, particularly in civil procedure, to enable him to adequately handle the great diversity of cases which come before the District Court of the Southern District of New York.[37]   Primary emphasis was placed on the first allegation, and virtually all the evidence introduced was in reference to it. The second allegation was accorded relatively minor attention. Working closely with the Association of the Bar, the ABA Committee opened the case for the opposition with statements by past ABA President Whitney North Seymour and Committee member Cloyd Laporte. Then the case was handled by counsel for the city bar group, who interrogated all the witnesses. As noted earlier, this arrangement was undoubtedly made to emphasize the opposition of the local group to counter the hostility of several senators on the Judiciary Committee toward the ABA Committee.[38]

---

[37] *Ibid.*, p. 41.

[38] *Ibid.*, p. 35. To Cloyd Laporte, Senator McClellan stated: "I am ready to turn him down if he has not the ability . . . if he is too temperamental . . . but I want facts; I do not want somebody's opinion based upon what somebody told them whose name they cannot give. I cannot go along with that."

From 1939–1960, Irving Ben Cooper had served as an Associate and then Presiding Justice of the Court of Special Sessions of the City of New York. That court is an intermediate criminal court with original misdemeanor jurisdiction limited to three-year jail sentences. It functions without a jury; three judges or one judge hear each case, depending on the seriousness of the offense, and decide both the law and facts. The most common cases deal with such offenses as narcotics violations, statutory rape, impairing the morals of a minor, unlawful entry, larceny, and gambling. A great number of defendants are below the age of 25.

Prior to 1951, when Cooper became Presiding Justice, and for a short time thereafter, the tribunal was forced to mete out sentences on the basis of meager evidence and without prior probationary reports. It had virtually no funds to provide for the needed services. Its docket was overcrowded and growing increasingly unmanageable. The problem was infinitely compounded by the large number of defendants who were indigent and unable to provide adequate legal defenses. Many cases were handled by the Legal Aid Society staff, which itself was undermanned and often unable to give personal attention to each case.

During his tenure on that court, Judge Cooper crusaded successfully to improve conditions, gaining for his efforts as well a national reputation:

. . . Wherever I could . . . I appeared before groups, civic groups, governmental groups, hoping to arouse their interest to the extent that the budget . . . would be reinforced so that additional personnel could be engaged to the end that there would be a surcease to this endless panorama of misery and operating in the dark.
The hit or miss method of dealing out shorter or longer sentences without the guidance of information concerning the offender, his character, his family, his associations, occupations and capacities, precludes any kind of sentencing pattern that would balance the possibilities of rehabilitation with the needs of protecting society. No city can justify risking the future of so many of its citizens and the very safety of the community in order to avoid increased budgetary provisions for auxiliary services to the courts.[39]

Judge Cooper often sat alone as the single judge in the Youthful Offenders' Part of the Court (exclusively after 1956, when he apparently refused to sit in the other parts), and it was here that his greatest efforts for reform were made, and his work here on which criticism

---

[39] *Ibid.*, pp. 294, 295.

was mainly based. Most of the defendants appearing in the Youth Part were first offenders; if they pleaded guilty to being a youthful offender, they would not incur a criminal record. If not, their cases would be transferred to the regular adult part where conviction meant a criminal record.

Judge Cooper found that many of these defendants were contemptuous of the court, if not of society as a whole; they were not usually candid with the probation officers, and often did not recognize the seriousness of the situation. Cooper "learned from past experience that those young people were on the way to becoming possibly potential criminals, and . . . had found that the so-called reasoned approach, the soft voice, was mocked and the subject of derision." [40] He decided that he would have to do something drastic to win the confidence of such offenders, to encourage them to make a full disclosure to the probation officers and to the Court:

It was a simple device. It was a judge's plea to the defendants not to fool themselves. And it worked. I spoke their language. What has wantonly been referred to as "an opportunity to hear myself talk" was an emotional plea to these young people that lasted from 30–35 minutes and that took more out of me than a day in a busy Federal court.

I tried to talk their language. I wanted . . . them to know that the judge would know something about their behavior. . . . I wanted as many as possible to have the benefit of the youthful offender treatment to the end that they would not have a criminal record around their necks from which they could not extricate themselves.

I felt that if we could deal with them as youthful offenders and save them the stigma of criminal records, that we would then be in a position to learn which ones would soon be rehabilitated and under the court's guidance and direction, and which ones must be committed for their safety and for the safety of the community.[41]

It was this single-minded pursuit of his goal which brought about the outbursts of temper charged against Judge Cooper. Witnesses testified that during the course of these pleas, "youthful offenders, unconvicted as yet, were called in open court 'punks,' 'bums,' 'flotsam and jetsam,' 'slime of the earth,' and were told that they would 'rot in jail' if it weren't for the candidate." [42]

Judge Cooper's exasperation and frustration with the ineffectiveness

---

40 *Ibid.*, p. 296.
41 *Ibid.*
42 *Ibid.*, p. 363.

of his court to properly handle even a fraction of the cases before it was also reflected in his impatience with customary courtroom procedures.   Lawyers who asked for delays (which meant in most cases that the defendant languished in jail in lieu of bond) to permit their appearance in other courts were publicly excoriated or ordered to appear in Judge Cooper's chambers forthwith for a dressing-down. Other lawyers who did not appear to Judge Cooper to be adequately representing the interests of their clients were banished from the courtroom.   Lawyers who refused to consent to the necessary guilty plea to receive youthful-offender treatment for their clients were abused and threatened with disbarment.   Courtroom personnel who whispered during the proceedings, or who in other ways caused a disturbance, received the same sort of treatment.   Witnesses testified that such behavior was so regular that the term "cooperized" became a part of the vocabulary of the Criminal Courts Building in New York City.[43]

Several of his fellow judges refused to talk to Cooper, or even sit with him on the bench.   One declared that "if you dissented on a ruling by Judge Cooper, as we were compelled in conscience to do, he felt that that was a personal affront to him; that you were questioning his judgment and integrity." [44] Similar incidents of Judge Cooper's temperament outside the courtroom were introduced into evidence. The brief submitted by the bar associations suggested that Cooper suffered from a persecution complex; that he believed that any action not exactly in accord with his way of operating the court was an attack on him and the Court.[45]

In his own testimony, Cooper was unable to satisfactorily explain many of these incidents, or even to remember some of them.   He denied that he had called defendants "slime of the earth," but admitted that he may have declared that "the public" regarded them as such.[46] While not denying that most of the alleged incidents of temper had taken place, he contended that the reports of his displays of anger were exaggerated.   He did admit to ordering several attorneys out of the courtroom.[47]

In concluding the case, the bar groups emphasized that when Cooper had resigned from the City Court in 1960, it was on the advice of his doctor, because "with his temperament" he could not avoid getting

---

[43] Such testimony is summarized in the Brief for the Opposition, reprinted in *ibid.*, pp. 361 ff.

[44] *Ibid.*, p. 364.   [46] *Ibid.*, pp. 370, 371.

[45] *Ibid.*, p. 365.   [47] *Ibid.*

stirred up.[48]   How could he then hope to take the wear and tear of a federal judgeship, they asked?

No one with the slightest objectivity and knowledge of the duties of a federal judge in the Southern District of New York can claim that it is an easy job.   The myriad of civil litigation of all kinds, as well as the complicated, lengthy, emotional and stirring trials of violations of the criminal law by highly placed and important members of the underworld in the City of New York belie any such belief.   So, too, does the history of the "Spy" and the "Communist Conspiracy" trials.[49]

In answer to a statement by Presiding Judge Sylvester Ryan of the District Court on which Cooper was presently serving via recess appointment (quoted in Chapter 2), Cloyd Laporte stated: "Of course, he is on good behavior.   He has known all along that he had this hearing and was going to have opposition, and I would be surprised if his temperament has not been exemplary." [50]   Other witnesses charged that "you can't judge a man on his honeymoon and certainly not on his courtship." [51]

A key factor in the bar associations' case was the support of the New York City press.   When Judge Cooper resigned from the Court of Special Sessions in 1960, he was the recipient of only the highest praise from the local newspapers as well as the same bar groups now opposing him.[52]   Indeed, in 1957, he had been chosen by *Life* magazine as one of America's most eminent jurists.[53]   When his nomination to the federal bench was announced, the *New York Times* heartily endorsed his candidacy.[54]   However, when the opposition of the three bar groups became known, the *Times* withdrew its support and, on the urging of Bernard Segal, opposed the nomination:

While the ABA is not infallible, its opinions command wide respect for competence and impartiality, and are relied upon heavily by the Attorney General and his deputy.   However, two of the new judges were nominated and confirmed in spite of the fact that the ABA found them "not qualified." This is two too many.   Granted that each of these appointees was able to adduce other endorsements in behalf of his candidacy, a flatly negative appraisal by a responsible committee of his peers ought—except in the most extraordinary cases—to lead to his rejection.   For this reason, we feel we must withdraw the endorsement of Irving Ben Cooper of New York, which we gave on the strength of his good work as judge of Special Sessions, but before

---

48 *Ibid.*, p. 47.
49 *Ibid.*, p. 366.
50 *Ibid.*, p. 43.
51 *Ibid.*, p. 48.

52 Quoted in *ibid.*, p. 249.
53 September 23, 1957.
54 September 25, 1961, p. 32.

learning that he has been designated "not qualified" by the judiciary committee of both the ABA and the Association of the Bar of the City of New York.[55]

Having accepted the veto role of the ABA Committee, the *Times* also accepted its full argument against Judge Cooper, and campaigned against his confirmation:

We remain convinced—and we regret it—that Judge Cooper's nomination should be disapproved. His integrity and zeal for reform are not disputed. But he is unqualified to serve on the Federal bench for two reasons: First, his demonstrated emotional instability and, second, his lack of the experience needed to deal with the immensely intricate and important cases that come before the court. He served about twenty-two years in Special Sessions— a local criminal court of limited jurisdiction—before his resignation in 1960 due to "anxiety, irritation, and strain."

The Senate Judiciary Committee should promptly recommend that approval of the nomination be denied. Action has already been too long delayed.[56]

The Case for Judge Cooper

The case for Judge Cooper was presented alternately by Congressman Celler, New York lawyer Theodore Kiendl, and by Cooper himself. Knowing that the burden of convincing the senators of Cooper's lack of qualification rested with the opposition, and that, as in any confirmation case, the impetus is initially in favor of confirmation, the Cooper forces concentrated on five points. *First,* they claimed that Judge Cooper's ten months of service on the District Court under a recess appointment had demonstrated that beyond any doubt he had both the temperament and the ability required. *Second,* they claimed that his outbursts of temper on the Special Sessions Court and resulting poor health were a result of the incredible problems of administering such a court, and could not be fairly considered as permanent disabilities. *Third,* they tried to impeach the testimony of many of the bar associations' witnesses by pointing out that in some cases the witnesses had long been feuding with Judge Cooper, and in others that the same witnesses who now attacked him had heaped praise upon him only a short time before. They produced an imposing list of public figures

---

[55] October 7, 1961, p. 22. Apparently this change in position was in part due to the efforts of Committee Chairman Bernard G. Segal, who criticized the original *Times* editorial and persuaded the editors to support the Committee against Cooper. Interview with Bernard G. Segal, October 30, 1962.

[56] *New York Times,* August 9, 1962, p. 24.

who backed Cooper and vouched for his integrity and ability. *Fourth,* it was stated that Cooper's testimony before the Senate Judiciary Committee indicated enough ability and composure to disprove all allegations. And *finally,* it was charged that the bar associations' appearance of monolithic opposition to Cooper belied the very divided nature of not only the members of the several judiciary sections involved, but of the whole bar membership as well.

There is no doubt that besides the support of Senators Keating and Javits, the most important (and probably crucial) argument in Judge Cooper's behalf was the uncontroverted statement by Judge Ryan that his conduct on the District bench prior to and during the hearings was eminently satisfactory. Before the hearings, and then twice again during them, Judge Ryan declared that Cooper's work on the Court was "excellent, efficient, competent, and courteously and patiently performed. During the past nine months, no word or complaint or criticism as to his judicial demeanor or work has reached me." [57] Three of Cooper's colleagues on the District Court commented that "he has conducted himself industriously, with competence and with fine dignity and a sense of proper conduct in the dispatch of his business in the Court." [58]

The brief submitted in Cooper's behalf criticized the ABA and Association of the Bar for claiming to have made a "painstaking" investigation when they did not even interview sitting members of the District Court. The ABA Committee's reasoning that you cannot judge a man on his honeymoon was ridiculed:

But if Judge Cooper were "emotionally unstable" as Mr. Marden claimed, or were addicted to the intemperate and irrational behavior attributed to him by Mr. Brownell . . . such traits could not have been kept concealed for a period of ten months from Chief Judge Ryan and his colleagues—as well as from the clerks in the District Court and the lawyers who appeared therein. . . . [59]

Evidence was introduced to show that a poll by the New York State Association of Trial Lawyers of attorneys who had participated in cases in Judge Cooper's District Court produced not one adverse appraisal, and a significant number of those queried—many who lost cases before Cooper—wrote letters endorsing Judge Cooper on the basis of their experience in his court. [60]

On the basis of this testimony, counsel for Judge Cooper was able

---

[57] *Cooper Hearings,* pp. 379 ff.
[58] *Ibid.*

[59] *Ibid.*
[60] *Ibid.*

to claim that incontrovertible evidence of instability was the result of the difficult administrative problems associated with the Court of Special Sessions and Judge Cooper's commitment to reform, rather than deeply ingrained characteristics. Judge David Peck, long a justice of the Appellate Division of the New York State Supreme Court, testified that:

I thought that Judge Cooper was a tense and intense individual, that I felt that the load of Special Sessions under all the conditions of work there was after a period of years a strain upon this man, and that I had found in my dealings with him in his deep concern for this court, and its administration that he was both tense and intense about it. And I felt that there was, therefore, some question as to whether in the performance of judicial duties he would have the poise and the patience which was highly desirable in a judge. I ventured the opinion at the same time . . . that I thought that the very different atmosphere of the Federal district court, where the pressure, the rush, and the volume and the nature of the business is quite different, that Judge Cooper, with his conscientiousness, with his dedication, would also have the discipline to overcome that intensity which I thought was desirable to overcome to be a judge.[61]

There were three types of responses to the charges leveled against Cooper by lawyers who had appeared before him, judges who had worked with him, and courtroom personnel. The defense tried to show that many of the critics who had led the praise for Judge Cooper upon his retirement had now turned against him. The Association of the Bar itself had twice endorsed him for reappointment in 1951 and 1956. Thus, their testimony was challenged as being of doubtful validity; it was claimed that their original appraisals of Cooper had been more timely and more accurate. It was also alleged that Special Sessions Justice Matthew Troy, who had testified against the candidate, had been motivated by previous differences with Cooper, and because he had been an unsuccessful contender for the position of Presiding Justice.[62] This impeachment of Judge Troy's testimony may have been a key factor in the rebuttal. Finally, backers of Judge Cooper tried to counteract the adverse testimony with a flood of supporting letters from prominent persons. In response to the introduction of these letters, ABA member Cloyd Laporte stated:

Our Committee has found from long experience that the least satisfactory way to obtain information about candidates for the bench is by correspondence. When one writes a letter about a candidate, he quite naturally feels

---

61 *Ibid.*, p. 20.
62 *Ibid.*, p. 393.

the letter may be shown to others and possibly may come to the attention of the candidate himself. The tendency in writing letters is to write only favorable letters and to gloss over the vital points in the candidate's qualifications. It is doubly true when, as we have been informed is the case here, the letters have been solicited with persistence and urging.[63]

Counsel for Judge Cooper criticized this position as evidencing an "arrogant disregard" for the views of such people.[64]

The case for Judge Cooper also gained credence from his own testimony, which, apart from the content of his answers to the various charges, was poised and devoid of any signs of temperament.[65] Judge Cooper conceded his short temper when on the Special Sessions bench, noting that it was a reaction to the human misery paraded before him. He testified that the strain of trying to reform that situation "had put a strain on my emotional being," but that he felt no similar strain in ten months on the District bench. He admitted that when lawyers presented their cases badly or failed to appear in behalf of their clients, "I would bring them up sharply. . . ." But he denied a host of specific allegations of his treatment of lawyers, and professed not to remember many others. Cooper was questioned closely by Senator Keating of New York on every minute phase of the charges against him. When the Committee had no further questions, Cooper asked for permission to make a statement, and took the "offensive" against the bar associations. He noted that both local groups had proceeded against him only after closely divided votes in their respective judiciary committees. The implication was clear that the opposition to Cooper was primarily the doing of the leadership of each group, which did not know him personally, and was not representative of the rank-and-file lawyers in the city. Then he charged that although it was public knowledge that the bar groups were going to oppose his confirmation, the nature of the complaint against him was not revealed until the hearings began. Furthermore, he charged that attempts by several friends of his, including Judge Peck, to find out the nature of the charges against him were fruitless. Finally, he "reminded" the Committee

. . . that present Associate Justice Byron White, then Deputy Attorney General, in full receipt of the position of the association, continued with his own independent inquiry, actually coming to New York with assistants from

---

[63] *Ibid.*, p. 34.
[64] *Ibid.*, p. 387.
[65] All quotations from here to the end of the section from *ibid.*, pp. 290–354.

his staff, continued with the inquiry, especially addressed to the complaints recorded by the Association of the Bar; and that a statement from his office was issued to the effect that the independent investigation warranted recommendation by the Attorney General to the President, and that I was so recommended.

Concluding his statement, Cooper claimed "that from the very first witness until the last witness it was conceded that there was nothing against my character, or my reputation or my integrity." Appropriately enough, the *New York Herald-Tribune* headlined the story of Cooper's testimony: "Battling Irving Ben Cooper: Will He Win?" [66]

Confirmation of Judge Cooper

Following the hearings, Senator Keating publicly endorsed Cooper and indicated that he would vote for confirmation. In a speech on the floor of the Senate, Keating acknowledged Cooper's temper, but declared that the incidents alleged were caused by conditions in the court, and did not represent any serious deficiency. If these occasional lapses were considered in the perspective of Judge Cooper's entire career and, *most important,* in light of his good service on the District Court, they could not be allowed to control the decision. "To my mind, the evidence that he has passed this test with flying colors must outweigh any lingering doubts about his qualifications." [67] In an interesting commentary on the confirmation function of the Senate, Keating declared:

In conclusion, I would like to emphasize that the Senate has not been called upon in this case to select a nominee for the Federal District court, but only to determine whether a nominee chosen by the President should be confirmed. In making this determination, we cannot delegate the difficult and delicate task of weighing all the evidence to any private organization, no matter how highly we esteem its work or weigh its conclusions. The evidence in this case might well have convinced the President that he should have rejected Judge Cooper's candidacy, but it is not sufficient to convince me that the President's decision should be vetoed by the Senate.

While I was not asked to advise with regard to this nomination, it is my judgment on the whole record that the President's nominee merits our consent and I shall vote for Judge Cooper's confirmation in the committee and in the Senate.[68]

---

[66] August 8, 1962, p. 1.
[67] U. S. *Congressional Record,* 87th Cong., 2nd Sess., 1962, CVIII, p. 17829.
[68] *Ibid.*

The Subcommittee then voted 3–2 to favorably report the nomination, with Senators McClellan and Johnston dissenting.[69]   The alignment for and against Judge Cooper was somewhat paradoxical in that the two senators clearly hostile to the role of the bar groups—particularly the ABA—accepted their arguments, whereas Senators Keating and Hruska, both advocates of a vigorous ABA role in the selection process, rejected their contentions.   The nomination was then approved by the full Judiciary Committee "in a voice vote to which there were no audible dissents," and subsequently approved by the entire Senate in routine fashion.[70]

The Lesson of the Cooper Case

The Irving Ben Cooper case illustrates the futility of expecting the Committee on Federal Judiciary to have a significant impact on the *deliberations* of the Senate Judiciary Committee.   Here was a case in which that Committee was least committed to a course of action, and most vulnerable to outside influence.   The nominee was supported by one senator from his state, and ultimately backed by the other.   But he was not sponsored by any senator and the Committee was not faced with the choice of overriding one of its colleagues.   Here was an unusual case in which the ABA and other bar groups were able to present the sort of derogatory evidence rarely available for presentation.   It is likely that the ABA would have been successful if Cooper had not received a recess appointment and been given the opportunity to "prove" himself.   But in all cases, the presumption of qualification rests with a candidate who is the choice of a senator of the President's party, or the choice of the administration.   For the ABA Committee to have a significant impact on the deliberations of the Senate Judiciary Committee would require the presence, in combination, of several favorable factors—a highly unlikely occurrence.

Its failure to block the nomination of Irving Ben Cooper was a bitter pill for the ABA to swallow, not only because a "not qualified" judge was confirmed, but because his confirmation highlighted its impotency at this stage of the nomination process.   The Cooper case effectively marked the present limits of the ABA Committee's influence at *all* stages of the process of selection, and it marked them much more narrowly than the Committee had hoped would be the case.   Of course, it is possible that the Committee's efforts in this case may not have

---

[69] As reported in the *New York Times*, August 31, 1962, p. 1.
[70] As reported in the *New York Times*, September 18, 1962.

been entirely futile. Its fight was undoubtedly a source of acute embarrassment to the administration, and if those who choose judges in the future do so with the awareness that "bad" choices will be exposed by the Committee, then the case of Irving Ben Cooper may stand as a monument to the success instead of the futility of the Committee's work.[71]

71 The following year the Committee reported that no appointments over its objections had been made.—"Report of the Standing Committee on Federal Judiciary," 88 *ABA Reports* (1963), 524.

7

⚜

CHANGING PATTERNS

OF JUDICIAL RECRUITMENT

The preceding chapters have concentrated on describing the impact of the ABA Committee on the process of selecting federal judges—its influence at the key points in the decision process. Emphasis has been placed on the Committee's efforts to become a mediate force in the selection process, a filter through which prospective judges must pass. But though these efforts, and the results so far achieved, are of importance in and of themselves, they must also be regarded as instrumental to the ultimate ABA objective of securing the recruitment as federal judges of persons with certain types of qualifications and certain types of views toward the role of "judge." Has the work of the ABA Committee resulted in the selection of better judges? Has it resulted in the selection of different types of judges? What are the likely implications of the work of the ABA Committee for the patterns of training and occupation in which aspiring judges are likely to engage?

THE SELECTION OF BETTER JUDGES

Has the ABA's Committee on Federal Judiciary been responsible for the selection of better judges? The major difficulty in attempting to answer such a question is that as yet there have not been developed reliable yardsticks for the measurement of desirable judicial attributes and desirable judicial behavior. We can measure some of the characteristics that judges or judicial candidates actually possess and some of the consequences that seem to flow from these characteristics. In so doing, of course, we may be contributing to efforts to develop accepted standards of judicial qualification. But at present political science has no specific answer to the question, "What is a good judge?" beyond the obvious answer that a good judge is one who acts in a manner with which we agree.[1]

Political scientists are not alone in their failure to specify the most desirable attributes of a good judge, or the most necessary qualifications for a prospective judge. The Committee on Federal Judiciary itself has never explicitly stated all the ingredients that it considers essential in the making of a good judge.[2] And few of our constitutions shed any light on the subject. Aside from citizenship and residence requirements—which are even excluded by the U. S. Constitution—only a few states list any substantive qualifications. Arkansas requires its judges to be "of good moral character" and Maryland prescribes that they be "distinguished for integrity, wisdom, and sound legal knowledge." Indiana and Nebraska require their judges to be "in good standing at the bar," and North Carolina disqualifies any judge who has been previously "convicted of a crime, felony, corruption, or malfeasance in office." [3]

Though unable to specify desirable judicial characteristics, political science is able to describe the attitudes toward such characteristics held by individuals and groups. Therefore, we can inquire if, in its own estimation, the ABA Committee has been responsible for the selection of better judges. Confirming the hypothesis advanced in earlier chapters, the data in Table 7.1 clearly indicate that the Committee has had little success in increasing the ratio of judges whom it considers to be either "exceptionally well" or "well" qualified. The Kennedy and Eisenhower percentages of judges in these categories were almost identical. In fact, if one breaks down by years the ratings of judges appointed during the Eisenhower Administration, the year 1960 (when the ABA's influence reached a peak) shows the lowest percentage of "well" or "exceptionally well" qualified ratings.[4]

What the composite figures in Table 7.1 do indicate, however, is that the ABA Committee *has* been able to effectively deter the nomination of "unqualified" or "bad" judges. It has not, of course, been able to eliminate them entirely (except during the last term of the

---

[1] See Rodney L. Mott, "Measurement of Judicial Personnel," 23 *New York University Law Review* (1948), 267.

[2] See pp. 107–108.

[3] Mott, *op. cit.*, p. 270.

[4] In 1960 the percentage was 42.9 per cent. From 1954–1959 the percentage varied from 52 per cent to 65 per cent. Full table appears in Joel B. Grossman, *The Role of the American Bar Association in the Selection of Federal Judges* (Ph.D. dissertation, State University of Iowa, 1963), p. 365.

TABLE 7.1

ABA RATING * OF JUDICIAL NOMINEES, 1953–1962

Rating †	Eisenhower	Kennedy
Exceptionally well qualified	61.7 { 17.1%	16.4% } 61.8
Well qualified	44.6	45.4
Qualified	25.1	30.0
Recommended (no other information)	6.9	0.9
Neither recommended nor opposed	0.6	0.0
Not qualified or opposed	5.7	7.3
	100.0%	100.0%
	(N = 175) ‡	(N = 110)

* All ratings were collected from the files of the Department of Justice.
† Ratings for the years 1953–1958 have been adapted to fit the rating system in use since that time. Thus, "especially" or "very" well qualified were equated with "exceptionally well qualified," etc.
‡ President Eisenhower actually made 181 nominations, but six were never submitted to the ABA Committee for evaluation.

Eisenhower Administration), but it has been able to hold the line with the transition in administrations. That the ABA was able to do this with the Kennedy Administration is most impressive in view of the fact that the new President had to work with twice as many senators of his own party than had his predecessor and thus had less flexibility of choice. Also, a change of both administration and party in control usually increases the value of patronage plums such as federal judgeships and there is less likelihood of a new President being able to cede a veto power to an outside group—as President Eisenhower had done in 1958. A President who needs his party or personal organization for future political battles—as President Eisenhower did not and President Kennedy did—will be much less indulgent toward outside groups making claims upon instruments of party control such as judicial patronage.

CHANGING JUDICIAL TYPES

Perhaps even more important, for purposes of analysis, than the quality of judges selected is their background. To know the type of judges whom the Committee has preferred, and to know the actual patterns of recruitment which its activities have fostered, is to have a more sophisticated knowledge of its impact on the judicial-selection process. The major purpose of the ABA Committee, after all, is to promote the nomination of judges of certain types whom it considers to be better qualified. But what is the rationale behind the ABA's preferences? Why is it that the ABA finds certain types of judges to be more congenial than others?

We have already suggested in earlier chapters the major background characteristics preferred by the ABA Committee. For District judges these include adequate legal training, legal *and* trial experience, a substantial period of private practice, and relative youth. For Circuit Court judges (who do not often preside at trials) the trial experience factor is minimized,[5] and in its place prior judicial experience on either a state or federal District Court is considered helpful though not essential. The requirements of adequate legal training and ability, some private practice, and maximum age are similar if not exactly the same. For judges of the United States Supreme Court, the ABA Committee considers adequate legal training and demonstrated high legal ability, possible prior judicial experience, prior public service, and suitable age as basic qualifications. For all three courts the Committee has campaigned for bipartisan or nonpartisan selection, and has sought judges of even temperament and detachment.

Some of these characteristics, such as degree and quality of prior trial or legal experience and judicial temperament, are not quantifiable on the basis of presently existing information, and must be temporarily excluded from our analysis. Others, such as political party affiliation, will also be omitted since—for reasons stated earlier—the ABA Committee is not in a position to consider them in specific cases. Four factors will be used as an index of the Committee's success in securing as federal judges certain character "types." These factors are age at appointment, extent of prior training, prior judicial experience, and previous occupation.

The Selection of Younger Judges

Has the work of the ABA Committee resulted in the selection of younger judges? The Committee on Federal Judiciary will not recom-

---

[5] There are several recorded instances of the Committee's rating a lawyer as "not qualified" for the District bench and "qualified" or "well qualified" for the Court of Appeals.

TABLE 7.2

AVERAGE AGE OF JUDGES AT APPOINTMENT, 1946–1962

Court	Truman	Eisenhower	Kennedy
Supreme Court	57.7	53.3	49.0
Courts of Appeals	55.4	56.0	54.1
District Courts	51.5	52.1	51.7
Average age	52.3	53.1	52.0
	(N = 115)	(N = 178)	(N = 110)

mend the nomination of any person who has reached his sixty-fourth birthday and, if the candidate is over 60, will make a positive recommendation only if the person is "well qualified" or higher. All recent Attorneys General have agreed with the general principle of this rule while refusing to be bound by it absolutely (cf. Sarah Hughes case, *supra*). As Table 7.2 indicates, only the average age of *Supreme Court* justices has dropped sharply from the mean of the Truman Administration—when the ABA Committee had not yet entered into its liaison with the Attorney General. But the real impact of the ABA Committee is seen in the data in Table 7.3. It shows a steady reduction in the number of nominees over the age of 60 for both the Circuit and District Courts, and a corresponding increase in the number of nominees in the 50–59 age bracket. It would appear that the ABA Committee has been quite successful in its campaign to reduce the number of judges who take office at a relatively advanced age and will therefore have to remain on the bench past the age of 70 in order to qualify for full retirement benefits.

TABLE 7.3

DISTRIBUTION OF JUDICIAL NOMINEES BY AGE, 1946–1962

Age	Courts of Appeals			District Courts		
	Truman	Eisenhower	Kennedy	Truman	Eisenhower	Kennedy
Under 40	0.0%	2.2%	0.0%	7.2%	2.3%	1.1%
40–49	30.0	13.3	17.6	33.3	29.8	33.0
50–59	30.0	51.1	58.8	38.5	54.2	54.9
Over 60	40.0	33.3	23.6	16.7	11.5	8.8
Unknown	0.0	0.0	0.0	4.2	2.3	0.0
	100.0%	100.0%	100.0%	100.0%	100.0%	100.0%
	(N = 20)	(N = 45)	(N = 17)	(N = 96)	(N = 131)	(N = 91)

The Selection of Better-Trained Judges

Has the work of the ABA Committee resulted in the selection of better-trained judges? There is, of course, some dispute as to what constitutes adequate professional training for a federal judgeship. The ABA Committee argues that a substantial amount of "pre-job" training, that is, trial experience, is a necessary prerequisite, whereas some Attorneys General have felt that "on-the-job" training, that is, little or no trial experience, is possible where the candidate is sufficiently able. The ABA has strongly supported the notion that prospective judges have as much formal training as possible; in fact, through its many non-judicial-selection activities, the ABA has given support to the practice of making a college *degree* a prerequisite for law-school entrance. It may be the willingness of law schools to accept this suggested entrance requirement as much as the ABA Committee's pressure on the Attorney General which is responsible for the marked increase shown in Table 7.4. The ratio of nominees with college de-

TABLE 7.4

JUDICIAL NOMINEES WITH COLLEGE DEGREES, 1946–1962

Court	Truman		Eisenhower		Kennedy	
Supreme Court	100.0%	(N = 3)	80.0%	(N = 5)	100.0%	(N = 2)
Courts of Appeals	50.0	(N = 20)	60.0	(N = 45)	64.7	(N = 17)
District Courts	48.9	(N = 96)	57.3	(N = 131)	69.2	(N = 91)

grees to those without has gone from 1:1 to 2:1 in the decade since the establishment of the ABA Committee's liaison with the Attorney General.

The increases in formal legal training are also attributable as much to other factors as to the influence of the ABA Committee. Of the 410 judicial nominees included in this study, 387 (or 94.4 per cent) had formal legal training, as compared with less than half that number a generation before.[6] With respect to these factors, it is probable that the ABA's role is one of reinforcing increasingly held norms about the ways in which both lawyers and judges should be schooled. During the period of 1946–1962, the percentage of Circuit nominees without formal legal training dipped from 10 per cent to zero, and the

---

[6] Rodney L. Mott *et al.*, "Judicial Personnel," 16 *Annals of the American Academy of Political Science* (1933), 149.

TABLE 7.5

JUDICIAL NOMINEES WITH PRIOR JUDICIAL EXPERIENCE, 1946–1962

Supreme Court

Experience	Truman	Eisenhower	Kennedy
More than 5 years	66.7%	20.0%	0.0%
Less than 5 years	0.0	60.0	0.0
No experience	33.3	20.0	100.0
	100.0%	100.0%	100.0%
N =	3	5	2

percentage of District nominees without formal legal training dipped from 5.2 to 2.2 per cent. It is not likely, regardless of the future influence of the ABA Committee, that these percentages will show significant increases in the future.

The Selection of Judges with More Judicial Experience

Has the work of the ABA Committee resulted in the selection of judges with more prior judicial experience or of more judges with prior judicial experience? Although most Committee members at any one time have never supported efforts of others to make some prior judicial experience a *legal* requirement for federal judicial office—and particularly for a Supreme Court position—they have always considered it to be an important factor in assessing the qualifications of prospective nominees. Although there is no necessary connection between the way a judge acts on a lower court and his behavior upon being promoted to a high appellate court, prior service does give the recruiter a unique view of the ways in which a judge is likely to handle the new role. An incumbent judge is much more of a known quantity than a lawyer—no matter how famous—who has never actually conducted a trial or written an opinion. Furthermore, a judge with prior experience on a lower court is more likely to have accepted at least the major norms of the judicial role; where he has not, as was alleged with Judge Irving Ben Cooper, the evidence of his inability or refusal to accept such a role is clear and unmistakable.

The data in Table 7.5 do not indicate that the ABA Committee has had more than a selective impact in promoting the nomination of judges with real or nominal prior judicial experience. Partly on the urging of the ABA, and partly due to other pressures, President Eisenhower did choose as his last four Supreme Court nominees men

TABLE 7.5 *(Continued)*

Courts of Appeals			District Courts		
Truman	*Eisenhower*	*Kennedy*	*Truman*	*Eisenhower*	*Kennedy*
55.0%	37.8%	52.9%	21.9%	19.1%	20.9%
10.0	17.8	5.9	6.3	7.6	12.1
35.0	44.4	41.2	71.9	73.3	67.0
100.0%	100.0%	100.0%	100.0%	100.0%	100.0%
20	45	17	96	131	91

with prior experience.   But in three of the cases (Harlan, Whittaker, and Stewart), the experience was purely nominal; each was appointed first to the lower federal courts and promoted shortly thereafter to the Supreme Court.[7]   There was actually a decrease in the number of judicial nominees to the Courts of Appeals with prior judicial experience, and the percentage of persons nominated for the District Courts who had prior experience increased slightly.   It is interesting to note that while the percentage of District judges who had prior experience increased, the percentage of those who had more than five years' experience decreased.   This phenomenon is at least in part attributable to the ABA's influence in lowering the maximum age at which such an appointment was likely to occur.   The pressure to find younger judicial nominees brings with it the inevitability of getting persons somewhat less experienced.

Given President Eisenhower's frequently articulated support of the ABA Committee's work, and his well-known support of the principle

---

[7] The following table lists the average years of judicial experience of those judges appointed since 1946 (of those who had any judicial experience):

Court	Average Years
Supreme Court	
Truman	6.5
Eisenhower	3.8
Kennedy	0.0
Courts of Appeals	
Truman	13.3
Eisenhower	11.6
Kennedy	16.0
District Courts	
Truman	10.4
Eisenhower	9.3
Kennedy	7.4

of prior judicial experience, his low percentage of Circuit nominees with more than five years' prior experience requires explanation. The most probable cause was the dearth of young Republican judges sitting on the federal district bench in 1953. Young District judges of the President's party are a natural source of supply for the Courts of Appeals, but after twenty years of Democratic administrations, the entire federal bench contained less than 20 per cent Republicans. President Eisenhower was able to meet his own standards by promoting his own District Court appointees to the Courts of Appeals after a short period of time.

The question of the desirability of prior judicial experience has received considerable attention in the last decade, arising particularly out of the controversies engendered by several Supreme Court decisions in 1954–1957. What is surprising is that the norm of prior judicial experience seems to be much more widely followed than would have been expected. Between 55 and 65 per cent of all Circuit nominations after 1946 went to persons with prior experience (35–50 per cent from the District Court), whereas between 25 and 35 per cent of all District Court nominations went to persons with previous judicial service on state or local courts. Even the Supreme Court nominations of Presidents Truman and Eisenhower showed considerable deference to the "requirement" of prior experience.

The Selection of Professional Lawyers

Has the work of the Committee resulted in the preferential selection of professional lawyers over lawyers whose careers have been pri-

TABLE 7.6

MAJOR OCCUPATION OF JUDGE AT NOMINATION

Supreme Court

Occupation	Truman	Eisenhower	Kennedy
Private practice	00.0%	00.0%	00.0%
Justice Department	33.3	00.0	50.0
District Courts	00.0	00.0	00.0
Courts of Appeals	33.3	60.0	00.0
State or municipal judge	00.0	20.0	00.0
Other	33.3	20.0	50.0
	100.0%	100.0%	100.0%
N =	3	5	2

marily political?   One of the major goals of the organized bar has been to promote the selection of judges who shared at least the professional values of the profession, if not the ideological preferences of its leaders.   The existing system of federal judicial selection, resting heavily on the recruiting resources of United States senators and state party organizations, has traditionally favored either the "political" lawyer or the "politically involved" lawyer.   It is this type of lawyer who not only generates sufficient visibility in his own behalf to announce his "availability" for judicial service, but whose services to the party support his candidacy.   The lawyer who makes little or no effort in his own behalf to obtain a federal judgeship is likely to remain a private citizen.

To fight this situation the Committee on Federal Judiciary has geared its standards for the District Court to favor professional, career lawyers.   Its emphasis on *trial experience* as the *sine qua non* of approval for a District Court nomination would, if accepted by the Attorney General and the senators involved, virtually eliminate the "political" lawyer, particularly the person whose only claim to the title of "lawyer" is the possession of a law degree.   The acceptance of such a standard would have the further desirable effect (from the ABA's point of view) of impeding the flow of Justice Department personnel from primarily administrative posts to the federal bench (excepting, of course, U. S. Attorneys and the staff of the Solicitor General).   As Table 7.6 clearly shows, the work of the ABA Committee parallels very closely a marked increase in the selection of lawyers from private practice and a decrease in the selection of lawyers from the Justice Department.   Although the Kennedy proportion of lawyers chosen for the District Court from private practice dips somewhat

TABLE 7.6 (Continued)

Courts of Appeals			District Courts		
Truman	Eisenhower	Kennedy	Truman	Eisenhower	Kennedy
20.0%	24.4%	17.6%	36.5%	57.3%	49.5%
15.0	15.5	00.0	14.5	8.4	1.1
50.0	35.0	47.0	00.0	00.0	00.0
00.0	00.0	00.0	00.0	00.0	00.0
10.0	13.3	11.7	18.9	20.6	27.4
5.0	11.3	24.7	40.1	13.7	22.0
100.0%	100.0%	100.0%	100.0%	100.0%	100.0%
20	45	17	96	131	91

from the peak of the Eisenhower period, it still represents a marked increased from the Truman period when the ABA Committee had not yet established its liaison with the Attorney General. President Kennedy made one District Court nomination and no Circuit Court selections from the Justice Department, a sharp drop from the percentages of either of the preceding administrations. Although this sharp drop reflected a dearth of Democrats in the Justice Department, it also indicates some measure of success of the Committee on Federal Judiciary in promoting the nomination of private practitioners. Much of the slack caused by bypassing the Justice Department was taken up by the state courts, which increased by 50 per cent as a source of judicial nominations.

It should be clear from the foregoing that the first ten years of the liaison between the Committee on Federal Judiciary and the Attorney General have seen small but marked changes in the patterns of recruitment for the federal judiciary—particularly at its lower levels. Other courts and the private practice of law seem to provide more than 75 per cent of the personnel for the federal judiciary, as opposed to just more than 50 per cent during the Truman Administration. Although the average age of judicial nominees has not changed, the number of judges who are chosen at advanced ages has dropped sharply. With the exception of the age factor, these changes all tend to reflect or reinforce the emphasis on professional values which the ABA Committee and the organized bar have sought to institutionalize in the judicial role. There is as yet no evidence linking these changes with altered patterns of judicial decision-making, but such patterns may emerge.

NEW PATTERNS OF JUDICIAL SOCIALIZATION

If these changes in the sources of judicial recruitment prove enduring, they are likely to be followed by corresponding changes in the career patterns of lawyers aspiring to the judiciary. Lawyers with ambitions for the federal bench are more likely to seek their training in private practice (with some side political activity, of course) or on the state courts than in the state legislatures, Congress, or the Justice Department. Such career pattern changes, if they occur, will mark the ultimate successes of the ABA drive. For it is the lawyers in private practice [8] or who sit on state benches who are much more likely to

---

[8] It is recognized that there are substantial differences even among lawyers in private practice, differences frequently attributable to the types of clients each represents

be receptive to the messages of the organized bar than their counterparts holding political office.

Of course, this process will also have a circular effect. As it becomes more evident that obtaining a federal judgeship depends as much on an evaluation by the ABA Committee on Federal Judiciary as it does on friendship or service to a senator or state party organization, prospective judicial nominees will be more likely to heed the preeminent values of the bar. They will have to learn those certain types of behavior which, through the efforts of the ABA Committee, have become the norms for judicial candidates. In short, they will be socialized for the judicial role in a manner at least partly prescribed by the organized bar. The exact extent to which these new patterns of socialization materialize will have to be determined in the light of future experience.

(e.g., "plaintiff's" vs. "defendant's" lawyers). But it is felt that these differences are less than those between lawyers in private practice and those with primarily political careers.

8

THE ROLE OF THE ABA

COMMITTEE: A SUMMARY

AND CRITIQUE

THE ABA COMMITTEE, 1964

Present Status

The institutionalization of the ABA Committee's liaison with both the Attorney General and the Senate Judiciary Committee is clearly the most obvious accomplishment of its eighteen-year existence. To be sure, its relationship with the Senate Committee is mostly nominal and its liaison with the Attorney General leaves room for considerable variation in the scope and extent of the powers it wields. The liaison first established in the waning days of the Truman Administration has continued through the Eisenhower, Kennedy, and Johnson administrations. Although its actual influence will vary with administrations, its formal position seems secure. The work of the ABA Committee has acquired a measure of legitimacy which has had significant implications for the selection process.

The most obvious of these implications is that for the first time a private group of national scope has become an integral part of the federal recruitment process. Many such groups, of course, operate regularly on the local level, and occasionally in the past national groups have exerted significant influence. But no national groups have actually been incorporated into the selection process. It is often no longer sufficient to convince merely a senator and the Attorney General of the desirability of a certain nomination; the ABA Committee must be consulted and, as often as not, satisfied before a nomination goes through.

The ABA Committee operates on the sufferance of both the Attorney General and the Senate Judiciary Committee, but it has nonetheless altered the previously existing distribution of recruitment power. It has curtailed some of the real (though not, of course, formal) power of the Attorney General while creating new types of power for him which have worked in favor of the Committee's goals. And the Committee has succeeded, in several instances, in limiting the senatorial prerogative.

The Committee's effective influence has been primarily, and is likely to remain, in the realm of setting minimum standards of qualification and determining types of acceptable prejudicial career patterns. Despite its success in several individual cases, the Committee has not yet achieved the power to control individual judicial nominations. In all likelihood, however, its influence over standards and prejudicial career patterns will prove its most effective weapon.

Fulfillment of ABA Goals

How well has the Committee fulfilled the original goals of the American Bar Association? The general objectives of the ABA in setting up the Committee on Federal Judiciary were to institutionalize the mediate role of the bar in the judicial-selection process. The Committee itself was charged with promoting the nomination of better judges and opposing the nomination of unqualified judges. And it was to carry on the traditional bar policy of "trying to get the selection of judges out of politics." As described earlier, the Committee was faced with an immediate dilemma. For if it was to be at all effective in either "institutionalizing" the role of the ABA or in promoting the nomination of good judges, it would have to work within the very systems which the parent organization was trying to modify. The Committee could not very well expect much cooperation from an Attorney General whose responsibilities for judicial recruitment were being assailed by the ABA itself. So the first decision which the Committee had to make was, in effect, to forsake one of the goals so dear to the hearts of many ABAers—the establishment of a "nonpolitical" system of selection paralleling the "Missouri Plan" used in several states. The goal of "nonpartisan" selection in a highly partisan political system is at best idealistic.

The ABA Committee has campaigned for a "bipartisan" principle of selection and was even able to convince President Eisenhower of its merits. But the party pressures on even the most willing of Presidents would make even bipartisanship a difficult goal to achieve. Congress could require, as a matter of law, that every other nomination go to a member of the party not in the White House, or that every court have a set ratio of members of each party. But the ABA Committee is limited to fight for this *general* principle; it cannot effectively fight for it in specific cases.

The verdict on the ABA's efforts to achieve an institutionalized role in the selection process must be favorable. The role that the Committee on Federal Judiciary has achieved falls short of the dominant role that some other bar groups have achieved at the state and local levels. But it is quite an accomplishment in the context of national politics and the judicial-selection traditions that preceded the Committee's liaison with the Attorney General. Congress has not seen fit to reinforce the ABA role by statute, and the Committee's power rests essentially on the indulgence of the Attorney General. Perhaps, then, its other accomplishments should be considered even more remarkable, since they must rest on a fluid base.

The ABA Committee has had somewhat less success in promoting the nomination of "better" judges, but it has so far done much better in establishing and enforcing minimum standards of qualification. It is perhaps ironic that its greatest successes have been at the District Court level and its least influence has been exercised at the Supreme Court level. For it was a series of conditions on the Supreme Court which stimulated the formation of the Committee, and it has been the Supreme Court which has been the target of unrelenting criticism from various sectors of the legal profession.

Any evaluation of the Committee is, in part, a function of one's initial premises or criteria for judgment. One who is not ready to accept any compromise with the ABA's broader goals is not likely to grant the importance of what the Committee has accomplished. Illustrative is the position of Loyd Wright, a former member of the Committee and past president of the ABA:

The work of this Committee, in my opinion, is useless. The fact is that we never . . . if ever block an appointment if the appointee is not disbarred. We are used, I fear, as a cat's paw for political Attorneys General who in turn are subject to pressures at levels never dreamed of by our forefathers. In fact, you will find in the Federalist Papers a statement that a senator would never dream of suggesting to the President who to appoint, but would content himself, through the appropriate committee, with advice and consent. It is my experience on the Committee, and in watching it carefully since off, that these appointments are political; the Supreme Court appointments are a disgrace, and unhappily and unfortunately, the degrading of the profession and of the Courts is not entirely the act of one political party.

. . . What the ABA ought to do is to exercise its great influence into getting at the root of the evil, to wit: the method of selection. I have advocated, since 1958, that the ABA propose to the Congress a creature of its legislative powers comparable to what we call in the profession the "Missouri System." Then the President would be compelled to appoint from a panel, selected not because of political indebtedness, but because of the experience, the ability, training, and ethical concepts of the proposed nominee.[1]

But Wright's assessment is, I think, unnecessarily harsh. His complaint that the ABA Committee never blocks a nomination unless the lawyer is disbarred is not true. And his dissatisfaction with the Supreme Court nominations of the past decade puts him at odds with the Committee's evaluations of those judges, which were of the highest order. As for his dismay that the predictions of Hamilton were inaccurate, it should be reiterated that Hamilton's words were never descriptive of an actual situation. From almost the first case, the senators have considered judicial appointments in their states as their prerogatives. This may be bad—but not simply because Hamilton said so!

Aside from its impact on the judicial-selection process, the Committee on Federal Judiciary may also have been an important contributing factor in the recent growth—both in membership and in political influence—of the American Bar Association. The work of the Committee has dramatized, as could no other organizational endeavor, the need and utility of a unified national voice speaking in behalf of all lawyers *and* the propriety of the American Bar Association being that voice. It was the increased prestige of the Committee within as well as outside the legal profession which led Chairman Bernard Segal to publicly refer to the ABA and the Committee as "*the* [emphasis mine] official spokesman of the organized Bar of the country in matters affecting the administration of justice in our courts." [2] Such a statement would hardly have been warranted a decade earlier.

In conclusion it might be said that the impact of the Committee on Federal Judiciary on the federal judicial-selection process has been selectively significant. It has achieved more than could have been realistically expected of it, but less than the ultimate goals of the organized bar. At this stage of its development, the long-range conse-

---

[1] Letter to author, February 14, 1963.

[2] U. S. Congress, House of Representatives, Committee on the Judiciary, *Hearings, Federal Courts and Judges*, 87th Cong., 1st Sess., 1961, p. 427.

quences of its work are uncertain. But its short-run successes do give promise of a more lasting impact.

THE COMMITTEE ON FEDERAL JUDICIARY: A CRITIQUE

The significant role that the ABA Committee has come to occupy in the judicial-selection process raises anew the problem of determining the legitimate role of a private group in the governmental process. There is no constitutional problem, since the Attorney General is free to seek advice from whatever sources he chooses, and to weight that advice in whatever proportions he desires. The Committee is equally free to press its claims on the Attorney General and, concurrently, on the Senate Judiciary Committee and individual senators.

But the question of legitimacy is not limited to the concept of constitutionality. It is much more firmly based in our democratic tradition of accountability and political responsibility for important political decisions. These traditions require that the important decision-makers be identified, and that in some manner—however indirect—their tenure as decision-makers and their actual decisions be subject to periodic review by elected public officials.

When a professional group such as the ABA claims the privilege of passing upon decisions of peculiar concern to the members of the profession, the need for considering questions of legitimacy is not lessened because the privilege has been granted. Nor is it lessened because professional organizations in our society have traditionally carried out quasi-public functions in a variety of spheres. To each individual case the criteria of legitimacy must be applied. But these criteria should certainly take into account not only the considerations of political responsibility described above, but also more practical factors such as the group's contributions to the stability, efficiency, or other aspect of the process of which it has become a part. In short, the question must be "to what extent is the continued quasi-public function of a professional group consistent with the requirements *and* needs of a democratic political system?"

The Committee as a Veto Group

Since the role of the ABA Committee may fluctuate with changes in administrations, the question of legitimacy will vary accordingly. For purposes of this analysis we will first consider the Committee in the "veto" group role which it came to occupy during the latter stages of the Eisenhower Administration. It was in this role and at this time that the Committee reached a pinnacle of power; and with that pinnacle the question of legitimacy was raised in most pressing fashion.

The grant of a veto power to the Committee on Federal Judiciary was no more or less than the ceding of partial control over the judicial-selection process to a private group. Furthermore, this control was given to a group which did not fully represent the political attitudes existing within the ABA or in the legal profession. The members of the Committee represent only a small (but dominant) class of lawyers— a class which has traditionally championed very conservative political values. And the American Bar Association itself claims less than half of all American lawyers as members.

More important, perhaps, is that the internal procedures by which the Committee screens prospective candidates magnify this nonrepresentative character. The Committee appears to be more selective than exhaustive in choosing the sources of its information, and the "informed opinion" which it solicits is transparently the opinion of a small segment of the legal profession. Its investigations and evaluations of each candidate are jealously guarded from public scrutiny with only its "ratings" publicly announced. Even the Attorney General whom the Committee serves is not privy to all the sources upon which the Committee bases its evaluations. Although it is probably true that the operations of the Committee fulfill a generalized expectation of most members of the legal profession [3] and the standards of qualification it espouses do not markedly differ from those widely subscribed to by lawyers, the fact remains that in no way is a "veto" power accorded to the Committee consistent with the norm of political responsibility—a norm which is certainly satisfied by the indirect responsibility of the Attorney General and the direct responsibility of the members of the Senate.

The American Bar Association, of course, does not make its claim to "veto" power on the basis that it represents the electorate, or even the entire legal profession. Its leaders claim that, by virtue of their special training and work with the court system, they, as practicing lawyers, are better able to choose judges than "political officials." They argue that the government would never permit its scientists to be chosen exclusively by officials without scientific training; why then should it allow its judges to be chosen without the benefit of similar

---

[3] See Joel B. Grossman, *The Role of the American Bar Association in the Selection of Federal Judges* (Ph.D. dissertation, State University of Iowa, 1963), pp. 82–88.

professional advice?[4]   The fallacy of this analogy, however, is that it assumes that technical competence—which might be more or less objectively measured—is of equal predominance in the task of the scientist and the judge.   But the average judge—and certainly the appellate judge—is much more of a policy maker than the average scientist, and the ultimate responsibility for whatever policy is made must rest with responsible public officials.   The products of scientific decision are open to verification by accepted methods.   Its premises are acknowledged, and its results are empirical.   But the judicial decision is the product of a greater array of forces, its premises are often inarticulate, and its results are not similarly verifiable.   The decision of the scientist is ultimately reviewable by public officials who are at least indirectly responsible to the electorate, whereas the reversal of a judicial decision by responsible elected officials (that is, Congress) is less easily done.   Furthermore, one basis of the compatibility of judicial policy-making with democratic theory is that this policy-making be ultimately subject to some form of political control.   Frequently this control takes the form of recruitment or the replacement of judicial manpower.   To permit this control to be dominated by a private group would have the undesirable effect of further removing the judiciary from public control.

Removing the process of selection and with it the entire judicial process from public control, or "politics," has long been a major goal of the organized bar.   Its ultimate success is quite dependent on the acquisition of a measure of legitimacy for its operations.   Such legitimacy has been proffered by several state legislatures in enacting versions of the "Missouri Plan" of judicial selection.   But in the absence of any congressional or constitutional specifications of the degree of control ceded to the ABA Committee, the legitimacy of its veto group role must remain in serious doubt.   Even its contributions to the selection process, which easily sustain a consultative role, are insufficient to adequately support a veto role.

The Committee as Advisor and Consultant

Insofar as its functions are limited to advising and consulting, the ABA Committee offends none of the traditional requisites of legitimacy.   In fact, in terms of its contributions to the stability and efficiency of the process of selection and to the nationalization and standardization of judicial qualifications, the Committee on Federal

---

4 Bernard G. Segal, "Federal Judicial Selection—Progress and the Promise of the Future," 47 *Massachusetts Law Quarterly* (1961), 40.

Judiciary could be said to be performing a valuable service. Its contributions to the stability of the process have come through its efforts to standardize the types of qualifications required for candidacy for judicial office. And it has contributed to the efficiency of the recruitment process by making available types of information which might otherwise remain obscure. In so doing, it has widened the alternatives of the Attorney General, permitting him in many cases to consider judicial fitness uninhibited by a variety of other considerations.

Contributing to the stability and efficiency of the Attorney General's role in the selection process is not, of course, an entirely selfless act on the part of the ABA Committee. The Committee has much more effective access to the Attorney General, and the freer *he* is of senatorial pressures, the more vulnerable he is to ABA pressures. And the qualifications for judicial office which the Committee hopes to standardize are qualifications that reflect its own values.

The inclusion of the organized bar in the judicial recruitment process as a consultant and advisor to the Attorney General and the Senate Judiciary Committee certainly makes sense. The legal profession already plays an active role in other sectors of the judicial process, such as in the formulation of rules of procedure for various court systems. In a group-dominated political system it could hardly be considered unusual, and certainly not illegitimate, for a professional organization to participate in the making of policy relevant to its area of specialization. Whether the participation of such a group is politically wise, or otherwise desirable, is another question entirely.

Ultimately, the question of the compatibility of the ABA Committee's exercise of power with accepted notions of democratic theory depends on the role that the Committee plays. If it remains, as it is today, *a* consultant of the Attorney General, no question of compatibility arises. That the Committee is occasionally able to persuade the Attorney General to block a nomination is of no particular concern. But when the Committee is permitted, either tacitly or formally, to veto prospective judicial nominations, there is reason for grave concern. For neither the methods by which the Committee operates nor the discrete interests which it serves qualify it for exercising *that* degree of control over the recruitment of judges.

FEDERAL JUDICIAL SELECTION: SOME ALTERNATIVES

This book has been about the efforts of the American Bar Association to achieve influence over the federal judicial-recruitment process. By focusing particularly on the most successful attempt of the past generation to alter the selection process, an effort has been made to characterize the interplay of political forces which make up that process and to explore the possible consequences of such interplay for the federal judiciary. But no description of the judicial-selection process, however brief, would be complete without some mention of the alternative modes of choice frequently suggested by reformers and disgruntled litigants alike. That the ABA Committee has not sought structural changes indicates only that it has found it more rewarding to work within the system. But others including the parent ABA have felt the need to call for a basic overhaul of the selection process.

Proposals for change in the method of selecting federal judges have not been lacking in any period of American history. Disappointed litigant groups particularly, but not exclusively, have frequently made proposals for change on the theory that "better" or "different" judges would have decided their own cases differently. Proposals made in the last decade are just illustrative of a continuing process.

Following the decision of the Supreme Court in *Brown v. Board of Education* in 1954, and the series of decisions by that Court in 1956–1958 upholding the rights of political offenders, there was a severe reaction in the Eighty-fifth Congress and numerous attempts were made to "punish" the Court by restricting its jurisdiction. Attempts were also made to reverse the import of specific Court rulings.[5] But far more numerous were the fourteen bills designed to alter in some way the process of choosing the judges themselves. Proposals were made to limit the terms of Supreme Court justices to twelve years, renewable with the consent of the Senate, to provide for the election of federal judges in the states where they serve, to provide for nomination by the President from a list of seventy-five submitted by the American Bar Association, to provide for the appointment of federal judges by the sitting judges of the highest state courts, and to require judicial nominees to have five years prior judicial experience.[6] There is little doubt that the incorporation of some of these reforms into the

---

[5] See C. Herman Pritchett, *Congress Versus the Supreme Court* (Minneapolis: University of Minnesota Press, 1960) and Walter F. Murphy, *Congress and the Court* (Chicago: University of Chicago Press, 1961). The best known of these attempts was the Jenner-Butler Bill, designed in part to restrict the appellate jurisdiction of the Supreme Court in areas where the Court had made controversial decisions. The bill was defeated 49–41 in the Senate in 1958.

[6] The bills, all introduced in 1957, were SJR 9 introduced by Senator Long (La.), HJR 119 introduced by Representative Grant, HJR 406 introduced by Representative Burdick, HJR 438 introduced by Representative Fisher, and S 1184 introduced by Senator Smathers.

selection process would lead to significant changes in the patterns of recruitment. Whether these changes would actually produce the results desired by their proponents is another matter entirely.

The rationale behind some of these proposed changes is as instructive as it is interesting. The proposal to provide for nomination by the President from a list of seventy-five names submitted by the American Bar Association paralleled the 1958 resolution of the ABA House of Delegates (described in Chapter 5) and was, of course, based on the ABA or "Missouri Plan" of selection adopted in several states. It was aimed at eliminating three allegedly objectionable features of the federal recruitment process: (1) the preference of "political" over "professional" lawyers; (2) the participation of the chief litigant in the federal courts—the Attorney General—in the process of selection; and (3) the reliance on partisanship as a basis for selection.

Bypassing the Attorney General

We have already discussed the first item listed. But the other two bear further attention. Bypassing the Attorney General in the judicial-selection process has been urged by some voices of the organized bar. The critics of the Attorney General see a conflict of interest in his dual role as chief litigant in the federal courts and recruiter of the judges before whom his cases will be argued. In the words of one critic, the Attorney General "pitches, catches, runs the bases, and selects the umpire." [7] Yet, overlooked is the fact that it is the Solicitor General and not the Attorney General who represents the government in court. The Attorney General rarely appears personally to argue a case, or even to prepare a brief, although he does make token appearances and supervises the preparation of cases. And the Attorney General supervises the work of U. S. Attorneys and others who appear for the government in the lower courts. Nonetheless, if the responsibility for recruiting judges is to remain anywhere in the administration, the Attorney General is probably the most knowledgeable and in the best position to effectively examine candidate qualifications. If the President were to make the nomination from a list of seventy-five submitted by a bar panel, he would still have to devise some process for screening the candidates, and if that function were not performed by the Attorney General, it would probably have to be done by the White House staff which, if anything, would be more likely to be

---

[7] Charles J. Bloch, "The Selection of Federal Judges," 41 *American Bar Association Journal* (1955), 510.

partisan than the Attorney General. Furthermore, the problem of conflict of interest would not be lessened by giving the organized bar the function of selecting a panel of names. If anything, the bar has at least as much of a stake in the judicial decision-making process as the Attorney General, although its interests are more diverse. It would certainly seem that if there is to be an inevitable conflict of interest, it is better that it be in the open and lodged in a public official than in a private group.

Eliminating Partisanship

The ABA's interest in bipartisan selection has been described in detail in earlier sections of this book. At this point, it might be pertinent to raise the question of the need for such a reform and its possible consequences. For example, there is no evidence indicating that partisanship per se causes a serious downgrading of judicial manpower. Attorney General William Rogers, a strong supporter of the bar position on other matters, commented in 1957 that

. . . Historically, and I suppose that it will be true prospectively, each administration appoints principally from its own party. That, in practice, has not proven to be a serious weakness in the system of selection of federal judges. The reason that the federal court system has worked well is that federal judges put aside all political considerations once they assume judicial duties.[8]

The quest for bipartisanship—always described as a temporary expedient pending the achievement of a nonpartisan system—can more properly be described as a calculated effort to strip the political robe from the selection process and thus make it more vulnerable to the influence of the organized bar. The downgrading of partisan and patronage considerations would not only be an effective solvent of the senatorial prerogative in the selection process, it would serve to boost the priority of other standards of selection such as prior judicial or trial experience. Both of these consequences would be quite advantageous to the American Bar Association. The breakdown of the senatorial prerogative would be of considerable aid to the ABA Committee on Federal Judiciary. And if prior judicial or trial experience were to be considered major qualifications for appointment, the ABA's role as advisor or consultant would be considerably enhanced. It must also be noted that the downgrading of the partisanship factor

---

[8] "Judicial Appointments in the Eisenhower Administration," 41 *Journal of the American Judicature Society* (1957), 40.

would not at all eliminate "politics" from the recruitment equation. "Politics" would still be involved, but it would be transferred from a public to a private forum.

But the argument against eliminating partisanship from the recruitment equation need not rest entirely on a negative base. It could be argued that considerations of partisanship (excluding only the more blatant uses of it) make a positive contribution to the rationality of the selection process. First, they insure that the selection process will be indirectly responsive to popular sentiment. More important, they insure that the important question of the social and political philosophies of the judicial candidate will be considered.

Although most judges appointed for life tend to shed previous party identifications, there is substantial evidence that prior political affiliation is associated with decision-making tendencies.[9] Since a proper and inevitable factor in the selection is not only the manner in which a judge will conduct his duties, but the types of decisions he will make, and since there are some fairly clear though not mutually exclusive distinctions between members of the two major political parties, political party label is often as good a key (though by no means an infallible one) to the mind of the prospective judge as is available. Although partisanship may be a pernicious influence in the actual rendering of judicial decisions, it *may* also be a desirable feature of the recruitment process. Partisanship may be less important to the selection of Supreme Court judges than it is to the selection of lower federal judges. For the greater scrutiny given to Supreme Court nominations affords a better picture of the "real" politics of the nominee, and party label may add little relevant information. But the process by which lower-court judges are selected does not afford the same deep perspective, and party affiliation may be an effective, albeit gross, index of the values of a prospective judge and of his predicted behavior on the bench.

Prior Judicial Experience

The question of a minimum number of years of prior judicial experience for high judicial office has been one of the most prominent in the controversy following *Brown v. Board of Education*. The proponents of this requirement, including most of the organized bar but not

---

9 See John R. Schmidhauser, "Judicial Behavior and the Sectional Crisis of 1837–1860," 23 *Journal of Politics* (1961), 615, and Stuart Nagel, "Political Party Affiliation and Judges' Decisions," 55 *American Political Science Review* (1961), 843–850.

the ABA Committee on Federal Judiciary, argue that judges with such experience are more likely to exhibit certain kinds of attitudes on the bench, particularly a healthy respect for precedents. Yet the available evidence would seem to point to exactly the opposite conclusion. Both the federal District Courts and the Supreme Courts of most states, where Circuit and Supreme Court judges would have to get their experience, are staffed primarily with "political" rather than "professional" lawyers. As noted earlier, a federal district judgeship, until the present, has been primarily the culmination of a successful political career, or a reward for unsuccessful political activity. Mere promotion from the federal District Court or from the state courts may not always produce a "lawyer's" judge. Furthermore, recent empirical research has contradicted recent assertions that judicial experience per se is the most effective way to "make an outstanding judge wedded to the system of precedents." [10] Professor John Schmidhauser states in a recently published study:

The notion that significant prior judicial experience predisposes justices to adhere to *stare decisis* is clearly without foundation. Indeed, to the extent that significant experience conditions attitudes toward *stare decisis* at all, those members of the Supreme Court who were members of courts within the American common law judicial tradition prior to their appointments to the high court were actually more prone to deviate from the institutional norm of adherence to *stare decisis* than were the justices who were not so integrated.[11]

Prior judicial experience is not only not likely to produce the results which its proponents claim, it is likely to have the further desultory consequence of reducing the flexibility of choice of those who must recruit our judges. Barring any adoption of a form of the Continental system of career training for the judiciary, it is clear that our lower courts do not have a monopoly of future judicial talent. In fact, the patterns of recruitment for lower federal and most state courts tend to emphasize those very factors which the proponents of prior judicial experience oppose.

That most of these proposed reforms of the selection process are feasible should not obscure the fact that in most cases they are also inadvisable. The existing selection system is far from perfect. But

---

10 Senator John Stennis (D., Miss.), quoted in U. S. *Congressional Record,* 84th Cong., 2nd Sess., 1956, CII, Part 6, p. 7277.
11 "Stare Decisis, Dissent, and the Background of the Justices of the Supreme Court of the United States," 14 *University of Toronto Law Review* (1962), 194.

it has the virtues of being flexible, predictable, politically responsive, and battle-tested.   Some aspects of these proposed reforms have been informally incorporated into the system via the ABA Committee on Federal Judiciary.   The consequences of their use on an informal basis can serve as a guide to further action.

INDEX

223